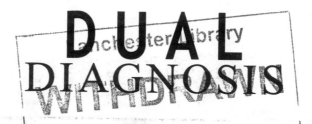

DUAL DIAGNOSIS

DUAL
DIAGNOSIS
An Integrated Approach to Treatment

Ted R. Watkins • Ara Lewellen • Marjie C. Barrett

Sage Publications, Inc.
International Educational and Professional Publisher
Thousand Oaks ▪ London ▪ New Delhi

For information:

Sage Publications, Inc.
2455 Teller Road
Thousand Oaks, California 91320
E-mail: order@sagepub.com

Sage Publications Ltd.
6 Bonhill Street
London EC2A 4PU
United Kingdom

Sage Publications India Pvt. Ltd.
M-32 Market
Greater Kailash I
New Delhi 110 048 India

Printed in the United States of America

Library of Congress Cataloging-in-Publication Data

Watkins, Ted R.
    Dual diagnosis: An integrated approach to treatment / by Ted R. Watkins, Ara Lewellen, Marjie Barrett.
        p.   cm.
    Includes bibliographical references and index.
    ISBN 0-7619-1557-5 (c) — ISBN 0-7619-1558-3 (p)
        1. Dual diagnosis.   I. Lewellen, Ara.   II. Barrett, Marjie.   III. Title.
    RC564.68 .W38   2000
    616.89—dc21   00-009856

This book is printed on acid-free paper.

01   02   03   04   05   06   07   7   6   5   4   3   2   1

Acquisition Editor:	Nancy S. Hale
Editorial Assistant:	Heather Gotlieb
Production Editor:	Sanford Robinson
Editorial Assistant:	Victoria Cheng
Typesetter/Designer:	Lynn Miyata
Indexer:	Cristina Haley
Cover Designer:	Michelle Lee

Contents

Preface

The service delivery systems in the fields of mental health and substance abuse have long been separated by both philosophical and methodological differences. Agencies that provide treatment services to the two groups are funded through different governmental bureaucracies and are staffed by persons who are oriented to one or the other but seldom both problem areas. Each field has its own methods. During recent years, there has been increasing awareness that many individuals have both mental illness and problems with substance abuse.

The growing body of professional literature relating to these dually diagnosed persons has been similarly divided, with materials published by mental health professionals tending to simply broaden the dominant mental health treatment models to include substance abuse as an add-on. Substance abuse practitioners have tended to attempt to stretch their treatment models to include substance abusers who also have mental illnesses. Numerous sources have acknowledged the need for a philosophy of treatment and accompanying methodology that truly integrate the expertise of the two fields. During the past 15 years, there has been a proliferation of research and scientific literature that is, in fact, breaching the gaps in the treatment of persons having dual diagnoses. The authors of the present book, experienced in both mental health and substance abuse treatment, build on recent research literature in the field of dual diagnosis treatment. We take the literature to a meta-systems level, identifying basic principles of human behavior and treatment methodology that are applicable to the treatment of both substance abuse and mental illness. Thus, the model presented is an integrated one in two ways. First, it integrates practice theory and research from the two fields of mental health and substance abuse treatment. Second, it proposes simultaneous *integrated* treatment in a single setting. This book is aimed at expanding the understanding and competence of professionals in both areas of practice: mental health and substance abuse. Trainees who are just beginning their professional experience will be oriented immediately to the commonalities of the two fields rather than to the parochial interests and techniques specific to either one.

The primary target readership of this book is professionals-in-training from the fields of medicine, nursing, psychology, social work, and other counseling disciplines who work with persons who have problems with both mental illnesses and substance abuse. We believe, however, that the book also will prove to be useful to current practitioners in the helping professions, whose training and experience have not prepared them for effective work with the challenging population of persons who have dual diagnoses of mental illness and substance abuse disorders. Although much of our theory is available in the technical journals aimed at researchers and academics, we have attempted to maintain a highly readable text within a consistent and comprehensible format that is more reader friendly for the professional student and general professional practitioner.

Chapter 1 gives the theoretical bases on which the model is developed—a biopsychosocial approach to understanding mental illness and substance abuse, a basic problem-solving framework for intervention, and the application of the elements and stages of change as delineated in the transtheoretical model of treatment. It is this triad of theory that builds the foundation for the detailed treatment model that is carried throughout Chapters 4 through 9.

Chapter 2 reviews much of the professional literature pertinent to the major issues and problems created by the coexistence of mental illness and substance abuse disorders. It describes the target problems toward which the treatment model that follows is aimed. Chapter 3 focuses on the complex process of assessment of clients who have both mental illness and substance abuse disorders.

Each of Chapters 4 through 9 presents the unique problems and treatment methods tailored to a specific mental illness when combined with substance abuse: schizophrenia (Chapter 4), major depression (Chapter 5), bipolar disorder (Chapter 6), major personality disorders (Chapter 7), anxiety disorders (Chapter 8), and primary substance abuse disorders accompanied by secondary mental illnesses (Chapter 9). These chapters follow a standard format that consists of the following:

1. A brief definition of the mental illness

2. The unique problems inherent in that illness combined with substance abuse

3. Assessment procedures relevant to the particular mental illness (including gender and ethnicity implications)

4. Prioritized treatment goals

5. A detailed treatment model including the nature of the helping relationship to be established; psychopharmacological considerations; applicability of psycho-educational services; treatment of symptoms in the cognitive-behavioral, affective, and coping dimensions; services needed for the family; employment and housing service requirements; and recommendations regarding support groups

Chapter 10, the final chapter, pulls together major conclusions from the earlier chapters and provides a grid that simplistically but visually shows the relationships among specific disorders, the stages of readiness for change, and techniques recommended for their treatment.

Introduction

Recognition of the extent of coexistence of mental illness and substance abuse disorders is recent, with few references in the professional literature dating back more than 15 years. The problem has been reported independently by treatment specialists in the mental health and substance abuse fields. The current professional literature regarding this phenomenon has been disparate in philosophy, perspective on assessment, treatment recommendations, and even basic terminology. This chapter identifies the perspective of the authors and, thereby, orients the reader to the material in the remainder of the book.

AUTHORS

The three authors of this book have career histories that include direct service and administration in a variety of service delivery agencies in which persons with mental illness, chemically dependent adults and minors, and persons with both disorders were served. More recently, we have moved to more academic, theoretical analyses of these problems while maintaining contact with the issues through the provision of clinical supervision, consultation, workshops, and professional education of practitioners currently working in the field and through limited ongoing clinical practice. Our interest in the phenomenon of persons having dual diagnoses, therefore, comes from both clinical experience and academic curiosity. We share with a number of contemporary scholars in the field (e.g., Carey, Drake, Evans & Sullivan, Kofoed, Minkoff, Osher, Pepper, Sciacca—all of whom are cited throughout this book) a belief that treatment of persons with coexisting mental illness and substance abuse disorders requires an integration of the theories that have proved to be effective in treatment of each of the separate disorders, with modifications required by the synergistic interaction of the two.

1

TERMINOLOGY

Coexistence of mental illness and substance abuse disorders is referred to in several ways in the professional literature. Medical journals most often use the term *comorbidity*. Psychological and social science literature generally uses *dual diagnosis* or *dually diagnosed*. A few scholars prefer *mentally ill chemical abuser, substance-abusing mentally ill*, or *mental disorders with chemical dependency*. Each term is justified by the particular focus of the writer, but such diversity of terminology complicates the process of literature search and, consequently, retards the development of a common body of knowledge of the phenomenon. We have chosen to use the term *dual diagnosis* throughout this book because, in spite of its lack of specificity, this is the terminology that is most widely used and, therefore, links us best with the work of others.

There is similar variability in terminology relating to the non-medically prescribed use of psychotropic drugs including alcohol. The lack of general acceptance of alcohol as a drug has resulted in frequent use of the redundant phrase *alcohol and drugs* or *alcohol and other drugs*. Some writers distinguish between drug use and drug abuse. Others, however, maintain that there is no acceptable use of nonprescribed psychotropic drugs and that the phrase *drug abuse* always should be used. The American Psychiatric Association's (1994) *Diagnostic and Statistical Manual of Mental Disorders* (*DSM-IV*) classification distinguishes between drug abuse and drug dependence on the basis of the extent to which the drug user suffers negative consequences of the use. Other terms that sometimes are used include *drug dependency, chemical dependency, alcoholism*, and *addiction*, preceded by the drug of primary use. Throughout this book, we use the term *substance abuse* to include any use of psychotropic substances that creates or exacerbates difficulties—medical, psychological, or social—in the user's life.

Biopsychosocial Model

From the 1960s into the 1990s, much of the literature and research on the etiology of both mental illness and substance abuse disorders focused on a single factor such as a genetic predisposition, early life experiences, peer influences, or cultural contexts. There are, consequently, bodies of research connecting each of those factors with the development of mental illnesses and with the development of substance abuse disorders, although no one factor can be demonstrated to be solely responsible for the disorder being studied. Treatment research and theory also often are limited in scope to a single method such as medical intervention, cognitive-behavioral treatment, family therapy, and the like.

During recent years, there has been a growing acceptance of the multifactorial nature of mental illness and substance abuse disorders, leading to the articulation of a biopsychosocial perspective. As implied by its name, this perspective assumes that the disorders in question have roots in some interplay among biological, psychological, and social factors.

The biological dimension refers to the brain chemistry problems (which may be genetic) that underlie both disorders.

> Just as some people are particularly sensitive to the effects of prescribed medications, the dual-disorder client may have a sensitivity to alcohol and street drugs that has to do with his or her body chemistry and particularly with the direct effects upon the brain. (Ryglewicz & Pepper, 1992, p. 279)

Some brains are especially vulnerable to the disorganizing effects of substance use, such as those of persons affected by learning disability or schizophrenia or of persons whose brains already are damaged by substance use. Many persons with mental disorders have such fragile brain chemistry that even social use of alcohol or drugs can destabilize them and cause psychotic episodes, perhaps resulting in unnecessary hospitalization. In addition, even casual use of alcohol and street drugs may bring on transient psychiatric problems in drug abusers, especially while they are actively using drugs or just after stopping use (National Institute on Drug Abuse, 1991).

The "psycho" in the biopsychosocial perspective of the etiology of the dual problems of mental illness and substance abuse disorders refers to psychological factors (e.g., early developmental experiences, personality traits, emotional states, cognitive styles) that result in the habitual patterns of perceiving, thinking, feeling, and acting that are related to the disorders (Gorski, 1994). "A person with a mental/emotional/personality disorder has, by definition, some impairment of ego functions involving one or more of the capacities for judgment, reality testing, impulse control, affect modulation, memory, mastery, competence, and so forth" (Ryglewicz & Pepper, 1992, pp. 279-280). Psychoactive drugs are, by definition, those that affect these ego functions.

"Social" refers to factors such as poorly developed social skills, family dysfunction, poverty, and membership in oppressed or deviant groups that may contribute to the etiology of mental illness and substance abuse and to problems that develop in work, social, and intimate relationships as a result of the disorders (Gorski, 1994). Persons with mental/emotional disorders are vulnerable socially, with their relationships and life situations often only tenuously maintained. Their social relationships tend to be nonreciprocal; that is, they involve much receiving and little giving (Westermeyer, 1985). Their families, friends, and lovers already have lived through too many crises related to the disorders and might not be willing to endure more. Persons who have used up too much of their "social margin" through episodes of their psychiatric illness might pay an extra-heavy price for getting into trouble with alcohol and/or drugs (Ryglewicz & Pepper, 1992).

Read, Penick, and Nickel (1993) state, "The biopsychosocial model has been used to 'explain' the substance use disorders and the other mental disorders separately. However, no theoretical system exists currently that was specifically designed to address the development of dual diagnosis subtypes" (p. 143). A number of recent studies, both theoretical and research based, have begun to address the problem and are cited in the relevant chapters of this book.

Authorities have repeatedly proposed that treatment programs should address the physiological, psychological, and social dimensions of the functioning of the client, but such a comprehensive approach is not yet routinely demonstrated in the practice of treatment of mental illness and substance abuse disorders. The biopsychosocial perspective is one of the three theoretical constructs that are the foundation of the current book. Within the discussion of each of the mental disorders in the following chapters, we address treatment issues related to the biological, psychological, and social dimensions of the functioning of the client. The different mental disorders are affected in each of the three dimensions to different degrees. For example, schizophrenia, often referred to as a thought (i.e., psychological) disorder, now generally is believed by medical researchers to be predominantly a biologically based illness with severe social consequences (Andreasen, 1994; Benes, 1995; Keefe & Harvey, 1994; Wilson, 1997). Effective treatment must address all three of the biopsychosocial spheres, with progress in psychological and social functioning often being dependent on biochemical intervention (Wilson, 1997). Personality disorders, by contrast, require greater emphasis on social intervention, with physiological and psychological methods playing more supportive roles. The presence of substance abuse in each of the mental disorders adds tremendous complications in the client's functioning and necessitates modifications in treatment protocols. The biological, psychological, and social components of substance abuse react synergistically with those of the mental disorders, many times requiring a change in the prioritization of interventive techniques. The biopsychosocial perspective provides a cognitive framework for approaching the problems and treatment of dually diagnosed clients.

Problem-Solving Approach

The problem-solving approach is much discussed in social work literature but is implicit in the methods of all of the helping professions. Based on the scientific method as articulated by Dewey (1939), it refers to a methodical movement from step to step in the helping process. It was brought into wide use in social casework by Perlman (1957), who conceived of it as a three-step process consisting of study, diagnosis, and treatment. Since Perlman's work, it has been further detailed to a sequence that includes assessment, planning, intervention, evaluation, termination, and follow-up (Hepworth, Rooney, & Larsen, 1997). Assessment in the case of the dually diagnosed client (discussed in greater detail in Chapter 3) must entail evaluating the biological, psychological, and social functioning related to the effects of the client's mental illness and the effects of the substance abuse, both qualitatively and quantitatively. Treatment can be only as good as the assessment on which it is based. On the basis of the findings of the assessment, a comprehensive treatment plan can be made. Simplistic as this might appear to be, it still is the case that many treatment programs attempt to fit the dually diagnosed client into a preset regimen developed for more traditional clients who have only one disorder. A good treatment plan includes a prioritized schedule of interventive techniques that are directed toward solving the specific problems in client functioning that have been identified in the assessment. It addresses issues shared by all dually diagnosed clients, clients having the same specific diagnoses as the client in question, and issues that are unique to the specific client being served.

The intervention step in the problem-solving process consists of the implementation of the methods and techniques specified in the treatment plan. There is a growing body of literature on the effectiveness of various treatment methods with clients having problems with either mental illness or substance abuse disorders, and there are some beginnings of validation of methods when used with dually diagnosed clients. Chapters 4 through 9 draw heavily from those studies that give empirical evidence of successful treatment.

The process of evaluation is used throughout the intervention step and periodically thereafter. Evaluation refers to the measurement of the client's movement toward the treatment objectives as specified in the treatment plan. It is a sort of compass that indicates to the treatment personnel whether or not they are going in the right direction. If the client is not making measurable progress or is regressing, then the need for a change of direction is clear. In practice, evaluation often is informal, with the treatment personnel making subjective judgments regarding whether or not a client has been helped by the interventions used. A major obstacle to the development of more sound treatment methods for persons with dual diagnoses is the lack of carefully documented outcome studies in which the effectiveness of various treatment efforts is reported. (See Ridgely & Jerrell, 1996, for a discussion of the difficulties inherent in attempting comparative outcome studies in agency settings.)

Termination refers to the winding down of the treatment process, in which closure is attained through a review of gains made by the client and clarification and reinforcement of strategies for relapse prevention. Particularly if the therapeutic relationship between the client and treatment personnel has been intense or lengthy, termination must include some focus on the client's emotional reaction to the cessation of therapeutic contacts with the personnel.

In the case of persons with mental illness, substance abuse disorders, or both, follow-up services are considered to be essential to the maintenance of gains made during the intervention stage. Follow-up services may take a variety of forms including periodic in-person contact with treatment personnel, agency follow-up groups, and referral to external groups such as 12-step groups. As with treatment planning and intervention, follow-up services need to be tailored to the specific needs of dually diagnosed clients because more generic methods might be counterproductive with this population. Recommendations for follow-up services for specific dually diagnosed populations are included in Chapters 4 through 9 of this book.

Transtheoretical Model

Prochaska and DiClemente (1984), after reviewing the literature on many types of psychotherapy, identified 10 core processes that are related to therapeutic change regardless of method and applied those processes to the treatment of addictive behaviors (Prochaska and DiClemente, 1986; Prochaska, DiClemente, & Norcross, 1992). Their transtheoretical model has become a foundation for much of the contemporary literature on treatment of substance abuse disorders. The 10 processes of change and brief definitions follow:

1. *Consciousness raising*. This means increasing the client's awareness of his or her behavior and its consequences. It is akin to the familiar concept of insight, and in the case of the dually diagnosed client, it would include making the client aware of the effects of substance use on his or her mental state.

2. *Self-liberation*. This means freeing the client from victimhood. Similar to "empowerment," self-liberation is enabling the client to recognize that he or she has choices and is not a passive victim of mental illness or substance abuse disorders.

3. *Social liberation*. This is providing a social environment that offers opportunities for the client to get needs met through nondestructive means.

It would include providing subsidized housing for the mentally ill so that they do not have to remain homeless or with dysfunctional families, establishing alcohol- or drug-free social and recreational options for persons with substance abuse disorders, and reducing the stigma for persons with mental illness or substance abuse disorders.

4. *Counterconditioning.* This means essentially "unlearning" the destructive behaviors that have become automatic responses to triggering events. For the substance abuser, it would be learning new behaviors to replace the alcohol or drug use. For the person with mental illness, it would be replacing symptomatic behavior with more socially appropriate behavior.

5. *Stimulus control.* This is the avoidance of emotional states or situations that tend to trigger undesirable behaviors. It might include avoiding friends with whom one has used drugs, staying away from situations in which drugs will be available, and avoiding stimuli that threaten one's emotional control.

6. *Self-reevaluation.* This means reassessing one's strengths and weaknesses in the light of new insights. An example of this would be helping a person with mental illness to see that the individual has many healthy aspects to his or her mind as well as the illness aspect. For the client with a substance abuse disorder, it might entail comparing one's current behaviors to those of the type of person one wants to be.

7. *Environmental reevaluation.* This is a new look at one's social environment, especially as it relates to one's own behaviors. The dually diagnosed client might recognize that his or her social rejection is a consequence of symptomatic behavior rather than others' inherent dislike of him or her. This also might mean assessing the effects of one's behavior on the well-being of his or her loved ones.

8. *Contingency management.* This means changing the consequences of behavior. The acting out dually diagnosed client might have been "excused" from unacceptable public behavior when holding him or her accountable would make such behavior less rewarding and less self-reinforcing.

9. *Dramatic relief.* This entails ventilation or catharsis. An opportunity to verbalize frustrations might be necessary before problem solving can begin. This is particularly important during the early stages of detoxification, when the substance-abusing client no longer can seek relief through drug use.

10. *Helping relationships.* This is the "therapeutic bond." The connection between client and helper provides support and encouragement to the client's change efforts. Social support in one's natural environment also promotes positive change. The sense of being understood and accepted is particularly meaningful to the dually diagnosed client.

The identification of these 10 processes is helpful in understanding how successful treatment occurs. They need not all be used, but it seems clear that therapeutic progress is not made without the use of some of them, and the more of these 10 processes that are used, the greater the chance of therapeutic success. We refer to these processes throughout the book to explain the essential elements in treatment methods and techniques.

Another dimension of Prochaska and DiClemente's (1984) transtheoretical model to which we refer in subsequent chapters is the "stages of change." Not all clients are in the same place with regard to their readiness to work on their problems with mental illness and substance abuse disorders. At the time of first contact with helping professionals, they may be in any one of the following stages:

1. *Precontemplative:* not aware or not acknowledging having a problem

2. *Contemplative:* beginning to recognize that something is wrong but not yet committed to doing anything about it

3. *Decision:* acceptance of the existence of the problem and commitment to do something about it

4. *Action:* actively seeking solutions that may include "home remedies," 12-step programs, and formal therapy

5. *Maintenance:* relapse prevention

Dually diagnosed clients may be at different stages of change with regard to their two disorders (Brody et al., 1996). That is, they may be in the maintenance or relapse prevention stage regarding their mental illnesses while they still are in the precontemplative stage regarding their substance abuse problems. The way in which one works with a client must take into consideration which stage the client is in. Any treatment model must incorporate strategies to ready clients for active change (Carey, 1996a). Methods of helping clients with dual diagnoses move from the stages of precontemplation and contemplation to a decision to begin the action stage are controversial. Substance abuse treatment personnel traditionally have considered their clients to be "in denial" when they are in the precontemplative and contemplative stages and have used aggressive confrontive techniques to push clients into the decision and action stages. As is discussed in Chapter 2, such aggressively confrontive techniques can be devastating to the client with mental illness that involves a fragile mental status. This has been a major source of conflict between treatment personnel from the substance abuse field and those from the mental health field. Motivational interviewing (introduced by Miller & Rollnick, 1991), a nonconfrontational method stressing self-efficacy and self-esteem, is making major inroads toward establishing less harsh methods in moving clients to accept their need for change. It is particularly appropriate with dually diagnosed clients who might not do well in emotionally charged interactions (Carey, 1996a).

A third dimension of the transtheoretical model deals with where one targets change efforts. Prochaska and DiClemente (1986) identify five levels at which intervention may be directed:

1. *Symptom/situational:* deals with the immediate stimuli that trigger symptomatic behavior and its consequences

2. *Maladaptive cognitions:* focuses on correcting the dysfunctional thought patterns that lead to the symptomatic behavior

3. *Interpersonal problems:* addresses difficulties the client has in dealing with the world outside his or her intimate circle (this may include issues related to the client's lack of social skills or a lack of acceptance on the part of the larger society)

4. *Family conflicts:* relates to dysfunction within the intimate circle of family and friends of the client (this dysfunction often triggers and feeds the symptomatic behavior)

5. *Intrapersonal conflicts:* deals with pain from deep intrapsychic problems rooted in early-life experiences and reinforced by continuing maladaptive affective responses

This scheme for identification of points of intervention is a part of assessment and treatment planning and is compatible with the biopsychosocial perspective. The transtheoretical model, then, deals with where the client is, which level of intervention is sought, and the elements that are necessary to bring about meaningful change. Individualized application of the model guides treatment with a high probability of success.

CONCLUSION

We have presented the three major theoretical elements that provide the foundation for our model of treatment of persons with coexisting mental illness and substance abuse disorders. The biopsychosocial perspective broadens our view to include consideration of the whole person; the problem-solving approach structures the process by which treatment proceeds; and the transtheoretical model provides labels and conceptual tools with which to analyze our therapeutic efforts.

Issues and Problems With Dual Diagnosis 2

The knowledge base in the area of dual diagnosis has grown out of the contributions of persons in the disparate fields of mental health and substance abuse treatment. Consequently, no single perspective has been agreed on, and there is considerable variation in the way in which the term *dual diagnosis* is defined, in reports of the incidence of persons having coexisting disorders of substance abuse and mental illness and how such persons should be treated. This chapter reviews some of the controversies in the field so as to set the stage for the treatment model that follows.

DEFINITIONS

There is considerable disagreement about just who should be considered dually diagnosed. This is predictable given that definitions of the individual categories of mental illness and substance abuse are not clear. If all persons meeting the criteria for any *Diagnostic and Statistical Manual of Mental Disorders* (*DSM-IV*) diagnostic category (American Psychiatric Association, 1994) are mentally ill, and if all persons who at times have problems related to alcohol or drug use are substance abusers, then the number of dually diagnosed persons is astronomical. Etiological factors also are an issue. For example, is the chronic substance abuser who has developed symptoms of mental illness mentally ill, or should the mental dysfunction be considered only a side effect of the substance abuse? Substance abuse may be viewed as one of the causes of a mental disorder or as a result of the mental disorder, and vice versa. One definitional problem concerns whether or not symptoms that emerge following the onset of substance abuse should qualify as an additional psychiatric diagnosis. For example, many behaviors associated with antisocial personality (e.g., frequent job changes, criminal activity, problems in interpersonal relationships) also are directly associated with a

11

protracted period of substance abuse. It has been argued that considering them in the diagnosis of antisocial personality has resulted in an overestimate of this disorder among substance abuse populations (National Institute on Drug Abuse [NIDA], 1991).

Historically, there has been considerable challenge to the categorization of substance abuse disorders as diseases separate from mental illness. It often is difficult to determine whether an individual's symptoms represent substance abuse or mental illness. For example, a primary depressive disorder may look like symptoms that are secondary to long-term substance abuse. An intoxicated person who hears voices may be in a transient psychotic state due to the alcohol or may be exhibiting symptoms of a mental state that preceded the alcohol abuse. Overdiagnosis can occur when treatment staff mistake the withdrawal symptoms of early recovery from substance abuse for the symptoms of a mental illness. Substance abusers who are in early recovery may be diagnosed as having dysthymia or a major depressive illness when in fact the depression is a normal part of the withdrawal process and will disappear with continuing abstinence.

The issue of whether substance abuse and mental illness are separate entities is related to assumptions regarding the causes of the disorders. Many mental health professionals have tended to view alcoholism and addiction as symptoms of an underlying psychiatric disorder rather than as illnesses in their own right. Consequently, these professionals have focused treatment on the "underlying" psychiatric problem, assuming that the substance abuse behaviors would disappear as the "real" problem was resolved.

Although chronic drug use sometimes causes mental illness by producing biological changes in the individual, that causal connection cannot be assumed. Another perspective regarding the origins of dual disorders is that both the substance abuse and psychiatric disorders may be the result of a third factor that can be biological, psychological, or social in nature. As discussed in Chapter 1, both mental illness and substance abuse disorders currently are seen as biopsychosocial conditions.

Both mental illness and substance abuse disorders vary over a spectrum from mild to severe and overlap with normal behavior. When both are present, the clinician must determine whether the person's problems are caused mainly by the substance abuse, by the psychiatric disorder, or by the interaction of the two.

SYMPTOM INTERACTION

Authorities in the fields of both mental health and substance abuse agree that the combination of the two disorders is more serious than either disorder alone. "The whole problem is greater than the sum of the parts, since the two disorders inevitably exacerbate each other" (Evans & Sullivan, 1990, p. 3) and interact in synergistic ways. For mentally ill individuals, any use of nonprescribed psychoactive drugs, including alcohol, may result in problems in functioning. "Alcohol and drug use places an additional and often overwhelming stress on an already shaky and stress-vulnerable system" (Ryglewicz & Pepper, 1992, p. 278).

INCIDENCE

Substance abuse is the most frequently coexisting disorder among seriously mentally ill persons. Whereas drug dependence is in itself a serious disorder, it frequently occurs in conjunction with, or secondary to, psychiatric disorders such as depression, organic impairment, and schizophrenia.

> Just as it has been recognized that primary substance abuse is frequently associated with other diagnosable psychiatric disorders such as sociopathy or attention deficit disorder . . . , we have also begun to become aware that many other individuals in our society with psychiatric or other problems also suffer, to varying degrees, from substance abuse. These problems may be considered secondary by various specialists or treatment personnel; but nevertheless, they are problems, and what disorder is primary or secondary in a given individual may often be very difficult to determine in a meaningful fashion. . . . Substance abuse is a formidable and frequently overlooked or disregarded problem in the treatment of schizophrenia and . . . also undoubtedly presents difficulties for persons principally undergoing treatment for other labeled disorders. (Alterman, 1985, p. vii)

There is an obvious overlap between the population of persons who are substance abusers and that of persons who experience serious and chronic psychiatric problems. Psychoactive drugs such as crack cocaine, heroin, and amphetamines have become readily available and affordable during recent years, and their usage has increased among the mentally ill as well as among the general population. Most mentally ill individuals have used psychotropic drugs at some points in their lives.

Regier et al. (1990) report that persons diagnosed with mental disorders have three times the risk of substance abuse problems as do those without mental disorders. Persons with schizophrenia and bipolar disorder are especially prone to disorders of alcohol and other drug use (Cuffel, 1996). Drake, Alterman, and Rosenberg (1993) report that the rate of alcohol use disorders among persons with schizophrenia is 10 times greater than that among nonschizophrenic persons. Estimates of the incidence of dually diagnosed patients vary widely. Different research studies suggest that up to 60% of all psychiatric patients also have substance abuse problems (Cohen & Levy, 1992). The estimates are even higher when only young adult mentally ill persons are considered, and in some settings the majority of young adult psychiatric clients have problems with substance use. Gorski (1994) reports that studies of relapse-prone chemical dependency patients show that more than 85% of them have coexisting personalities or mental disorders.

Much of the variance in estimates of the incidence of the coexistence of mental illness and substance abuse is related to the specific diagnostic category of the mental illness reported. Several authorities have observed that the specific mental disorder of the individual drug abuser seems to be related to the type of substance chosen for abuse, and some have suggested that this fact supports a theory of drug abuse as a form of self-medication. More recent research, however, has failed to find such a symptom-substance association (Cuffel, 1996).

Additional factors that may be associated with differences in the proportions of psychiatric diagnoses seen among substance abusers are gender, primary drug of abuse, and socioeconomic status. The lack of standardization of diagnostic procedures and the different mixes of gender and socioeconomic levels make it impossible to draw conclusions about the relative frequencies of different diagnoses among the various substance abuse samples.

A major impediment to gathering valid figures concerning the prevalence of coexisting substance abuse and mental problems is the biases of treatment personnel. Substance abuse personnel tend to interpret symptoms of mental illness as by-products of the drug use. On the other hand, mental health professionals often dismiss substance abuse as only peripherally relevant to mental health treatment. In reality, it often is impossible to determine, in emergency or intake situations, whether the primary cause of aberrant behavior is mental illness, substance abuse, or an interaction of the two.

In spite of the factors discussed heretofore, it is clear that the substance abuse research samples generally have higher proportions in every mental disorder category than do the general community samples. The one diagnostic category that is most dramatically overrepresented among substance abusers is the antisocial personality disorder. Substance abusers have much higher rates of this disorder than do nonusers, regardless of the factors of gender and socioeconomic status (NIDA, 1991).

There seems to be an increase in the dually diagnosed population. It is uncertain whether this is a genuine increase related to heavier drug use (beginning at earlier ages and accompanied by family and socioeconomic problems), heightened awareness and better detection procedures, or both. Younger individuals may be at greater risk for developing multiple disorders compared to individuals born at an earlier time (Read, Penick, & Nickel, 1993). It also has been suggested that the combination of deinstitutionalization and increasing acceptance of drug use has resulted in more persons with mental illness, particularly young persons, being at large in the society where street drugs and alcohol are readily available. Cutler (1993) states that current methods of treating the severely mentally ill strip them of the relative comfort of their hallucinations and delusions and then thrust them into the stark reality of life outside the hospital with minimal social supports. "It isn't surprising that many of them turn to . . . substances that are readily available" (p. 194). Large numbers of homeless, a lack of community services, decreased funding for mental health and drug abuse treatment, the refusal of many specialized programs for the treatment of mental illness or substance abuse to admit dually diagnosed patients, and generally poor coordination of service all contribute to an accumulation of the untreated in the community (Cohen & Levy, 1992).

WHERE TO TREAT

Persons with dual diagnoses are expensive patients to treat in financial, as well as human, terms. They make disproportionate use of medical, legal, and social services (often under emergency conditions) and require substantial administrative and treatment staff time. In addition to the time and resources required for their treatment, dually diagnosed clients are frustrating to treatment staff in traditional mental health or substance abuse programs because they have poor prognoses (Schmidt, 1991). They have extremely high rates of recidivism (Gorski, 1994), create more problems of acting out behavior and poorer medication compliance compared to patients with only one disorder (Drake & Wallach, 1989; O'Hare, 1992), and have more than the usual ability to disrupt staff relations. Standard procedures that are effective with most other clients do not work well with this group.

Treatment issues have been complicated by the rapid changes in funding for health care in general and for behavioral health care in particular. Concern over cost issues has resulted in more stringent restrictions on reliance on inpatient services. Consequently, outpatient treatment has become the most frequently used method, reducing the level of external control over client behaviors and increasing reliance on client motivation. This state of affairs increases the importance of the therapeutic alliance, the development of which may take months or years (Carey, 1996b). This alliance is in part dependent on the auspices of the treatment program, that is, whether it is a mental health program or a substance use treatment program.

Despite the often similar appearances of substance abuse and mental illness, programs for treatment of mental illness and those for treating substance abuse usually are separate. Governments have separate departments for mental health services and for alcohol and drug services. Benefit levels for treatment of the two sets of disorders usually are different, and staff training is separate. Funding for nontraditional programs is scarce.

Achieving a valid diagnostic assessment and developing an appropriate treatment plan are difficult with dually diagnosed clients. Orlin and Davis (1993) developed a Dual Diagnosis Assessment Form, which assists in clarifying the relatedness of the client's psychiatric and substance use disorders.

As a part of assessment, the clinician must determine whether the client will benefit more from services from a mental health facility, a substance abuse program, or a special program for dually diagnosed clients. Often, the diagnosis and treatment are determined by the bias of the professional who sees the client rather than by the client's needs. A dually diagnosed person may be barred from treatment because he or she does not fit into the diagnostic category of a specialized program. "Typically, this client is the dual-problem victim of a single-problem program and receives appropriate attention to one but not both of his or her problems—the psychiatric disorder *or* the substance abuse" (Ryglewicz & Pepper, 1992, p. 78). Mental health staff typically have been inattentive to problems of substance use and abuse. Their assessment of substance use has been limited to determining whether the client uses alcohol or drugs enough to be sent to the substance abuse system for treatment or whether the substance abuse is within the norms of our society.

> Some mental health professionals refuse to treat alcoholics and addicts, even those with a coexisting psychiatric disorder, seeing them as resistant to traditional mental health approaches or as unlikely to benefit from treatment as long as they continue to use substances. If they do treat them, these professionals sometimes tend to focus only on the coexisting psychiatric disorder. (Evans & Sullivan, 1990, p. 6)

Although most dually diagnosed clients, especially those with Axis I diagnoses, are treated exclusively in the mental health system (Carey, 1996a, 1996b), Minkoff (1996) recommends more traditional addiction treatment for those dually diagnosed clients who have substance dependence rather than substance abuse disorders. Several factors have been suggested as contributing to the lack of appropriate response of mental health professionals to such clients. Training for the mental health professions usually does not include significant content regarding the use of or dependency on alcohol or drugs or regarding the assessment or treatment of substance abuse. Mental health treatment programs seldom have formal assessment procedures for substance abuse, and when substance use is recognized, it may be benignly viewed as merely self-medicating and essentially ignored while the psychiatric problems are addressed. Mental health treatment personnel often do not subscribe to the goal of abstinence that might be needed by clients whose illnesses are easily exacerbated by even minor amounts of substance use. Treatment philosophy is likely to be supportive rather than confrontive (Schmidt, 1991). When a serious substance abuse problem is recognized, it may result in a referral to a substance abuse treatment program without psychiatric treatment. If the client is not referred, then sequential treatment of one disorder and then the other may be used rather than concurrent coordinated treatment. Such sequential treatment is likely to be ineffective because of the interactive nature of the two disorders. Sometimes, improvement of one of the disorders through treatment is even associated with the worsening of the other diagnosed problem.

On the other hand, some substance abuse counselors either do not recognize psychiatric disorders in their clients or underestimate the need to treat the psychiatric disorder in dually diagnosed clients. Ryglewicz and Pepper (1992) point out that the problems in this instance parallel those of the mental health system's difficulties in coming to terms with substance-abusing clients. Education for the treatment of substance abuse does not include extensive training in psychopathology. Symptoms of mental illness often are misinterpreted as resistance to treatment or denial of a substance abuse problem. Substance abuse treatment facilities seldom include psychiatric evaluations and differential diagnoses except, perhaps, after the client already has been labeled as treatment resistant or as a treatment failure. Symptoms of severe anxiety or depression sometimes are interpreted as by-products of the substance abuse or abstinence from it. When the client's mental illness causes atypical response to substance abuse treatment, the staff are more likely to refer to a psychiatric program than to modify their substance abuse treatment protocol to better accommodate the dually disordered client. In addition, substance abuse treatment programs seldom are attuned to the need for outreach; in fact, they may rely heavily on the client's persistence in finding service as a sign of the client's readiness for treatment. The dually diagnosed client often requires outreach, individualized treatment, and adaptations of the usual protocol for sustained and successful treatment. The typical program's emphasis on abstinence might cause the personnel to reject the mentally ill client who cannot maintain abstinence because of erratic motivation and difficulty with reality testing, judgment, and goal-directed effort (Ryglewicz & Pepper, 1992). Often, the mentally ill substance abuser needs months or years to achieve abstinence (Drake, 1996). "The motivational, harm reduction, client empowerment approach must continue—step by slow painful step—as the client explores whether absti-nence is important . . . to him" (Minkoff, 1996, p. 309). Programs that insist on total abstinence from all drugs are especially troublesome when the client requires psychotropic medication, which many substance abuse coun-selors view as mood altering and, therefore, undermining to a person's recovery.

In view of the preceding paragraphs, it is apparent that the separation of programs for the treatment of psychiatric disorders and substance abuse, and the lack of cross-trained staff, results in clients emerging from either source of treatment with unmet needs and the experience of failure.

> It is also a "system failure" that reinforces the lack of a perceived con-nection between substance use or abuse and the persistence or worsen-ing of psychiatric symptoms. . . . Failure of the treatment system to respond adequately to the needs of dual-disorder clients has three aspects: (a) limitations within the mental health system, (b) limitations within the substance abuse system, and (c) lack of integration between the two systems. (Ryglewicz & Pepper, 1992, p. 80)

TREATMENT

The significant economic, social service, and health care delivery problems presented by the population with both mental illness and substance abuse problems have resulted in a dramatic increase in the amount and types of clinical treatment offered to these persons. One type of treatment structure has been treatment in psychiatric programs using substance abuse profes-sionals to provide educational or treatment groups as "add-ons" to the men-tal health treatment. This also has led to the addition of urine monitoring and breathalizers to better track the progress of clients with substance abuse problems. Some therapeutic community treatment programs for drug abus-ers have opened up their programs to mentally ill abusers. This has necessi-tated a softening of confrontive techniques and a shift away from the hard-line resistance to the use of psychotropic medicines of many drug treatment programs.

Newer models attempting simultaneous treatment of both disorders are being tried in some settings. These models are based on the similarities of the two disorders: extremes in behavior and impairment of functioning in numerous areas, chronicity and relapse, denial, multifactorial etiology, social isolation, inattention to physical health, negative impact on the family, loss of control, and a sense of helplessness. Another impetus for simultaneous treatment of both disorders is the cyclical nature and interplay of the disorders; each problem exacerbates the other so that progress in the treatment of one disorder is unlikely to be long-lasting without bringing the other illness under control as well. During the past decade, large numbers of both public and private hospitals have opened specialty units for the treatment of mentally ill substance abusers. Elements in the treatment may be drawn from both psychiatric and substance abuse programs, combining individual, group, and family therapy; educational groups for clients and families; and introduction to self-help groups.

Some of the newer integrated programs pull literature and theory from the substance abuse field into mental health treatment settings on behalf of dually diagnosed clients. For example, the usefulness of the stage-wise or readiness for change concept in intervention has been demonstrated (Drake, 1996; Osher & Kofoed, 1989). "Our work documents that dually diagnosed clients are first engaged in treatment, next develop some motivation for pursuing reduction or abstinence, then acquire skills and supports consistent with leading an abstinent lifestyle, and finally work on anticipating and managing crises and relapses" (Drake, 1996, p. 312). Particularly with dually diagnosed persons with severe mental illness, harm reduction approaches (which do not demand a commitment to total abstinence from alcohol and drug use) and intensive case management are proving to be appropriate (Drake, 1996). In addition, Miller and Rollnick's (1991) motivational interviewing has proved to be highly appropriate with dually diagnosed clients (Carey, 1996a; Minkoff, 1996). Later chapters in this book cover the application of these innovative treatment principles.

Psychoeducation is a new approach that has been gaining momentum with dually diagnosed populations. Its nonjudgmental didactic format provides patients with information that they can use to understand and protect themselves (Brody et al., 1996). Its work through the cognitive dimension of the client's functional ability complements psychotherapy's use of the emotional dimension and evokes little resistance. Orlin and Davis (1993) suggest topics for psychoeducational groups: defining mental illness and addiction in terms that clients can understand and accept, theories of etiology, triggers for relapses, symptoms of mental illness and addiction, progression and patterns, family roles and involvement, good drugs and bad drugs, social and political issues in mental illness and addiction, and treatment planning. Psychoeducation provides an opportunity to stress the serious life problems that result from substance use so that clients can see the ways in which their use exacerbates their psychiatric symptoms. This insight enables clients to recognize when symptomatic behavior is beginning to occur so that they can get assistance before complications become too serious.

Some aspects of dually diagnosed clients' mental illness, especially those with schizophrenia, may reduce the effectiveness and appropriateness of traditional self-help groups in the community such as Alcoholics Anonymous and Narcotics Anonymous (Carey, 1996a; Drake, 1996). DiNitto and Webb (1994) report on a psychoeducational group therapy program called Good Chemistry, which teaches clients to make more appropriate use of self-help groups, permits discussion of both mental illness and substance abuse, and reinforces the benefits of maintaining mental stability. This includes following medical recommendations regarding psychotropic medications and staying sober and clean. In addition, some settings are sponsoring groups of Dual Recovery Anonymous, a 12-step organization specifically modified to better meet the needs of persons with dual diagnoses.

RESEARCH

The increased clinical attention to this population is matched by the increase in the number and diversity of research efforts. Empirical research is rapidly replacing clinical observation and anecdotal reports as the main source of information about dually diagnosed persons and their treatment needs (Cuffel, 1996). Systematic research has been facilitated by improvements in diagnostic criteria and by the development of structured diagnostic interviews such as the Diagnostic Interview Schedule, the Psychiatric Diagnostic Interview (revised), the Schedule for Affective Disorders and Schizophrenia, and the Alcohol Research Center Intake Interview (Read et al., 1993). The Addiction Severity Inventory Index scale has been used to identify substance-abusing psychiatric patients and is considered the single best predictor of treatment outcome for substance-abusing populations. In general, patients with the highest levels of psychiatric problems have the poorest outcomes, whereas those with the least severe problems are most likely to improve regardless of the type of treatment they receive (NIDA, 1991).

Further research has explored the effects of the length of time in treatment, comparing the effectiveness of therapeutic community and methadone maintenance programs for substance abusers with various levels of severity of mental illness and other variables. Results seem to indicate that greater length of time in treatment increases the likelihood of positive change in all levels of clients and in both therapeutic communities and methadone maintenance programs, with one notable exception: Severely mentally ill clients worsened over time when treated in the therapeutic community programs. This negative outcome is thought to be related to some of the characteristics of the therapeutic community model: sanction against the use of psychotropic medications, use of paraprofessionals and ex-addicts as counselors, and punitive and embarrassing confrontational group encounters. Although these techniques have proved effective with opiate abusers without serious mental illness, today's high-severity patient often is younger, uses more non-opiate drugs, has few social and personal supports, and is more psychologically fragile (NIDA, 1991; Schmidt, 1991).

These research efforts will enable clinical personnel to make much more sound differential treatment decisions. However, there still is considerable measurement and criterion variability, and this remains a focus of ongoing research and reviews by professional standards committees.

There still is much to be done in researching dually diagnosed clients and their treatment. Scientifically validated knowledge about dually disordered individuals still is very limited. "This paucity is particularly true about the natural long-term course of these disorders and which kinds of treatments are more effective for which diagnosed conditions" (Read et al., 1993, p. 123). Both basic research and outcome studies can contribute greatly to this field.

> Program evaluation and outcome research are always complicated endeavors, and perhaps especially so when the presenting problems are multifaceted. Participating staff believe in what they do and frequently hear informal accounts of their former clients' successes. However, observation, anecdotes, and intuition are not adequate substitutes for organized empirical studies, and systematic collection of history, intake, and follow-up data has now begun. . . . Relevant criteria of success include frequency and duration of psychiatric hospitalizations and chemical dependency treatments; quality and length of abstinence; general medical care utilization; occupational functioning; financial independence; legal conflicts; satisfaction in interpersonal relationships; self-esteem; and personal and social responsibility. (Harrison, Martin, Tuason, & Hoffmann, 1985, p. 389)

The combination of the growth of awareness of the dually diagnosed population and the continuing difficulty in finding appropriate and effective services for these persons has resulted in the development of advocacy groups such as Addiction Intervention With the Disabled and the Institute on Alcohol, Drugs, and Disabilities. These groups are pressing for substance abuse treatment adapted or designed specifically for multidisabled clients (DiNitto & Webb, 1994).

RECOMMENDATIONS

In spite of rapid progress in the field, surprisingly little is known about how most effectively to treat dually diagnosed individuals. The statement of Evans and Sullivan (1990) a decade ago still is apt:

> Debate still exists about the best approach for counseling the chemically abusing or dependent individual and, in some cases, persons with certain psychiatric disorders. Dually diagnosed individuals can intensify this debate. . . . The available literature and research, although beginning to grow, are still limited. (p. xii)

Although it often has been observed that dually disordered clients are likely to be disruptive to the standard operations of either substance abuse or psychiatric treatment programs, DiNitto and Webb (1994) point out that detoxification in psychiatric hospitals seems preferable in most cases. This is because dually disordered clients may present special management problems in community-based detoxification programs. This general recommendation, however, is subject to change based on many factors.

The professional literature clearly shows that the population having coexisting and interdependent problems with substance abuse and mental illness is a diverse one. Often, this diversity is not recognized when programming decisions are made or when a specific client is being referred for treatment. A single uniform model appropriate for all dually disordered clients is not feasible.

> What is needed . . . is a systematic analysis that will help clinicians to complete a differential assessment, determine the appropriate level of care, design a general holistic treatment plan that will support the management of common or overlapping symptoms, and develop a disorder-specific treatment plan that will address the unique symptoms of each disorder. (Gorski, 1994, p. 51)

We believe that this book is a step toward meeting that need.

CONCLUSION

Much of the literature gives a perhaps negatively biased view of treatment of dually disordered persons. Cohen and Levy (1992) put a positive spin on the process: "Dealing with mentally ill chemical abusers is always a story about human renewal. It is also about pluck, innovation, counterculture, outrageousness, and belief in the human spirit" (p. 11). What more could a therapist want?

Harrison et al. (1985) state,

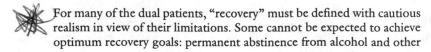

> For many of the dual patients, "recovery" must be defined with cautious realism in view of their limitations. Some cannot be expected to achieve optimum recovery goals: permanent abstinence from alcohol and other

drugs, a future free of psychiatric hospitalization, a return to the workforce, and stable interpersonal relationships. Rather, recovery for some patients must be measured in terms of less frequent and less destructive encounters with chemicals, increased intervals of abstinence and satisfying sobriety, compliance with medication maintenance and fewer hospitalizations, less injurious behavior, and increased social responsibility and self-esteem. (p. 372)

There are several policy issues that need resolution if mental health services to substance abusers are to be effective. First, the artificial boundary between mental health and substance abuse services must be breached or eliminated entirely. The connection between substance abuse and mental status is apparent to all who work in the field. Policies against crossover services (e.g., mental health agencies that refuse service to substance abusers, funding channels that withhold funds for such services) are unethical and should be challenged legally. "Stricken by the disease of chemical dependency and suffering from a psychiatric disorder, the dually diagnosed individual is not well armed to deal with systems' conflicts" (Evans & Sullivan, 1990, p. 10). Some beginnings are being made in bringing the two services together. Some state mental health agencies now are employing persons with expertise in substance abuse treatment to help them serve the dually disordered population more effectively.

Unfortunately, the current crisis over managed care and problems with high costs to insurance companies creates a climate in which there seems to be some effort to cut costs by excluding groups of persons who need service. This leaves the dually disordered client vulnerable to exclusion, although rationally, the client with mental illness and substance abuse problems should be eligible for both services rather than neither.

But in the best of worlds, special expertise and special services and facilities would be available specifically for the dually disordered client. These services would be staffed by persons with dual training (i.e., expertise in mental health and substance abuse treatment). Such training would break down much of the distrust (and even contempt) that some professionals in the two fields show for each other. This has implications for professional training programs because, at the present time, there is little cross-training in any of the helping professions. Special facilities must not be discriminated against in licensing or third-party payments (O'Hare, 1992; Schmidt, 1991).

A framework for continued research and program development is needed. Research funding should be a high priority. The present time is one of extensive experimentation with different models of service to persons with coexisting mental illness and substance abuse problems. A national research agenda that can set a framework for state, local, and private efforts could go far in correcting and clarifying the mass of contradictory and, for the most part, pessimistic perspectives on this needy population.

▌ QUESTIONS FOR DISCUSSION

1. Are there terms that can be used to identify persons with coexisting mental illness and substance abuse problems that are less pejorative than those currently in use?

2. Discuss ways in which membership in a minority or an ethnic cultural group may further complicate the identification and treatment of dually disordered individuals.

3. In what situations would it seem to be preferable that detoxification services be provided in a community setting rather than an institutional setting?

4. How would you prioritize research goals for the next decade regarding issues of dual diagnosis?

5. Are there social justice issues in the current system of service delivery to dually diagnosed clients? Identify and discuss them.

Assessment and Differential Diagnosis of Dual Disorders

3

This chapter examines assessment issues for treatment providers of dually disordered clients. In the ideal setting, treatment providers should be members of a professional team of psychiatrists, nurses, social workers, psychologists, and rehabilitation specialists. Each member of the team establishes a genuine helping relationship with clients, collects data relative to his or her expertise vis-à-vis the client's strengths and barriers to achieving them, and organizes the information into a meaningful written evaluation of the client's status. All of the multidisciplinary evaluations are integrated into a comprehensive assessment. However, many treatment providers (e.g., those in rural settings) are responsible for collecting all of the data, evaluating the data, and writing assessments without the benefit of other disciplines' expertise. The purpose of this chapter is to familiarize members of treatment teams and individual treatment providers with terminology and cross-disciplinary explanations of signs and symptoms so as to perform competent and comprehensive assessments of dually disordered clients.

Diagnosis is a specialized form of assessment that "focuses on symptoms and assigns persons to categories" (Rauch, 1993, p. xiv). Decisions about diagnoses of mental disabilities and substance-related disorders are based on standards set forth in the *Diagnostic and Statistical Manual of Mental Disorders* (*DSM-IV*) (American Psychiatric Association [APA], 1994). Although diagnoses are primarily performed by medically trained physicians, other treatment team members and treatment providers without medical backgrounds must be familiar with the terminology and concepts of diagnosis to effectively serve their clients and, in some cases, to assign diagnoses. The first part of this chapter is devoted to the *DSM-IV* multiaxial system for understanding clients' symptom profiles. We also strongly believe that assessments of dually disordered clients must draw on the expertise of both mental health and chemical dependency knowledge bases. Therefore, the second half of the chapter presents a psychiatric rehabilitation assessment strategy often seen in mental health settings and a readiness for change model commonly applied to addictions and dual diagnosis treatment settings. A case example is given to depict an example of a dually disordered client—underdiagnosed—who relapsed without an accurate diagnosis, rehabilitation strategy assessment, and readiness for change assessment.

BACKGROUND

Descriptions of persons with coexisting mental illness and substance use or abuse have appeared in the literature since the early 1970s (Lara, Ferro, & Klein, 1997). Who are these clients? Some terms used in the literature include a mentally ill chemical abuser (MICA) client, a substance-abusing mentally ill (SAMI) client, and a dually diagnosed client. Professionals in mental health and chemical dependency settings may use words such as *manipulative* and *borderline* to describe the most difficult clients in their caseloads. Ryglewicz and Pepper (1992), however, suggest that the term *dual disorder* most appropriately emphasizes the variety of clients who fall into this population. They identify four subtypes:

1. Persons with a primary mental illness with episodic psychoses without the use of substances

2. Persons with psychiatric disorders other than brain disorders such as severely impaired personality disordered clients who become psychotic only when using substances

3. Persons with primary substance abuse or dependence and personality immaturity and dysfunction

4. Persons with primary substance abuse or dependence who have problem symptoms after withdrawal (p. 277)

UNIQUE DIAGNOSIS
AND ASSESSMENT ISSUES

A major problem in diagnosis and assessment of dually disordered clients is that a primary diagnosis often is unclear, particularly within the current managed care environment of rushed evaluation and referral for treatment. Clients with dual disorders have multiple diagnoses and problems (Lehman, 1996). A transtheoretical approach to assessment avoids the problem of relying on a single clear definition of the problem that might not exist (Kirst-Ashman & Hull, 1997). In theory-free interdisciplinary assessments, treatment professionals should address both psychiatric and chemical dependency issues simultaneously. Acute crisis management always should be available; however, this chapter emphasizes the need for a comprehensive interdisciplinary assessment after detoxification or withdrawal from substances or after a psychological crisis with potential for violence has passed. In later chapters on specific disorders, we address both short-term crisis assessment and long-term assessments.

Dual disorders present complex management challenges for both clients and treatment providers. The following four dimensions bring together rehabilitation and relapse prevention strategies:

1. Differential diagnosis as a critical element of meaningful assessment

2. A biopsychosocial grid for assisting in accurate diagnoses

3. A rehabilitation assessment focusing on client strengths as well as needs

4. Assessment of readiness for change as an important strategy for relapse prevention

The multidisciplinary treatment team or individual treatment provider is responsible for integrating each of these dimensions into an interdisciplinary assessment. The following case example provides an illustration of a dually disordered client who relapsed following decreased functioning in multiple areas of her life.

CASE EXAMPLE

Merrill, an attractive 22-year-old African American college student, had a sudden change in behaviors during the middle of her senior year. She went to class ill groomed, began laughing inappropriately during lectures, and at times stared vacantly out the window. Her class attendance dropped, and when seen by friends outside of class, she seemed unaware of their reactions to her strange behaviors. After 2 weeks of the onset of these symptoms, Merrill required hospitalization for dangerous delusional behaviors, deterioration in self-care, and inability to manage day-to-day living needs.

Following discharge from the hospital, Merrill revealed that her deterioration in functioning occurred around the time she had shared some pills with a roommate. She reported that she had experimented with friends' prescribed and recreational drugs in an attempt to deal with the stress of midterms. She also quit taking her own prescribed medication. Professionals, friends, and family members spent months in support of Merrill's return to her previous level of functioning. What information could have been helpful to prevent this relapse? Why did she and her support network fail to consider substance use as a cause of her symptoms? Does she have a substance-related disorder, or did the substance use or abuse precipitate a psychiatric crisis related to a major mental illness or personality disorder?

DIFFERENTIAL DIAGNOSIS

Although many combinations of mental and substance abuse disorders are possible, the most common subtypes seen in mental health and chemical dependency treatment programs come from the following *DSM-IV* classifications:

1. *Axis I disorders:* psychotic disorders, mood disorders, and anxiety disorders co-occurring with substance-related disorders

2. *Axis II disorders:* personality disorders seen in combination with Axis I substance-related disorders

3. *Axis III disorders:* medical conditions that mimic or precipitate mental disorders on Axis I or II

4. *Axis IV:* psychosocial and environment problems co-occurring with substance-related problems such as cocaine dependence with incarceration and unemployment or alcohol dependence with problems such as threat of job loss, pending divorce, and living alone (Ryglewicz & Pepper, 1992)

Each axis of the multiaxial *DSM-IV* diagnostic classification system (APA, 1994) provides a source of information about unique client characteristics, behaviors, physical conditions, and psychosocial issues affecting clients' ability to function effectively in their environments. The following is an overview of each axis with an emphasis on differential diagnoses of major mental illnesses, primary substance-related disorders, personality disorders, and medical conditions. In a brief review of Axis IV and Axis V, psychosocial and environmental problems are listed and the Global Assessment of Functioning is introduced.

Axis I Clinical Disorders

Psychotic disorders, mood disorders, and anxiety disorders are the Axis I disorders often seen to co-occur with substance-related disorders. These disorders are serious mental illnesses and are the focus of the treatment provider's plan of action.

Psychotic Disorders

The psychotic disorders are schizophrenia, schizophreniform disorder, schizoaffective disorder, delusional disorder, and brief reactive psychosis (APA, 1994). "In *Psychotic Disorder Due to a Medical Condition and in Substance-Induced Psychotic Disorder,* 'psychotic' refers to delusions or only those hallucinations that are not accompanied by insight" (APA, 1994, p. 273, italics in original). Thought disturbances, hallucinations, bizarre behaviors, and general deterioration represent a common profile of symptoms seen in persons with psychotic disorders. Because these symptoms are stereotypical of mental deterioration, clients usually are referred to mental health treatment settings. However, many mental health professionals underdiagnose co-occurring alcohol and other drug use (Woody, 1996). This is what happened to Merrill, who was a client in a local mental health center. Merrill reported that she was having problems, but her physician blamed her deterioration on her failure to take an antipsychotic medication as prescribed. The physician and other members of the treatment team did not probe to determine whether Merrill had been using any other substances. This placed Merrill at high risk of medical complications, psychological risks of suicidal and violent behaviors, and social risks such as homelessness and victimization.

What issues are critical when psychoses are substance induced and not related to a psychotic disorder? For example, "vivid auditory, visual, and tactile hallucinations are plausible side effects of a 5-day, high-dose cocaine binge" (Ries, 1994, p. 76). A major consideration is to know the type and amount of drug consumed. With stimulants, psychoses are unusual unless used in high doses coupled with deprivation of food, sleep, or other environmental stressors. On the other hand, sedative and hypnotic withdrawal often causes hallucinations and delusions. Similarly, hallucinogens often arouse delusions and mood disturbances, but clients usually are aware that they are under the influence of drug-induced disturbances (Ries, 1994).

Many clients who have been homeless or who have been in other health-endangering environments have symptoms that look like psychotic disorders but are caused by neurological dysfunction such as brain hemorrhage, central nervous system infections, pneumonia, AIDS-related issues, diabetes, or hyperthyroidism. Dually disordered clients such as Merrill need more intensive medical evaluation than do clients with single mental disorders. High-risk clients with acute symptoms need to have immediate access to medical assessments.

Mood Disorders

The mood disorders are major depression, dysthymia, bipolar disorder, cyclothymia, mood disorder due to a general medical condition, and substance-induced mood disorder (APA, 1994). Symptoms of mood disorders are characterized by extreme disturbances in emotions accompanied by physiological changes. Clients may be overly agitated or overly depressed or may experience both extremes at different periods of time. Related physiological changes often affect sleep, energy, food intake, and ability to concentrate. Among alcohol and drug abuse clients, mood disorders and anxiety disorders are more prevalent than co-occurring psychotic disorders. They are seen most often with methadone and heroin drug users (Regier et al., 1990).

Clients in addiction treatment settings might not be diagnosed with mood disorders. One reason is that diagnosis is complicated by drug impairment that mimics depressive symptoms. Another reason is that professionals in chemical dependency treatment settings often are untrained in clinical diagnoses of mental illnesses.

Intoxication, chronic use, and withdrawal from substances all may precipitate symptoms that appear the same as those of a major mood disorder. For example, with sedative intoxication, persons may experience acute episodes of depression from a few hours to a few days. With chronic use, episodes may last weeks or months. During withdrawal, emotional states can intensify, causing suicide ideation and suicide attempts (Ries, 1994).

Time is the most critical ally in determining whether changes in mood are primarily related to substances or to a mental disorder. However, in many treatment settings, providers have limited time before they must determine the most appropriate referral agency based on the presenting problem. Therefore, it is essential that the initial screening include questions related both to substance use and to history of symptoms related to mood disorders (Lehman, 1996). In the long term, if symptoms of depression still appear intense after 1 month of detoxification, then a depressive episode might be the most likely diagnosis (APA, 1994).

Mood disturbances may indicate serious medical conditions such as malnutrition, anemia, hyper- and hypothyroidism, dementia, brain disease, lupus, HIV/AIDS, postcardiac condition, stroke, and medication-induced depression or mania. Changes in mood also may be related to medications for hypertension, hypotension, diet pills, and some neuroleptics. Lehman (1996) urges professionals to use brief questionnaires such as the National Health Interview Survey (National Center for Health Statistics, 1991), a checklist of diseases and symptoms, to help rule out medical problems.

The population of clients with coexisting major depression and substance use presents an enormous risk for successful suicide attempts. Scales such as Littrell's (1998) Assessment of Lethality in Suicidal Persons are valuable tools for nurses, social workers, physicians, and other staff who assess high-risk clients. All professional staff should be familiar with crisis intervention techniques and services.

Anxiety Disorders

The anxiety disorders include panic disorder (with or without agoraphobia), agoraphobia without history of panic disorder, specific phobia, social phobia, obsessive-compulsive disorder, posttraumatic stress disorder, acute stress disorder, generalized anxiety disorder, anxiety due to a medical condition, and substance-induced anxiety disorder (APA, 1994). To qualify as an anxiety disorder, symptoms must be other than the normal fearful reactions that are appropriate in the face of danger. Extreme nervousness, tension, fear of dying or losing one's mind, and accompanying physiological signs such as shortness of breath, sweating, and elevated blood pressure are some of the symptoms of anxiety disorders.

Ross, Glaser, and Germanson's (1988) study of 501 patients entering addiction treatment reports that anxiety disorders are prevalent among more than 60% of persons treated in addiction centers. In chemical dependency programs, these persons often present to clinicians as junkies, potheads, and related negative stereotypes dismissed by professionals as treatment resistant. If not in addiction settings, they seldom receive health or mental health care. This population includes those from slums, those from correctional facilities, and the working poor (Hudson, 1990). The Epidemiological Catchment Area studies (Regier et al., 1990) further indicate that women, persons under 45 years of age, those separated or divorced, and persons from lower socioeconomic groups have higher rates of anxiety disorders than do other individuals.

According to Hudson (1990), persons with anxiety disorders self-medicate with alcohol and drugs to overcome extreme fright, literally the fright of death itself. On the other hand, there is substantial evidence that anxiety disorders are induced or exacerbated by the use of alcohol and drugs (Anthenelli & Schuckit, 1993). Addiction treatment providers are familiar with the painful anxiety symptoms associated with withdrawal, particularly from depressants, opioids, and stimulants. However, these symptoms may be misdiagnosed by mental health treatment providers and other professionals who have not worked with clients in withdrawal.

Because anxiety is so common among clients in addiction centers, it is possible to discount symptoms that can be life threatening. Clients who appear to be having problems with their environments (APA, 1994) may be undergoing withdrawal, and this can be extremely dangerous. For example, withdrawal from benzodiazepines can cause seizures. Other medical problems that treatment providers should have medically assessed are heart and respiratory conditions, neurological problems, and HIV/AIDS-related conditions.

Another serious danger of anxiety symptoms, especially when seen with accompanying depression, is suicide. As when working with mood disordered clients, it is critical for staff working with anxiety disordered clients to be familiar with assessment of suicide risk and with involuntary and voluntary crisis intervention.

Substance-Related Disorders

The substance-related disorders include disorders related to the taking of a drug of abuse (including alcohol), to the side effects of a medication, and to toxin exposure. . . . Drugs of abuse are grouped into 11 classes: alcohol, amphetamines, caffeine, cannabis, cocaine, hallucinogens, inhalants, nicotine, opioids, phencyclidine (PCP), and sedatives, hypnotics, or anxiolytics. Over-the-counter medications, prescribed medications, and poisonous substances, gases, etc. can also cause the symptoms associated with substance-related disorders. (APA, 1994, p. 175)

The symptoms are cognitive, behavioral, and physiological (APA, 1994). For example, a stereotypical profile of an alcohol-related disorder is irrationality, slurred speech, and incoordination. However, persons who exhibit these symptoms are not necessarily addicted, and addicts do not always have impaired functioning. To clarify differences, the authors of the *DSM-IV* (APA, 1994) divided substance-related disorders into two groups: substance use disorders (dependence and abuse) and substance-induced disorders (intoxication, withdrawal, delirium, dementia, amnestic, psychotic, mood disordered, anxiety disordered, sexual dysfunction, and sleep disordered).

Gorski (1994) insists that "psychosocial therapies will fail as long as chemically dependent patients keep damaging their brains by putting alcohol and drugs into their bodies" (p. 50). Regardless of the primacy of a diagnosis on Axis I, mental disorder or substance-related disorder, he proposes that effective treatment cannot begin until the brain is free of alcohol and drugs. Others who work specifically with mentally ill substance abusers argue that extra tolerance is needed for clients with "double trouble" (McBride, 1988). Abstinence is not the primary goal of assessment and treatment for persons with severe and persistent mental illness who also have a substance-related disorder. Sciacca (1987) describes initiatives in which progress is defined by how much insight clients have into their problems, particularly how alcohol and drugs affect their mental illness. Alcohol and drug-screening tools that encourage clients to answer questions about their drug-taking behaviors include the Short Michigan Alcoholism Screening Test (Selzer, Vinokur, & Van Rooijen, 1975), the Drug Abuse Screening Test (Skinner, 1984), and the Addiction Severity Index (McLellan,

Luborsky, Woody, & O'Brien, 1980), among others. Appleby, Dyson, Altman, McGovern, and Luchins (1996) examine the reliability and validity of the Chemical Use, Abuse, and Dependence Scale (CUAD) (McGovern & Morrison, 1992). Appleby et al. (1996) report that the CUAD reliably identified substance abusers from nonabusers among psychiatric clients.

Some professionals are concerned about the honesty of their clients' answers to questions on these instruments. Early research designed to determine the reliability and validity of clients' self-reports suggested that professionals can have confidence in their clients' answers when they are detoxified, rapport has been established with the interviewers, the questions are clear, and the clients know that confidentiality will be upheld (Skinner, 1984). In addition, it always is important to corroborate information with family and friends.

Axis II Personality Disorders

The personality disorders are paranoid, schizoid, schizotypal, antisocial borderline, histrionic, narcissistic, avoidant, dependent, obsessive-compulsive, and not otherwise specified (meets the general criteria with no criteria for a specific disorder or meets the general criteria with a disorder that is not in the classification such as passive-aggressive) (APA, 1994).

The *DSM-IV* (APA, 1994) groups the personality disorders into three clusters:

1. *Cluster A:* persons who appear odd or eccentric and include the paranoid, schizoid, and schizotypal personality disorders

2. *Cluster B:* persons who appear dramatic, emotional, or erratic and include the antisocial, borderline, histrionic, and narcissistic personality disorders

3. *Cluster C:* persons who often appear anxious or fearful and include the avoidant, dependent, and obsessive-compulsive personality disorders

The clusters represent patterns that persons display in the ways in which they think about themselves and interact with the world. However, all persons have set patterns of behaviors.

> The essential feature of a personality disorder is an enduring pattern of inner experience and behavior that deviates markedly from the expectations of the individual's culture and is manifested in at least two of the following areas: interpersonal functioning or impulse control. (APA, 1994, p. 630)

Axis III Medical Problems
(which can precipitate or mimic mental disorders)

Axis III provides treatment providers a reminder that medical conditions must be ruled out prior to making judgments about mental illness or substance use and abuse. Some conditions that may be confused with psychotic disorders are neurological disorders, infections of the central nervous system, pneumonia, AIDS-related complications, and endocrine disorders such as diabetes and hyperthyroidism. Warnings of serious immediate medical emergencies are "acute confusion, disorientation, or memory impairment; unusual visual, olfactory, or tactile hallucinations; and signs of physical illness (such as fever, marked weight loss, or slurred speech)" (Ries, 1994, p. 79).

Mood disorders, particularly in the elderly, often signal a serious medical condition that requires a thorough medical assessment. Some of the conditions that cause depression or mania are malnutrition, anemia, hyper- and hypothyroidism, dementia, brain disease, lupus, HIV/AIDS-related problems, postcardiac condition, and stroke.

Clients with anxiety disorders often believe that they have serious medical conditions. Because their fear is a hallmark of their anxiety disorders, professionals might overlook medical conditions while focusing on psychological issues. Medical problems that may create anxiety symptoms are those affecting the cardiovascular and respiratory systems, hematological and immunological disorders, and endocrine dysfunction. Disease states also can create symptoms of generalized anxiety or panic. They include acute cardiac disorders, cardiac arrhythmia, hyperthyroid conditions, brain disease, and HIV infection and AIDS (Ries, 1994).

Axis IV Psychosocial and Environmental Problems

Persons with dual disorders are vulnerable to relapse when their social worlds and physical environments are not stable. Axis IV from the *DSM-IV* (APA, 1994) provides treatment providers with prompts regarding problem areas in clients' external worlds. The problems grouped into categories are as follows:

Problems with primary support group

Problems related to the social environment

Educational problems

Occupational problems

Housing problems

Economic problems

Problems with access to health care services

Problems related to interaction with the legal system or crime

Other psychological and environmental problems (pp. 29-30)

Axis V Global Assessment of Functioning

In most clients with dual disorders, the overall level of functioning with regard to psychological, social, and occupational functioning is severely impaired. Axis V provides ratings of clients' current functional status where 0 is inadequate information and 100 is superior functioning in a wide range of activities. Clients who score below 50 on the 0-100 scale are at high risk of additional deterioration without psychosocial interventions (APA, 1994).

Despite the helpfulness of the multiaxial diagnostic system, many problems in differential diagnosis are due to the overlapping symptoms of subtypes of dual disorders. Furthermore, differences in clinical training among staff working primarily in substance abuse programs or primarily in mental health programs interfere with accurate diagnoses. The following biopsychosocial assessment grid proposed by Gorski (1994) uses a symptom grid to help clarify diagnoses.

BIOPSYCHOSOCIAL ASSESSMENT

The goal of Gorski's (1994) biopsychosocial grid (Table 3.1) is to prevent relapse caused by underdiagnosis, misdiagnosis, and overdiagnosis. For example, in the case example, Merrill's labile mood, inappropriate behaviors, and breakdown of daily living skills could typify either symptoms of disorganization seen in persons with schizophrenia, symptoms of bipolar illness, or deterioration associated with chronic use of substances. Her symptoms also could be related to an enduring personality pattern in which typical coping skills no longer are effective in the face of stress. Gorski provided a grid to help delineate chemical dependency, mental disorders, and personality disorders based on physical symptoms, psychological symptoms, and social symptoms.

In Merrill's case, misdiagnosis through failure to confront substance use could have been avoided using Gorski's (1994) grid to determine symptoms related to substance use. Pepper and Ryglewicz's (1984) warning during the 1980s still is valid today: "We can no longer use an assessment of

TABLE 3.1 Diagram: General Reasoning Structure of the Biopsychosocial Assessment Grid for Dual Disorders

Disorder	Chemical Dependency	Mental Disorder	Personality or Style
Physical symptoms	What are the physical symptoms of chemical dependency?	What are the physical symptoms of the primary mental disorder?	What are the physical symptoms of the personality style or discord?
Psychological symptoms	What are the psychological symptoms of chemical dependency?	What are the psychological symptoms of the primary mental disorder?	What are the psychological symptoms of the primary style or discord?
Social symptoms	What are the social symptoms of chemical dependency?	What are the social symptoms of the primary mental disorder?	What are the social symptoms of the primary personality style or discord?

SOURCE: Gorski, T. T. (1994). A suggestion for conceptualizing dual diagnosis: A systematic analysis to help cut through the confusion and mismanagement. *Behavioral Health Management, 14,* 50-53.

whether a patient is significantly affected by alcohol or drug use on our usual standards for 'moderate' or 'excessive' use" (p. 155).

For clients who already have fragile brains, any nonprescribed drug use is too much. Rigorous evaluations designed to distinguish between substance use and substance abuse should not be the focus of assessment of mentally ill chemical abusers (Pepper & Ryglewicz, 1984).

What is an effective focus for providers of treatment for persons with mental illness and substance-related disorders? Assessment instruments are being drawn from rehabilitation strategies such as those used with the severely disabled who have had strokes, head injuries, and the like. These strategies focus on assessing client functioning rather than on client pathology. Scales evaluate clients' daily living activities such as self-care, mobility, and work behaviors. Some models include outcome measures such as clients' self-assessments of health and quality of life.

PSYCHIATRIC REHABILITATION ASSESSMENT STRATEGIES

The emphasis of psychiatric rehabilitation strategies is on client strengths rather than disabilities and on skill training rather than curing the illness. This does not negate the advances in treatment, particularly in psychopharmacology. However, proponents of rehabilitation argue that psychosocial deficits, and not mental illness itself, maintain clients in sick roles where substance use plays a large part. Rehabilitation should be part of the overall strategy of treating these persons and their illness.

Assessments used in rehabilitation models often are called functional assessments because they measure specific abilities to perform socially with family and friends, as members of the community, in workplaces, and at home as independent adults. Patrick and Bergner (1990) developed an assessment for persons with chronic illnesses based on domains related to health quality of life indicators: opportunity, health perceptions, functional status, and impairment. Within this model, treatment providers focus on the clients' strengths as well as on their needs. The following assessment questions are adapted from this model for inclusion on a functional assessment:

1. What strengths does your client have for withstanding stress? Are there needs that could add to the client's skills in coping?

2. How has your client's illness affected relationships with family and friends?

3. On a scale of 1 to 10, how often does your client worry about having an illness?

4. Describe your client's job competencies.

5. What are the biggest barriers your client has to being a competent employee?

6. What activities or behaviors does your client use that positively engage other persons?

7. Are there behaviors or activities that offend friends, family, or others close to your client?

8. What has been your client's most successful role (e.g., employee, student, family member)?

9. What has been your client's least successful role?

10. What (or who) are your client's strongest sources of community support?

11. Check your client's skills in the following areas:

    ◆ Drives a car

    ◆ Knows how to use public transportation

    ◆ Cares for own physical needs at home including eating well, bathing, and grooming

    ◆ Manages own finances successfully

    ◆ Assumes responsibility for taking prescribed medications

      ➤ Protects self from victimization or high-risk behaviors

      ➤ Reads and writes well enough to communicate effectively

12. For each of the preceding abilities, list limitations of or barriers to skill achievement.

Patrick and Bergner (1990) probe for social, psychological, and physical aspects of client functioning. They also review the domain of impairment, both objective and subjective measures of clients' medical status. Measures are self-report, physical examination, laboratory and other diagnostic tests, and longevity.

If Merrill had been administered a functional assessment at the time she saw her psychiatrist, she might have reported problem areas in her life such as the stress of taking midterms and even the fact that she shared Quaalude with a friend. In addition, laboratory tests might have detected changes in blood levels due to substances other than her prescribed medication.

Sex, ethnicity and race, and socioeconomic status are critical assessment variables that give treatment providers clues regarding environmental problems in clients' lives. For example, women with dual diagnoses, such as Merrill, might have backgrounds of sexual victimization and poverty (Alexander, 1996). Both substance use and presentation of their mental illness might be linked to female issues of coping with untenable traumatic experiences. African American women have the added complexity of living in an American culture with expectations for persons to conform to a white middle class standard of behaviors.

A holistic assessment is essential for dually disordered clients with a multitude of complex overlapping biopsychosocial issues. Rapp, Shera, and Kisthardt (1993) also suggest that data on clients need to come from clients themselves whenever possible. Rehabilitation instruments need to be relative to client perspectives including clients' self-evaluations, which seem to have been lost in many assessment strategies.

Summary of Assessment Tools

     ◆ Client self-evaluation

     ◆ Laboratory tests

     ◆ History of past and recent sexual trauma

     ◆ Cultural issues related to race and ethnicity

     ◆ Gender-related problems

     ◆ Functional assessment

These strategies, often used in mental health settings, are not successful without assessing and treating clients simultaneously for substance use. The following relapse prevention approach is based on current progress regarding clients' motivation to change.

Readiness and Motivation for Change

What makes clients want to improve the quality of their lives? Psychiatric rehabilitation goals suggest that giving persons mastery over their own "internal drives, their symptoms, and the demands of their environments" is motivating (Lamb, 1994, p. 1016). Prochaska, DiClemente, and Norcross (1992) agree. In their proposed transtheoretical model of change, they suggest that habit changes occur across five vacillating stages that treatment providers must address so as to apply appropriate interventions at the times when clients are most receptive. The five stages are (a) precontemplation (known as denial or extreme resistance to change), (b) contemplation (when cognitive dissonance may occur between wanting to continue old behaviors and wanting to change), (c) preparation to change (when small changes may be attempted but with no clear goals for the future), (d) action (when deliberate goals to change habits are made), and (e) maintenance (when progress has been significant but triggers still are strong to return to old habits).

Osher and Kofoed (1989) developed a similar stage-wise approach for dually disordered clients in the process of recovery. The stages—engagement, persuasion, active treatment, and relapse prevention—emphasize the need for treatment goals to match clients' motivation to change.

In both models, the basis of readiness for change during the first stage, precontemplation or engagement, resides in the helping relationship with treatment providers. If clients believe that they are being coerced, or if providers are not genuinely committed to their clients' progress, then clients may terminate before intervention begins. Prochaska and DiClemente (1986) suggest, "If clients believe the therapist cannot identify with them because the therapist is of the wrong gender, ethnic background, social class, or sexual orientation, then clients will not feel free in therapy" (p. 22). Freedom is the first step in moving clients from the precontemplation stage to the contemplation stage of readiness for change. With freedom comes the willingness to hear and process information. Osher and Kofoed (1989) do not recommend confronting substance use at this time. A focus on current symptoms is the level where Prochaska et al. (1992) prefer to begin because it starts at the level of clients' perceptions of the presenting problem.

Propelling clients from denial of problems into contemplation of change or persuasion might not be related to the interventions applied as much as to the developmental or environmental changes naturally occurring in persons' lives. For example, middle-aged clients facing issues of aging and the consequences of their negative behaviors may be more open to contemplating change than would 20-year-olds. External circumstances, such as divorce and the death of a spouse, also may move persons toward desiring change. How can treatment providers help? Cognitive approaches vary with the individual client and the nature of his or her mental illness. For example, most mental health professionals believe that clients with schizophrenia have cognitive dysfunctions that prohibit deep probing and historical insights. On the other hand, the preferred treatment for mood disorders and some anxiety disorders is based on cognitive restructuring of irrational beliefs and thoughts about the self and the world.

Feelings of competence and self-efficacy can be used to help most psychiatric clients prepare to take action. Prochaska and DiClemente (1986) suggest value clarification techniques, which ask clients what types of persons they want to become. "When it comes to action, skill acquisition and utilization are most important for therapeutic progress" (p. 23). For clients with schizophrenia, this is the time to engage them in social skills training groups that use structured role-plays, skill rehearsals, and related behavioral interventions. For other clients such as those with anxiety disorders, the action stage is the time to focus on communication skills enhancement so as to strengthen interpersonal relationships.

To maintain sobriety and control over a mental illness is an enormous challenge for both clients and treatment providers. In the past, families have not been included as major supporters and members of the treatment team effort. During the maintenance or relapse prevention phase, clients need family, friends, and the community to provide a maximum impact strategy, Prochaska et al.'s (1992) basic strategy across all levels of change. At this time, family psychoeducation is especially helpful for clients with severe and persistent mental illness such as schizophrenia. Some clients without family and social supports need to have their environmental situations reevaluated (e.g., appropriate housing with social supports, clinical supports, availability of drug-free leisure time activities).

Rollnick, Heather, Gold, and Hall (1992) developed a readiness for change questionnaire to help clients and treatment providers identify starting points for self-change and treatment-directed change. The Substance Abuse Treatment Scale (McHugo, Drake, Burton, & Ackerson, 1995) is a scale for persons with severe mental illness assessing progress in recovering from substance abuse while in treatment, based on the model of recovery developed by Osher and Kofoed (1989). Subsequent chapters in this book, which address specific mental disorders, also have supportive literature such as the Motivation-Based Treatment model for applying readiness for change to the population of clients with schizophrenia and alcohol or drug dependencies. In other chapters, the readiness for change model has not been clinically tested with the specific populations. However, we suggest ways in which the model might be applied to other Axis I and Axis II dually disordered clients.

To sum up the variables that are critical to a comprehensive assessment,

> Differential Diagnosis + Medical Screening + Functional
> Assessment + Gender-Based and Cultural Considerations +
> History of Past and Recent Sexual or Physical Trauma +
> Motivation or Readiness for Change Assessment +
> Laboratory and Drug Screening Tests + Client
> Self-Evaluation = Transtheoretical Approach to Assessment.

CONCLUSION

A transtheoretical approach does not dictate what assessments and interventions to use with individual dually disordered clients. It does, however, provide important guidelines that help treatment providers to interact with their clients genuinely, professionally, and with the most comprehensive information available to the clients and treatment providers. This chapter emphasized comprehensive assessments including a thorough understanding of the *DSM-IV* diagnostic codes and differential diagnosis issues. Short-term assessment considerations were briefly mentioned but are highlighted later in individual chapters on specific populations. Long-term assessment considerations combine psychiatric rehabilitation goals with motivation-based readiness for change goals. In both models, the clients' perceptions and choices are as central as the professionals' objective assessments. The example given for assessing psychiatric rehabilitation concerns is a functional assessment that emphasizes quality of life across biopsychosocial domains. The relapse prevention assessment presents Osher and Kofoed's (1989) and Prochaska et al.'s (1992) motivational stages of progress through recovery.

◼ *QUESTIONS FOR DISCUSSION*

1. What factors are most important to consider in making a differential diagnosis?

2. What is the Substance Abuse Treatment Scale, and how can it help providers to identify appropriate treatment goals?

3. Give some sample questions that might be found on a functional assessment.

4. What do relapse prevention and psychiatric rehabilitation assessments have in common?

5. How do culture- and gender-based issues affect assessment and diagnosis issues?

6. What should be included on a comprehensive interdisciplinary assessment?

Schizophrenia and Substance-Related Disorders

Schizophrenia is a disease of the brain that most researchers believe has a genetic basis. This disorder also has been linked with traumatic events during childhood and viral infections during pregnancy, although there is no empirical evidence to support these linkages. The most likely explanation is that biological or psychosocial events set off the alarm of a gene clock transmitted from parent to child. Events such as accidents, illness, and changing hormones during puberty all may affect the onset of schizophrenia. However, current research and thinking is that individuals and families do not cause schizophrenia.

The substance-related disorders that co-occur with schizophrenia may be substance induced (e.g., alcohol intoxication) or substance use disorders (e.g., caffeine-induced sleep disorder). Some believe that clients with schizophrenia try to control their hallucinations and other uncomfortable symptoms through self-medicating with alcohol and other drug use. Persons who may abuse nonprescribed substances manage the negative side effects of prescribed antipsychotic medications. Kosten and Ziedonis (1997) report findings that may link schizophrenia and substance abuse to a shared genetic predisposition.

The result of nonprescribed drug use of any type in persons who already have biochemical abnormalities of the brain creates significant management issues. Chemical dependency programs seldom are equipped to deal with the special needs of persons with severe mental illness, and "patients with schizophrenia who are being treated in mental health settings often have undetected substance abuse" (Kosten & Ziedonis, 1997, p. 182).

This chapter provides information that bridges the gap between addiction interventions and treatment for major mental illnesses. We use a transtheoretical approach to assessment and intervention. The transtheoretical approach, proposed by Prochaska and DiClemente (1986), proposes 10 basic change processes that help clients to avoid relapse. Within this model, change depends on clients' readiness to participate in the treatment process. An accurate diagnosis and psychosocial assessment is critical to planning appropriate interventions. Assessment consists of differential diagnosis, evaluating clients' functioning across biopsychosocial domains, highlighting client choices as well as needs identified by treatment providers, and gauging clients' stage of readiness for change. The following case example demonstrates some of the critical issues faced by treatment providers for persons with coexisting schizophrenia and substance-related disorders.

CASE EXAMPLE

Elaine spends most of her day listening to the radio in an apartment that she shares with her common law husband, Frank. Her parents disapprove of her relationship, and she seldom sees them or anyone else. She remains home alone waiting for Frank to return in the evenings. Sometimes, she hears disturbing messages on the radio telling her that she is God's messenger who must change the world. When she tells Frank, he makes fun of her and says that she is crazy. Drinking makes her feel like she is not crazy. One night after drinking for several hours, she heard God talking to her, even though the radio was not turned on. She ran out of the house trying to escape God's messages. This time, the voice said to kill Frank. Elaine was picked up by the police and transferred to the emergency room of the local county hospital. She was reeking of alcohol and speaking incoherently. She had no identification with her and claimed that she did not have any family.

DEFINITIONS

In the *Diagnostic and Statistical Manual of Mental Disorders* (*DSM-IV*) (American Psychiatric Association [APA], 1994), schizophrenia and other psychotic disorders are classified as major mental disorders recognizable by the presence of active psychoses for at least 1 month and a disturbance for at least 6 months. Psychoses include hallucinations with no insight into their basis, disorganized speech, disorganized behaviors, and catatonic behaviors. Clinicians may observe inappropriate expressions of emotions, motor behaviors, thinking, and perceptions. These same symptoms, however, also may be features that are substance related or related to bipolar illness, particularly during the manic phase.

Substance-related disorders are in two groups: (a) substance use disorders, dependence, and abuse; and (b) substance-induced disorders, substance-induced intoxication, withdrawal, delirium, persisting dementia, persisting amnestic disorder, psychotic disorder, mood disorder, anxiety disorder, sexual dysfunction, and sleep disorder (APA, 1994).

UNIQUE PROBLEMS

One of the unique problems of coexisting schizophrenia and substance-related disorders is determining what causes psychoses. Clients may laugh inappropriately, cry, lash out, or talk to someone who is not there. Often, it is difficult to determine what is causing the psychotic episode—the mental disorder, the substance use or abuse, or a combination of the two. Occasionally, psychoses also may be related to a medical condition. Fine and Miller (1993) stress that "one cannot deduce the existence of a preexisting psychiatric illness based on presenting psychotic symptoms" (p. 64). Other causes, such as substance-related psychoses or psychoses due to medical conditions, must be ruled out.

Increasingly, clients with histories of substance abuse also have histories of recent or past experience with sexual or physical trauma associated with their substance disorders (Goodman, Dutton, & Harris, 1995). If this assessment and diagnostic consideration are ignored, then clients with severe mental illness and substance-related disorders may become even more victimized by undertreatment and underdiagnosis.

Differential Diagnosis Considerations

Layne (1990) suggests that professionals can determine the difference among persons with schizophrenia, those with a substance-related disorder, and those with bipolar illness through careful examination of the following issues:

◆ Schizophrenia has a constant course that continues to worsen when untreated. Bipolar illness, on the other hand, typically has alternating courses of highs and lows. The highs may look like schizophrenia in an agitated phase. Determining the correct diagnosis takes time and an accurate long-term history. Persons who appear to return to normal are more likely to have bipolar illness or a substance-induced disorder than to have schizophrenia.

♦ Permanent psychoses or organicity caused by long-term use of substances is rare.

♦ Substance-induced psychoses disappear after 2 to 4 weeks of abstinence. "A return of psychoses suggests schizophrenia" (p. 175).

♦ Although schizophrenia has many faces, the classic profile of a person with schizophrenia differs from that of a person who primarily abuses substances. For example, "substance abusers are less isolated, better able to intellectualize, and more rational than persons with schizophrenia" (p. 175).

When persons present with active psychoses, accuracy of long-term diagnosis is not possible until enough time has passed for persons to be substance free for at least 3 or 4 weeks.

ASSESSMENT

Short-Term Assessment Considerations

Drake, Rosenberg, and Mueser (1998) urge practitioners to use a battery of substance use tests to detect the high rate of substance use disorders among persons with severe mental illness such as Elaine. For interviews that are with the client, they suggest the following procedures:

1. The screening portion of the Structured Clinical Interview for the *DSM-IV*

2. A calendar method to document use patterns during recent months (Sobell et al., 1980)

3. A brief checklist to assess consequences of substance use

4. A history of past and present moderate alcohol use

5. General procedures in the clinical interview that allow the client to relax and ensure confidentiality (in conjunction with laboratory assessment)

6. Repeat self-report assessments on a regular basis (Spitzer, Williams, Gibbon, & First, 1990, p. 127)

Assessment of the lethality of suicide ideation is critical. "We should be mindful that the statistics involving suicide and schizophrenia state that 20% to 50% of all people with schizophrenia attempt suicide, and 10% die by suicide" (Littrell, 1998, p. 1). Littrell (1998) reports that more than one half of persons who succeed in killing themselves had made threats to do so prior to the acts. Furthermore, more than one third had been to see physicians on the days of their deaths. Unfortunately, most persons have not contacted other sources of professional help. What cues can professionals use to assess the risk of suicide?

The following cues are critical: (a) direct verbal threats (e.g., "I won't be here tomorrow"), (b) indirect verbal threats (e.g., "What happens to my body when I am gone?"), (c) engaging in dangerous acts (e.g., taking an overdose, standing on a high windowsill), (d) getting rid of possessions and making a will, (e) having a plan with violent intent (e.g., threatening to use guns, jumping, hanging, car crash, or drowning), (f) having the availability of means, (g) having made previous attempts, (h) having family or friends who have succeeded in suicide attempts, (i) having poor judgment or impulsivity, and (j) using alcohol or drugs (Littrell, 1998). In addition, acute stressors (e.g., the sudden death of a loved one) can increase the threat of suicide. Persons who are isolated, feeling hopeless, and depressed are especially vulnerable (Littrell, 1998).

Professionals need to be in touch with family, friends, and other close collaterals to obtain information that persons in crisis might not be willing or able to give. The focus of the relationship with clients should be not on intense questioning but rather on maintaining closeness and giving feelings of hope.

Some professionals worry that they should not bring up suicide or homicide issues unless the client brings them to their attention. However, Littrell (1998) reports that "mentioning suicide will not put the idea into a person's head" (p. 3). There are many valuable assessment tools that are significant predictors of suicide threats. Littrell's Assessment of Lethality in Suicidal Persons is short, well organized, and easily administered without overwhelming clients with probing questions.

As in all assessments, high-risk conditions should be considered from a biopsychosocial approach. In addition to the psychological risk of suicide, medical conditions that could be life threatening need to be ruled out. These conditions include withdrawal, delirium tremens, neurological disorders, infections, AIDS-related complications, and endocrine disorders (e.g., diabetes, hyperthyroidism). Social risks include homelessness, victimization, incarceration without treatment, and inadequate food and proper nutrition.

Lehman (1996) recommends that agencies implement screening procedures that include routine questions regarding medical problems. He gives two types of examples: reviews of specific diagnoses and symptoms and general health status measures. Examples include the National Health Interview Survey (National Center for Health Statistics, 1991) and the Medical Outcomes Short Form (Ware & Sherbourne, 1992).

Both Axis IV and Axis V of the *DSM-IV* (APA, 1994) provide useful measures of psychosocial functioning that may be exacerbating substance and mental illness disorders. Lehman and Burns (1996) also developed a questionnaire that can be used in a range of mental health, physical health, and social service settings.

Summary of Types of Short-Term Assessment Instruments

◆ Substance severity instruments

◆ History of past and recent alcohol use

◆ Suicide lethality scale

◆ Laboratory tests

◆ Consequences of substance use

◆ Medical screening tests

◆ Psychosocial assessment

Long-Term Assessment Considerations

In keeping with recent rehabilitation goals for persons with persisting mental illness, assessments for long-term planning should be customer driven. One of the most important conceptual considerations is for treatment providers to set priorities within the choices of persons with dual disorders as well as within the treatment team's identified interventions. For example, Elaine might say that her priority is keeping busy during the day to avoid hearing negative messages on the radio. Keeping active also might help her to acquire skills for avoiding drinking at night while waiting for Frank to return home.

Quality of life assessments are valuable assessment instruments because they focus on opportunities for satisfaction in day-to-day environments while simultaneously monitoring illness and substance behaviors. Keith and Lipsey (1993) list four domains of health-related quality of life:

(1) opportunity for healthy living including reserves to withstand stress; (2) health perceptions of clients including self-ratings of satisfaction in physical, psychological, and social areas of their lives; (3) functional status across social roles including feelings of being valued by others and actual participation in the family and community; and (4) impairment status including subjective complaints, symptoms, laboratory data and records, and actual survival. (p. 45)

Included in quality of life issues are social and cultural considerations. If clients continue to live in stressful environments, then relapse is almost certain to occur. Westermeyer (1995) suggests that clients can be given more effective services if the following cultural considerations are evaluated:

♦ Is the client alienated from his or her own cultural group, either religious or ethnic?

♦ What does the client's cultural group prescribe as accepted substance use?

♦ What aspects of treatment (e.g., Alcoholics Anonymous) either support or run counter to the client's cultural expectations of treatment?

Gender-based studies also point out that women such as Elaine have female-specific treatment issues related to coping styles for dealing with their illnesses. Because women generally are older at age of onset than are men, they might have unidentified lost opportunities in areas of relationships, jobs, and child rearing (Kulkarni, 1997). These areas could be significant quality of life indicators.

Rehabilitation assessment instruments sometimes are called functional assessments because they emphasize evaluating everyday functions such as preparing meals, getting ready for work, interacting meaningfully with family and friends, and participating in the community. A typical rehabilitation assessment instrument might include some of the following areas of evaluation.

Questions Typically Found on Rehabilitation Assessment Instruments

1. What symptoms create the most problems for you?

2. What do you do to cope with these symptoms?

3. What are your major sources of support?

4. What relationships at home bring you the greatest satisfaction? The least?

5. Rate yourself in the following areas on a scale from 1 to 10 (with 1 being the *least satisfied* and 10 being the *most satisfied*):

    ↠ Home environment feels safe and comfortable.

    ↠ Transportation is adequate.

    ↠ Finances are managed effectively.

    ↠ Work, school, or other major activity is meaningful.

➤ Relationships with family and friends are supportive.

➤ Medication works consistently.

➤ Medications have few negative side effects.

➤ Treatment providers are easily accessible.

Functional assessment instruments are abundant, but not all of them emphasize client perspectives and client strengths. For example, the checklist type of assessment seldom gives clients or treatment providers enough information to evaluate the unique needs and strengths of individual clients. Therefore, a functional assessment should be a part of a more comprehensive psychosocial assessment.

Summary of Long-Term Assessment Considerations

♦ Customer-driven wants and needs

♦ Functional assessments

♦ Quality of life assessments

♦ Cultural issues

♦ Gender-based issues

TREATMENT GOALS

In both chemical dependency and medical disease models of mental illness, the most effective programs are multidimensional and multitheoretical. The U.S. Department of Health and Human Services' Center for Substance Abuse Treatment recommends the goal of integrating services within a single umbrella whose mission is to prevent relapse (Ries, 1994). Programs should include multidisciplinary teams cross-trained in medical and psychosocial interventions, assertive case management in home environments, psychoeducational components for clients and families, 12-step programs sensitive to the needs of dually disordered clients, medication intervention, and psychosocial rehabilitation services. Recent studies also recommend that programs should have an individualized cognitive, behavioral, and social network focus (Drake, Rosenberg, & Mueser, 1996; Jerrell & Ridgely, 1995).

TREATMENT MODEL

The treatment model combines interventions found to be effective with persons with schizophrenia and adds Prochaska and DiClemente's (1986) relapse prevention strategies. Within this model, interventions are most likely to succeed if they match the client's readiness for change. The client's active involvement and direction of his or her treatment support the customer-driven aspect of psychiatric rehabilitation programs.

READINESS FOR CHANGE

Prochaska and DiClemente (1986) point out that "therapy progresses most smoothly if both the client and the therapist are focusing on the same stage of change" (p. 7). Therefore, of primary importance is an assessment of the client's readiness for change prior to planning for long-term management of both the mental illness and the substance disorder. Osher and Kofoed (1989) observed stages of change over the course of recovery of persons with dual disorders: engagement, persuasion, active treatment, and relapse prevention. Similar to the stages presented by Prochaska and DiClemente (precontemplation, contemplation, preparation for action, action, and maintenance), each of Osher and Kofoed's stages determines the type of treatment goals that are most likely to succeed.

In the first stage, precontemplation, Elaine may be particularly difficult to reach because her illness, schizophrenia, affects her ability to accurately interpret her experiences. However, the treatment team can help Elaine commit to treatment through active outreach to establish a trusting relationship. For example, Elaine experienced the negative event of being arrested and hospitalized following a drinking episode. Treatment team members can empathize with her feelings about her experience and learn about what she sees as most important in her world. During this stage, substance use behaviors should not be addressed directly. Some clients also need practical assistance during this stage such as help in finding shelter, clothing, and other supportive resources.

During the next stage, contemplation, the goal is to help Elaine realize how substance use or abuse has contributed to loss of control over her life. She should be encouraged to begin making connections among her addictive behaviors, how they affect her illness of schizophrenia, and resulting negative life events. Also, a sense of hopefulness can come from family interest and involvement in Elaine's treatment and her participation with others in group treatment.

During the contemplation phase, the biggest threat to the client is the risk of harming self or others in the absence of insight into the nature of dual illness. Some clients need to be involuntarily hospitalized or committed to community treatment so as to keep them and others safe.

Another treatment goal during this phase should be shifting both the client and the treatment team's efforts in the direction of taking control over environmental problems such as Elaine's development of social skills and finding meaningful activities while her husband is away from home. Clients who take prescribed psychoactive medications during this time are able to progress more readily to the next stage of change than are clients who do not comply with medication guidelines. However, coercion and threats are not as helpful as is explaining why medications are critical to getting well.

Progressing to the next stage, action, clients have an awareness of how their behaviors affect the nature of their problems but often have relapses. A relapse can be viewed as "opportunities to learn more about what each individual will need to achieve sustained abstinence" (Mueser, Drake, & Noordsy, 1998, p. 136). During this stage, clients are open to educational interventions or raising their consciousness through psychoeducation groups, self-help groups for the special concerns of dually disordered clients, family problem solving, and nonconfrontive supportive therapy interventions.

During the final stage, maintenance, the goal is for clients such as Elaine to evaluate what they value in their lives and to maintain awareness of their vulnerability to relapse. Elaine values her relationship with Frank, and this could be used to help motivate her to maintain sobriety.

Taking action to change her psychic problems of hearing negative messages from God and her addictive behaviors of drinking when she is lonely might be particularly difficult for Elaine. "There is limited information on motivation to quit among individuals with schizophrenia" (Ziedonis & Trudeau, 1997, p. 229). The Motivation-Based Treatment (MBT) Model, using Prochaska and DiClemente's (1986) stages of change, was the focus of a recent study of 497 persons with schizophrenia or schizoaffective disorder in an outpatient mental health clinic (Ziedonis & Trudeau, 1997). The results reported that many variables affect motivational levels to quit using substances.

Elaine is in a high-risk category to fail. Clients over 40 years of age in the Ziedonis and Trudeau (1997) study were less motivated than younger clients to stop drinking. Severity of the mental illness and/or substance disorder also was a possible important factor. The MBT model matches readiness for change with specific interventions. For example, during the maintenance stage, Elaine's goal is to maintain sobriety. Her successes may increase her feelings of control over her life, enabling her to handle future triggers. "Dual diagnosis relapse prevention uses the behavioral learning principles of role-playing, modeling, coaching, presenting positive and negative feedback, and assigning homework" (Ziedonis & Trudeau, 1997, p. 236). This makes it imperative for Elaine's treatment team to keep her active in out-patient programs and to avoid isolation. Elaine is likely to relapse if she remains inactive at home. She is a candidate for prevocational and vocational training and socialization programs. Attending 12-step programs designed specifically as offerings in mental health settings with other dually diagnosed clients also may be beneficial to Elaine. Finally, Elaine's desire to make her relationship with Frank work requires that Frank understand the nature of her illness. Prochaska and DiClemente (1986) believe that this may be central to maintenance, that is, realizing one's goals to "be the kind of persons one wants to be" (p. 10).

HELPING RELATIONSHIP

During each of the stages of change, helping clients to make real changes in their lives depends on a helping relationship that is nonconfrontive and supportive rather than threatening and coercive (Prochaska & DiClemente, 1986). Social workers, therapists, and other members of treatment teams often get discouraged when clients do not choose to alter their drug behaviors. On the other hand, when clients have successes, clients need to feel that their own efforts are more important than their helpers' efforts. The most effective helpers encourage clients to make a connection between their own actions and outcomes in their lives. For some clients at high risk of relapse, contingency management and stimulus control are helpful interventions. However, clients should not be made to suffer natural consequences, such as incarceration and homelessness, as a result of behaviors related to their illnesses. Sciacca (1987) stresses that "treatment staff do not seek to catch patients in lies . . . or to use punishment as a method of control. . . . Helpers need tolerance, patience, and above all a strong understanding of issues relevant to mental illness" (p. 1).

PSYCHOPHARMACOLOGICAL CONSIDERATIONS

Ries (1993) recommends that psychopharmacological considerations should focus on three issues:

1. What is the abuse potential of the medication?

2. What characteristics of the medication may help sobriety or recovery?

3. What characteristics of the medication may hinder sobriety or recovery? (p. 115)

Ries (1993) reports that antipsychotics, the most effective group of drugs to treat schizophrenia, pose no threat for abuse. The greatest threat to clients is unwanted side effects that cause them to turn to alcohol or drugs to feel better. Anticholinergics may help to remove some of the more uncomfortable side effects. However, Ries warns that clients might turn away from the treatment team that uses antipsychotics for acute management of drug-induced psychoses. Instead, he recommends using benzodiazepines during the first few days or weeks following substance withdrawal. They should not be used long term because of their high dependence qualities including anxiety during withdrawal.

COGNITIVE-BEHAVIORAL DIMENSIONS

Hogarty and Flesher (1992) offer a note of caution as well as a suggestion. In treating clients with schizophrenia, the treatment team should focus on the functional aspects of everyday life rather than on the elementary processes of cold cognition. Penn (1991) further explains that the issue for rehabilitation centers on the need for clients to understand how their behaviors affect social relationships and vocational functioning. Psychodynamic approaches not only are inappropriate but might even be damaging to persons whose psychiatric illnesses affect brain structure and functioning.

Some valuable interventions are psychoeducation (short informational presentations in clear and concrete terms), consumer support groups, and consumer empowerment strategies (Rapp, Shera, & Kisthardt, 1993). These strategies include increased opportunities for clients to set their own goals and to actively participate in the community through choosing meaningful vocations, educational opportunities, independent living, and a support network of family and friends.

COPING SKILLS

Many clients lack adequate coping skills due to poor health, homelessness, little or no family support, and joblessness. Removing these barriers can enable clients to build functional ways of coping. Moxley and Freddolino (1990) suggest that assisting clients in prioritizing their needs, not the needs of the treatment team, fosters positive steps toward change. Prochaska and DiClemente's (1986) process of self-liberation is a similar strategy involving helping clients to understand the power they have over their own lives. Applying this strategy to dually disordered clients, DiNitto and Webb (1994) describe a consumer group therapy program that encourages discussion of mental illness and drug use and reinforces remaining free of alcohol and drugs so that prescribed medications can work effectively. Other groups are self-run by clients. For example, some consumer groups provide training on schizophrenia and other major mental illnesses to community providers such as the police, social workers, and medical workers. In these groups, consumers are given authority over important decisions in the active running of their groups.

The stress-vulnerability-coping-competence model of Liberman (1998) suggests that persons with schizophrenia relapse in the face of inadequate strategies for handling stress. Furthermore, in persons with schizophrenia, the tolerance for stress is more limited than in other individuals. Consciousness raising is the process of change (Prochaska & DiClemente, 1986) that can aid clients with schizophrenia and substance-related disorders to learn effective coping strategies. Consciousness raising refers to increasing a person's awareness of destructive behaviors and why the drug taking (or other dysfunctional behaviors) persists. A major intervention for consciousness raising is psychoeducation. Orlin and Davis (1993) suggest that the following topics may be especially helpful in psychoeducation groups: defining schizophrenia and addiction in consumer terms, discussing triggers for relapses, discussing good and bad drugs, raising family issues, and noting sociopolitical issues that contribute to illness.

Stimulus control is the process used by consumers to avoid alcohol and drug triggers in their environments. It can be taught in psychoeducation groups, in weekly support meetings, or in social skills training groups. Smith, Schwebel, Dunn, and Melver (1993) define skills training as "a structured intervention [that] employs modeling, role-playing, and *in vivo* practice in a manner analogous to teaching a motor skill such as dancing" (p. 967, italics in original).

For fragile clients, stimulus control might not be adequate, particularly during the early stage of denial of illness or addiction. Clients might need intensive case management such as the assertive community treatment model pioneered by Leonard Stein and more recently modified to include a mobile program (Thompson, Griffith, & Leaf, 1990). In this model, treatment team members work cooperatively as crisis workers, assertively reaching out to clients at high risk of relapse. With assertive team interventions, consumers are encouraged to seek help in the face of environmental stressors including triggers to use nonprescribed medications.

INTERPERSONAL SKILLS

Interpersonal skills are strengthened through the development of peer support networks and self-help groups such as Support Together for Emotional and Mental Serenity and Sobriety (STEMSS) (Bricker, 1988, 1989). For example, group facilitators might request clients to list what situations have been the most aversive to them. Clients exchange "war stories" and ask their peers for ideas on how to avoid dangerous situations. The emphasis is on peer and treatment team support rather than on confrontation (Ries, 1994).

Rapp and colleagues (1993) discuss the empowerment paradigm for consumers with severe mental illness. In this paradigm, self-help and peer-help groups are individual-level interventions. However, they also stress the need for broader perspectives at the family level, in organizations that serve clients, and at the community level. They offer examples including public educational campaigns to reduce the bias against hiring persons with mental illness and vocational rehabilitation counselors being included on treatment teams.

Interpersonal skills also may be strengthened through communication skills training programs that provide clients with the language to identify feelings and symptoms that may trigger alcohol and illicit drug use. These skills may be included in consumer psychoeducation groups, 12-step groups designed specifically for clients with coexisting schizophrenia and substance-related disorders, or other skills training groups.

FAMILY RELATIONSHIPS

Rehabilitation strategies have reversed the recent trend to view family members as part of the problem of persons with mental illness. Replacing this bias, family members have become important cohorts of the treatment team. Whether the family will support treatment or undermine it may significantly affect the course of both schizophrenia and alcohol and drug use. Family psychoeducation is an important approach for providing consumer support in the community. Anderson, Reiss, and Hogarty (1986) identify the following processes common to family psychoeducation programs: support, information, skills, and family therapy. Topics of programs include problem-solving strategies for handling crises, behavioral strategies for limiting stressful interactions, information regarding the overlapping nature of mental illness and addictions, and information regarding how to effectively work with community service providers.

ENVIRONMENTAL INTERVENTIONS

Social liberation is a process of change (Prochaska & DiClemente, 1986) that relates to changes in clients' environments such as increased social interactions and employment opportunities. Social skills training, also used to help clients develop functional coping skills, has enabled many clients with schizophrenia to form new friendships, manage households, and pursue meaningful interests. Recent studies further suggest that persons do not require recovery in psychiatric functioning to perform jobs with a high level of competence (Lamb, 1994). Persons with schizophrenia and substance-related issues are at higher risk of cognitive dysfunction than are other diagnostic groups. However, jobs that do not require complex problem-solving ability might restore a sense of self-esteem, employing the "well aspects" of persons rather than the illness aspects.

Social liberation also involves the attitudes of family and significant others toward the person with dual disorders. Anthony and Liberman (1986) suggest role-plays that provide direct feedback to clients regarding their social role interactions. A role-play could be valuable in providing feedback regarding the effects of alcohol and substance use behaviors on family, friends, peers, and employers. Anthony and Liberman emphasize that highly directive behavioral techniques work most effectively for clients with severe and persistent mental illness such as schizophrenia.

AFFECTIVE DIMENSIONS

"Self-evaluation is said to be an emotional and rational appraisal of the pros and cons of overcoming substance abuse" (Barber, 1994, p. 36). Poor self-esteem is one of the emotional hallmarks of persons with severe and persistent mental illness as well as persons with addictions. San Blise's (1995) radical reframing is a particularly helpful model for redirecting consumers' appraisal of themselves and of their dual illnesses. She describes a conversation with a client: "Are you saying I have schizophrenia? Thank God! I thought I was losing my mind" (p. 20). This separation of the mind from the illness of the mind allows clients to focus on the healthy aspects of their functioning. It also appears to be closely tied to the roots of 12-step programs that focus on substance abuse as a disease rather than a moral shortcoming.

Dramatic relief, or ventilation, is a therapeutic technique that may serve to unlock pent-up emotions. With persons with schizophrenia, however, encouragement of loss of emotional control is not recommended. Instead, dramatic relief should help to provide such persons with labels for the emotions that already are on the surface. Stating to the client that he or she may be feeling some anger and frustration at having been arrested again for disorderly conduct gives the client some clarification of the tempest of emotions that he or she might be experiencing. This reduces the likelihood of the client turning to illicit drugs for relief, perpetuating the cyclical pattern of relapse.

SUPPORT GROUPS

Support groups should be used throughout the stages of change regardless of a client's readiness for change. During the early stages, a client such as Elaine learns why her life has gotten out of control. Later, she might make new friends to support her in her recovery and maintenance. Bricker and his associates began using support groups for persons with coexisting schizophrenia and substance abuse problems in 1984. The groups are informally called "double trouble." Formally, they are called Support Together for Emotional and Mental Serenity and Sobriety (STEMSS). Based on the original 12-step programs, STEMSS uses six steps to recovery. Evans and Sullivan (1990) have published workbooks that treatment providers can use to begin their own dual diagnosis "double trouble" groups.

CONCLUSION

Despite the fact that more than half of clients with schizophrenia also have coexisting alcohol or other drug dependence, few programs are designed to manage both issues simultaneously. In recognition of this problem, some programs are using assessment and treatment strategies that combine goals for psychiatric rehabilitation with relapse prevention. This chapter presented an overview of the strategies beginning with a case example to aid in practice application.

Students and practitioners can further pursue effective assessment and treatment techniques through educating peers, supervisors, administrators, and community members about the special needs of persons with coexisting schizophrenia and substance disorders.

◧ QUESTIONS FOR DISCUSSION

1. Why is drug use of any type particularly dangerous to persons like Elaine who have a dual disorder?

2. How do stages of readiness for change affect treatment goals and therapeutic relationships?

3. What types of questionnaires should be included in short-term assessment and screening procedures? In long-term assessments?

4. To assist Elaine in maintaining sobriety and control over her mental illness, what combination of treatment programs should she attend?

Depression and Substance-Related Disorders

This chapter deals with substance abuse and two mood disorders: major depressive disorder and dysthymic disorder. These disorders are in the *Diagnostic and Statistical Manual of Mental Disorders* (*DSM-IV*) chapter on mood disorders (American Psychiatric Association [APA], 1994). The term *mood* refers to a prolonged emotional state that colors the whole of a person's life. A mood disorder is a pathological elevation or disturbance of mood and includes episodes of depression or mania (or both, as in bipolar disorder).

DEFINITIONS

Major depressive episode is a mood episode that is a cluster of symptoms that occurs together for a discrete period of time, mostly all the time, for 2 weeks. The person feels depressed, has a loss of pleasure in or indifference to all activities, and has feelings of worthlessness and inappropriate guilt. Accompanying these moods and feelings are recurrent thoughts of death and suicide. Physiological signs include changes in sleep, appetite, and weight patterns. Symptoms of psychomotor agitation or retardation may occur. Fatigue, loss of energy, and inability to concentrate also are symptoms.

The *DSM-IV* (APA, 1994) lists nine symptoms of which at least five must be present including depressed mood or loss of interest or pleasure. In addition, the symptoms must cause some impairment in social or occupational functioning. These symptoms cannot be accounted for by other causes such as substance abuse, major life changes, and traumatic events. Major depression requires evidence of one or more episodes.

Dysthymic disorder requires the presence of a depressed mood most of the time for a period of 2 years in addition to the presence of two or more symptoms of depressive episode except suicidal ideation (APA, 1994). This disorder is considered a milder form of depression. However, dysthymia can be severely debilitating because of its chronicity. As Markowitz and Kocsic (1994) write,

> The dysthymic individual must struggle daily and perennially against depressed mood, low energy, guilt, pathological social awkwardness, and lifelong pessimism [that have impaired] social and vocational functioning. [These individuals] become . . . selfless workers . . . in attempts to counterbalance their sense of worthlessness . . . [and] are socially isolated and withdrawn, feeling empty and unworthy. (p. 210)

These authors continue to assert that persons with dysthymia lead lives of quiet desperation and often report chronic suicidal ideation. They are at high risk for comorbid conditions. The co-occurrence of dysthymia and major depression is referred to as *double depression.*

In both cases, mood disorders are not attributable to medical conditions and cannot be accounted for by other causes such as substance abuse, major life changes, and traumatic events. Medical conditions that can either precipitate or mimic mood disorders include the following:

◆ Malnutrition

◆ Anemia

◆ Hyper- and hypothyroidism

◆ Dementia

◆ Brain disease

◆ Pancreatic cancer

◆ Lupus

◆ HIV/AIDS

◆ Postcardiac condition

◆ Stroke (especially in the elderly) (Cohen & Levy, 1992)

Both prescribed and over-the-counter medications can cause or precipitate depression or conditions that mimic psychiatric or substance abuse disorders. A number of drugs may precipitate or mimic depression. The general effect of alcohol, barbiturates, and opioids is a slowing down of the psychomotor processes. However, in acute intoxication, an initial phase may be euphoria followed by relaxation, sedation, apathy, and drowsiness. In especially high doses, these drugs can cause mood lability as well as mental and psychomotor impairment.

Substance abuse requires a person to exhibit a pattern of use that leads to clinically significant impairment or distress so that such use results in the following outcomes within 1 year: (a) failure to fulfill major role obligations, (b) use of substance when it is physically hazardous, (c) use in spite of recurrent legal problems, and (d) continued use in spite of psychosocial problems caused by the use (APA, 1994).

Substance dependence requires that a person meet at least three of the following requirements within 1 year: (a) tolerance, (b) withdrawal, (c) drugs taken in larger amounts or over longer periods of time, (d) persistent desire and unsuccessful attempts to cut down on or control use, (e) spending a great deal of time getting or maintaining supply and using or recovering from effects, (f) giving up or reducing all other activities in favor of using, and (g) continued use in spite of negative physical, social, and psychological consequences (APA, 1994).

The *DSM-IV* requires a clustering of symptoms within 1 year as well as duration qualifiers for both abuse and dependence. *Duration* refers to the repetitiveness of symptoms as represented by the following terms: recurrent, often, and persistent (APA, 1994).

UNIQUE PROBLEMS

Alcoholism often has been associated with depression. Many clinicians believe that patients with recurrent depression use alcohol to treat their depression, whereas others hold that depression may be a product of alcoholism (Hirschfeld, Hasin, Keller, Endicott, & Wunder, 1990). The Epidemiological Catchment Area (ECA) study in 1990 (Regier et al., 1990) found that people with major depression were nearly 2 times more likely to have a substance abuse problem and 1⅓ times more likely to be diagnosed with alcohol dependence. The same study found that nearly 40% of those with alcohol problems were depressed and that, among people with other drug disorders, half reported symptoms of psychiatric disorders. O'Boyle and Hirschfeld (1994) concluded that the "use of alcohol should be suspected in those patients who are in treatment for depression" (p. 150).

During the early stages of substance withdrawal, people may exhibit symptoms of depression. The same ECA study reported that the prevalence rate for depression among alcoholic women was higher than that among men. Coryell, Winokur, Keller, Scheftner, and Endicott (1992) report that, among those with unipolar depression, 1 in 5 men and 1 in 10 women had an additional diagnosis of alcoholism. Other populations (e.g., Native Americans, HIV patients, patients maintained on methadone, elderly people) have a high risk for depression (Regier et al., 1990).

Grant (1995) reports from a 1992 national study that "the comorbidity of drug use disorders and major depression is pervasive in the general population" (p. 493). She continues,

> Among those with a past year drug use disorder, 18.17% experienced major depression, a comorbidity rate significantly greater than the population base rate of current major depression (3.33%). . . . Nearly 9% of the respondents with major depression reported a drug use disorder during the past year, a comorbidity rate significantly greater than the population base rate of drug abuse and dependence combined (1.54%). (p. 493)

Grant (1995) also reports that these rates are lower than the average rates reported in the treated sample (18% to 30%), suggesting that "comorbidity of drug use disorders and major depression is related to professional help seeking" (p. 493). Cook, Winokur, Garvey, and Beach (1991) found that alcohol was a risk factor in chronic depression. O'Boyle and Hirschfeld (1994) conclude that alcohol use should be suspected in persons who present for treatment for depression. This means that an accurate assessment of drinking behavior should be made. These authors quote from another study showing that depressed persons are likely to report fair to poor physical and emotional health, alcohol or drug abuse, and suicide attempts. Marital discord and financial dependence also were common.

The results of a study by Klerman and colleagues (1996) indicate that temporal trends in the rates of major depressive disorder are not fully explained by drug or alcohol use. Analysis indicates three risk factors for depression: (a) family history of affective illness, (b) comorbid drug or alcohol abuse or dependence, and (c) being female. Those with comorbid drug or alcohol abuse were twice as likely to develop major depressive disorder. Nevertheless, the temporal trend is evident in both people with and those without comorbid drug or alcohol abuse.

Schutte, Hearst, and Moos (1997), in a three-wave study spanning 3 years, find that baseline depression was associated with less alcohol consumption 1 year later among women and men. However, later on, more depression predicted heavier drinking for women. For both men and women, heavier drinking predicted more subsequent depression. These authors conclude that depressive symptoms play a dual role in the course of problem drinking, triggering change or maintaining chronicity. They further state that which role is active might depend on the stage of change for that person. They argue that clinicians "should consider what stage of change an individual is in when trying to evaluate the potential role of depressive symptoms on the course of problem drinking" (p. 401).

CASE EXAMPLES

Aaron came to treatment when he was 26 years old. He recently had moved into a large metropolitan area to take an important new job and was concerned that his inability to sleep during the night would interfere with his work. For some time, he had been unable to sleep for more than 3 or 4 hours at a time. His appetite was sluggish, but he was not concerned about this because he was trying to lose weight. He talked about the importance of getting back to doing his workouts.

Aaron related that he had been treated for depression 2 years earlier following the accidental death of his friend. He discontinued treatment when he thought that he should be over his grief. He added that, prior to the death of his friend, Aaron had been a cocaine user. The death of his friend, who also was a user, shocked him into giving up drugs. Since that time, Narcotics Anonymous (NA) has been his major social support. However, his NA group members do not believe that he should take any medication for his depression. Aaron says that alcohol never is a problem for him, but he drinks three or four beers every night for relaxation and to help him sleep.

Beatrice (Bea for short) is representative of a more chronic patient. She always has been unhappy. She is 45 years old and has been in the mental health system for nearly 20 years. She has carried a dual diagnosis for most of that time, but in this round of treatment she presented as depressed over family issues. She was from an abusive home and had married an abuser who, in a drunken fight, shot and killed her father. While her husband was in prison, she lived with her grandmother, who had been her major nurturer. Bea had two children to raise on her own and was not prepared for work, but she was eligible for Aid to Families With Dependent Children (AFDC). Through that system, she was referred to mental health/mental retardation for both anxiety and depression. Substance abuse was not addressed at that time. Bea's drinking was sporadic. She had episodes of binge drinking that consisted of going to bars on weekends, getting drunk, and waking up with people she did not know. Her relatives took care of the children.

By the time her children left home, Bea had been hospitalized several times for drug or alcohol overdoses that were viewed as suicide attempts. Her problems worsened with the discontinuation of her AFDC and the death of her grandmother. About 10 years ago, she was critically injured in an automobile accident. As a result, she eventually became eligible to receive disability compensation based on her mental illness and physical condition. This qualified her for a wide array of social services. With those benefits came the responsibility for navigating complex systems, and her mental illness deprived her of coping skills. She eventually found another distant relative to live with but who was abusive to her. Bea's life had become a constant struggle, and she used her medication and alcohol to cope. She withdrew into sleep and video games. She stopped tending to her health and nutritional needs.

She presented for treatment on referral from Adult Protective Services as a result of her repeated complaints about abuse that she had received from a relative. She clearly needs to find another place to live. Her first interview came near the anniversary of her family members' deaths, and she cried through most of the session. At present, she fits the earlier definition for dysthymic disorder.

Biopsychosocial problems for both Aaron and Bea include disturbances in sleep and appetite and also weight patterns common in depression as well as in alcohol and other drug intoxication, chronic use, and withdrawal. In addition, Bea suffers from chronic pain due to an injury to her back. Taking prescribed medications is a problem frequently encountered by persons with dual disorders. In Aaron's case, his NA group does not advocate taking any type of drugs. Bea misuses her drugs and loses track of when she takes them. Maintaining a regular pattern of taking medications is complicated by her erratic sleep patterns.

Bea's and Aaron's problems also are common in the grief process; a depressed person and a grieving person might appear the same. However, for both persons, the deaths of significant persons are removed enough in time for some of the symptoms to have abated, although both might still have unresolved issues to face with respect to the loss of those persons. Both are socially isolated.

Bea and Aaron present gender differences in the manifestation of both depression and substance abuse. Schutte, Moos, and Berman (1995), following a review of studies, report that the relation between depression and drinking differs between men and women. Depression appears to precede drinking problems in women, whereas men more often experience depression as a result of drinking. In their study, Schutte and colleagues found that the use of alcohol predicted an easing of depression in women, whereas depression predicted a reduction of drinking in men. They state, "Among women, heavier alcohol consumption predicted lower levels of depression over the course of one and three years. This suggests that alcohol consumption is part of a process related to the successful alleviation of depressive symptoms" (p. 817).

For men, depression predicted less alcohol use later on. Schutte and colleagues (1995) hypothesize that level of social interaction may account for this, particularly if men's drinking behaviors are associated with social activities. What this study shows is that alcohol use attenuates symptoms of depression for women rather than leading to more depression, whereas the opposite is true for men. They conclude that "the negative cycle between depression and drinking behavior may not be as immutable as proposed by others" (p. 819).

ASSESSMENT CONSIDERATIONS

Initial assessment first should determine whether the illness is life threatening and then should initiate appropriate short-term intervention methods. When the crisis has passed and the person is stabilized, a thorough assessment may take place. Such an assessment may require several sessions.

Assessment is a joint endeavor between the practitioner and the person with the problem. The assessment may include a diagnosis of specific illnesses, in these cases, depression and substance abuse. When the person presents without a medical diagnosis, then the practitioner makes the diagnosis as appropriate and as a part of the assessment. This occurs as the person's story unfolds and is told to the listener. The role of the practitioner is to listen and to assist the person in describing and exploring his or her situation.

A biopsychosocial assessment focuses on physical, psychological, and social symptoms of both depression and substance abuse. As mentioned in Chapter 3, Gorski (1994) recommends using a grid of symptoms so that the practitioner can differentiate between substance abuse and depression symptoms and can see the symptoms that are common to both disorders. The practitioner evaluates and gives meaning to the symptoms, sometimes naming factors that impinge on the person's situation. A critical piece of the assessment process is to discover why the person seeks assistance and what meaning the person ascribes to the situation. Finally, the assessment process should uncover what the person wants from assistance and what vision he or she has of a life without the problem.

DEFINING THE PROBLEM

Arriving at a differential diagnosis is an outcome of the process of defining the problem(s). The process includes determination of which illness came first, the length and severity of depression and of substance use, and consideration of medical illnesses. Transient substance-induced depressive symptoms will disappear in time. Substance-induced symptoms of depression may abate within 2 to 4 weeks (Dorus, Kennedy, & Gibbons, 1987). In the absence of waiting for the symptoms to abate, a thorough history of problems is helpful, as is information from family and friends. Likewise, a medical history and a good medical workup are warranted.

Features that distinguish substance abuse symptoms from "true" depression include the following:

♦ Depression predates onset of regular substance abuse.

♦ Depression has persisted during previous times of abstinence.

♦ Depressive symptoms are chronic.

♦ Depression emerges during a period of stable substance use.

♦ There is a positive history of depression or anxiety disorder.

♦ Characteristic mood anxiety symptoms that are present (e.g., severe suicide ideation, agoraphobia, social phobia, obsessions or compulsions) are not typically produced by drug toxicity or withdrawal.

♦ Types of drugs involved may or may not induce a mood disorder. (Nunes, Deliyannides, Donovan, & McGrath, 1996)

A patient with refractory depression might minimize the extent of substance abuse. A careful history should be taken, even if the patient denies abuse. The person needs to be carefully educated about the contribution of the substance to his or her depression. Family members or other collateral persons should be consulted. A trial of abstinence is recommended to observe whether or not symptoms improve. Care must be taken in the approach of substance abuse because some persons believe that limited substance use provides a respite from depression. The mood-elevating effects of most substances are short-lived, and tolerance develops so that the lift that once was felt no longer is easily attained. "Patients are pursuing the memory of a stronger [lift] experienced during initial use" (Nunes et al., 1996, p. 316) at a time when the lift is minimal. In addition to questions about the usual substances, the clinician should ask questions about unusual substances and prescription medicines (especially benzodiazepines), nicotine, and caffeine (p. 316).

Rapid assessment measures, such as the Beck Depression Inventory (Beck & Beamesderfer, 1974) for depression and the CAGE (Mayfield, McLeod, & Hall, 1974) and Michigan Alcohol Screening Test (Selzer, 1971) for substance abuse, are useful.

People with dual diagnoses react in different ways. Some might be angry that they have two diseases or disorders with which to contend. Some might focus on one disorder and avoid dealing with the other. Many persons with dual diagnoses and their families look for a cause-and-effect relationship between mental illness and chemical dependency. These patients' mental illness is viewed as an excuse to use drugs, and they avoid dealing with chemical dependency by focusing on the mental illness. Rubinstein, Campbell, and Daley (1990) conclude that it is important to assess people's thoughts, perceptions, and feelings regarding their dual problems. "This requires empathy on the part of the professional and the belief that denial and misinformation will continue to result in poor treatment outcomes" (p. 102).

Both problems and persons are best understood within the context of their development. The "social" part of a biopsychosocial assessment gives attention to the person's social environment and how this environment affects the problem (in these cases, depression and substance abuse). For example, among African Americans, being young and in fair to poor health was the strongest predictor of depression in a study by Brown, Ahmed, Gary, and Milburn (1995). Furthermore, this group was the least likely to receive clinical treatment in the study.

Who Is Involved in the Problem Situation?

Assessment of the family and friendship systems is important to determine the impact of the dually diagnosed patient on these systems and the impact of family and friends on the patient. Further assessment aims to discover the role that the family and friends can play in treatment and recovery as well as possible family treatment goals (Rubinstein et al., 1990). Family and friends are an integral part of assessing the environment of the client. As was pointed out earlier, dually diagnosed persons often come with marital discord and financial dependence.

Many people who are the most vulnerable and most at risk are situated in environments that are perceived to be destructive and intrusive and that have a disruptive impingement on these people's lives. However, Saleebey (1992) states,

> No matter how a harsh environment tests the mettle of inhabitants, it can also be understood as a lush topography of resources and possibilities. . . . In every environment, there are individuals and institutions who have something to give, something that others . . . need: knowledge, succor, an actual response, or simply time and place. (p. 7)

Social and physical environments must be assessed for strengths and limitations.

◆

itially was treated for depression, it was during the early
the death of a friend, and he had given up his cocaine
hat several months on Prozac had improved his mood to
decided that he did not need to remain on medication.
e was able to find a good job and leave his hometown.
visit his parents and old friends occasionally, but he now
is living apart from family and old friends. He has not made new friends outside of his NA group.

Less is known about Bea's first diagnosis. She apparently managed her family responsibilities well until her grandmother died. It is possible that drinking had masked her depression. She is rather isolated at this time.

The Person With the Problem

A person is not a diagnosis. Cowger (1992) outlines five areas for assessing a person's strengths: (a) cognition that focuses on thinking, perception, and understandings that are specifically related to a person's culture; (b) emotion that ranges from being in touch with feelings, to the appropriate control of affects, to feeling positive about life; (c) motivation that includes willingness to seek help and change such as taking responsibility for oneself; (d) coping that includes the range of coping skills available such as what the person has done in the past to "fix" the problem; and (e) the interpersonal area that includes a list of 24 items ranging from having friends to being resourceful. These items assist the practitioner and person in considering those strengths that may be used in coping with the problem situation.

Assessment of the person includes consideration of his or her culture. Maser and Dinges (1993) state that instruments designed to reach a diagnosis according to *DSM-IV* criteria miss the patient's strengths. Such instruments "fail to differentiate symptom severity and functional impairment, which may be crucially important in adequate treatment of culturally different patients" (p. 418). They recommend a focus on Axis IV of the *DSM-IV*, psychosocial stressors that afford an "elaboration into the cultural domain" (p. 419). Furthermore, they add that Axis V, global assessment of functioning, "holds considerable promise for expanding our understanding of cultural influences" (p. 419).

Lipton (1997) agrees that attention should be given to how stressors are assessed and experienced in specific cultural contexts. He states,

> The idioms of distress resulting from the experience of stress, such as depression and culturally more specific illness (e.g., *ataques de nervios*,

an attack of nerves, or *susto,* fright), should be examined at the level of the individual in his or her cultural . . . setting. (p. 110)

He concludes that culture is not simply a variable to be controlled but rather the context from which analysis proceeds.

Depression is identified by distressful symptoms, and distress is defined and tolerated differently among cultures. In cultures where suffering is valued, the person might not recognize depression as an illness. In cultures where suicide is prohibited, the person might have heightened anxiety around suicidal thoughts (Young, 1997).

In traditional cultures, depression often is understood as spirit possession. Carmelita, a Hispanic woman, talked about the voice that told her to take a knife and cut herself. "But I knew not to obey the voice," she related. Somatic complaints have been reported as symptoms of depression by non-European cultures. In the Asian tradition, depression is attributed to physical causes, whereas the Western patient accepts depression as psychological in nature. Chinese patients, for example, are more comfortable with a diagnosis of neurasthenia than one of depression (Ware & Kleinman, 1992). These persons present with a variety of somatic complaints. Native Americans from different tribes present with different symptoms, but often with alcoholism and feelings of social loneliness (Manson, Shore, & Bollin, 1985; O'Nell, 1993).

Thus, the practitioner should carefully attend to somatic complaints and the person's use of metaphors to express his or her complaints. As Young (1997) points out, "Differences between the patient's and clinician's values systems often make it difficult for the clinician to appreciate the importance of face saving, loyalty to family, and tradition in other cultures" (p. 42). The practitioner also needs to know when to apply universal norms versus cultural norms in differentiating between normal and abnormal behavior, considering etiological factors, and implementing appropriate interventions (Lopez et al., 1989). Of critical importance is the careful assessment of migration experiences and the pre-immigration life of the person.

TREATMENT GOALS

The overall goal is to assist the person in the process of recovery and the ongoing management of the illness. A general goal of treatment is to return the person to his or her previous level of functioning or to a level as close to "normal" as possible. The focus of treatment is on lessening the symptoms of depression and on abstinence from substances (particularly controlled substances) and serious reduction in drinking behavior. As with many dually diagnosed conditions, abstinence for a period of time is necessary for an accurate diagnosis of depression.

Treatment goals change through the process of treatment as people move through the stages of change, making adaptations in their lives to compensate for and cope with the life changes that illness and treatment require. Often by the time persons get help with their illnesses, they have experienced many changes in their lifestyles and social relationships. Thus, the goal is to help people to adjust to new lifestyles, to develop full understandings of their illnesses, and to manage their illnesses and prevent relapses. With some patients, this takes several cycles of treatment, relapse, and treatment.

For Aaron, this is his second course of treatment. His initial diagnosis and treatment occurred in the middle of bereavement processes and, for him, reinforced the belief that his depression was transient. Indeed, in his case, this second episode of depression also confirmed the diagnosis because the major depressive episodes occurred close together. He is removed enough from his friend's death that he can begin to believe (and understand) that he has a chronic illness. Aaron was limited to only six treatment sessions paid by his employee assistance plan. However, his family has offered to subsidize his sessions at a not-for-profit agency.

For Bea, the goal of treatment is for her to manage her life and illness better. Returning Bea to a higher level of functioning than she had before she began this cycle of treatment is an achievable goal. Fortunately, she has available unlimited treatment sessions through Medicaid.

Depressed patients have the capacity to form relationships so that psychotherapy is an option if people have the means to afford it. This means that people may go in and out of treatment as they move through the processes of change.

Outcomes

Five outcomes of treatment for depression have been defined and operationalized (Frank, Kupfer, Wagner, McEachem, & Cornes, 1991; Frank, Prien, et al., 1991):

◆ *Response:* significant level of improvement (responder is qualitatively different from a nonresponder)

◆ *Remission:* few signs of illness remaining

◆ *Relapse:* symptomatic exacerbation occurring after a response but before achieving sustained remission

♦ *Recovery:* sustained period of remission representing resolution of episode

♦ *Recurrence:* new episode of depressive illness following recovery (Riso et al., 1997, p. 134)

Riso and colleagues (1997) operationalized these definitions in a study of about 200 patients who were evaluated prior to treatment, during treatment, and during a 3-year follow-up. All five definitions demonstrated moderate to excellent validity.

TREATMENT MODEL

The transtheoretical model (Prochaska & DiClemente, 1986) is a psychotherapeutic model developed to treat addiction. The three-dimensional model was presented in Chapter 1. The model can be used with diverse treatment orientations such as interpersonal psychotherapy (IPT), which is based on psychodynamic theory, and cognitive behavioral therapy (CBT).

Thase et al. (1997) conducted a meta-analysis of original data of 595 patients with major depressive disorder in six different treatment protocols. They found evidence to support the widespread clinical impression that combining psychotherapy and antidepressant pharmacotherapy was far superior to using psychotherapy alone for treatment of severe recurrent depression. The two forms of psychotherapy that have been studied and shown to be efficacious in treatment of depression are IPT and CBT (Elkin, 1994). IPT also is recommended for treatment of dysthymia (Markowitz, 1997).

IPT is a present-oriented interpersonal approach to treatment of depression that considers social environment as important in the development and course of depression. Originally developed for use in a maintenance treatment trial, IPT has emerged as a standardized, empirically validated treatment for depression (Frank & Spanier, 1995). IPT focuses on four interpersonal areas: (a) grief, (b) interpersonal role disputes, (c) role transitions, and (d) interpersonal deficits (Weissman & Markowitz, 1994). Fifteen years after the original development of IPT, Frank and colleagues (1990) developed a specific IPT protocol for maintenance. Further clinical trials proved IPT-maintenance (IPT-M) to be empirically valid (the protocol is described in Spanier & Frank, 1997). IPT has the goal of bringing about remission, and IPT-M has the goal of sustaining wellness.

CBT is a short-term therapy developed by Beck, Rush, Shaw, and Emery (1979) for the treatment of depression. CBT is predicated on the assumption that the core difficulty in depression is a particular disorder of thought that leads to emotional and behavioral symptoms of depression.

CBT uses three general approaches to treatment: (a) didactic techniques, (b) cognitive techniques (eliciting and testing of automatic thoughts), and (c) behavioral techniques (role-playing and homework assignments). Meichenbaum (1995) lists seven tasks of therapy: (a) developing a therapeutic alliance and helping people to tell their stories, (b) educating people about their illnesses, (c) helping people to reconceptualize their predicaments into specific problems, (d) teaching people coping skills, (e) encouraging people to conduct personal experiments, (f) ensuring that people take credit for their own work, and (g) conducting relapse prevention.

READINESS FOR CHANGE

Readiness for change is one dimension of the transtheoretical model (Prochaska & DiClemente, 1986) and includes five stages. Assessment of readiness for change is essential so that the practitioner and person are working in the same stages. Furthermore, Barber (1994) suggests that the targets of intervention would differ depending on the stages of change. For example, during the precontemplative stage, the person and practitioner work on the micro or family system level. During the contemplative stage, the focus still is on small systems. But during the action stage, the emphasis broadens to all persons and systems with whom the person interacts. During this stage, the focus also is on lifestyle and behavioral changes. Maintenance focuses on all systems adding social supports and environmental changes (Barber, 1994). Rollnick, Heather, Gold, and Hall (1992) developed a short readiness for change assessment instrument.

As Aaron presents for treatment, he is in the precontemplative stage in terms of his addiction and mental illness. He has been able to stay free of drugs but does not realize the danger posed in using beer as a sedative. He still sees his depression as related to his grief. Coming for treatment is recognition that all is not right with his life. He is lonely and wants to have a normal life. Aaron is in the maintenance stage with his cocaine addiction.

Aaron is referred to a physician for assessment and treatment of depression. He meets most of the criteria for depressive diagnosis. Returning with prescriptions in hand, Aaron is tenuously moving to the contemplative stage. Beer drinking can be addressed. The goal during the contemplative stage would be to create a foundation for treatment, promote and sustain motivation, and develop goals.

Bea has carried her diagnosis for many years and is fluent in a discussion of symptoms, diagnosis, and medications. She appears to be in the maintenance stage of her depression. However, she "wears" her diagnosis and disability, and she uses illness as a defense against taking better care of herself, placing her still in a precontemplative stage. With her binge drinking, she is in the precontemplative stage. During this stage, the practitioner should promote discussion and reflection, develop awareness, and offer interpretation where indicated.

HELPING RELATIONSHIP

Therapeutic bonds are important for the depressed patient. However, Aaron and Bea have recent losses and have few social relationships. They might have problems in defining the limits of the relationship with the therapist. From the beginning, the parameters of the relationship should be discussed with respect to number of visits to expect, conditions of emergency contacts, and terms of rotation for interns and residents. This is particularly important for people with multiple losses.

Some studies estimate that at least 40% of the variance in outcomes of all forms of psychotherapy can be accounted for by the strength and quality of the therapeutic relationship (APA, 1993). Frank (1974) identifies six factors in the therapeutic relationship: (a) an emotionally charged confiding relationship, (b) a therapeutic rationale acceptable to the person, (c) the provision of new information, (d) a strengthening of the person's expectation for help, (e) the provision of successful experiences, and (f) the facilitation of emotional arousal. All of these relationship aspects are appropriate with depressed persons to varying degrees, depending on the stage of change. The last aspect, facilitation of emotional arousal, is dealt with separately in the process termed *dramatic relief.*

On the helping relationship, Saleebey (1992) comments, "The practitioner must be genuinely interested in, and respectful of, clients' accounts, narratives, the interpretive slants they take on their lives" (p. 6). He continues to say that the person is best known not through his or her troubles but rather as someone who knows things, has ideas and energies, and can do some things. A person who seeks help wants to know that he or she is cared about and that the practitioner respects the person and believes in him or her. Saleebey continues, "You can build little on . . . pathology and problem, but you may build an enduring edifice out of strength and possibility inherent in each individual" (p. 7).

The practitioner is a collaborator with the person with the problem. The practitioner might have specialized knowledge needed by the person as well as a vision of wellness that the individual might not yet possess. However, the client with the problem is his or her own expert on the client's own situation. Respect for this expertise must be conveyed to the client through the relationship.

Connected to the strengths perspective is the concept of empowerment. This concept focuses on helping the person to discover power within himself or herself, the family, and the community. To accomplish this task, the following are necessary:

◆ Instigating a collaborative (i.e., mutual, consultative) stance

◆ Helping to give voice to, and acknowledging the authenticity of, the individual's story, values, and beliefs

◆ Recognizing the individual's efforts and successes in surviving despite rootlessness

◆ Giving attention and making links to possible communities of interest where the individual's strengths are respected and can begin to flourish (Saleebey, 1992, p. 9)

PSYCHOPHARMACOLOGICAL CONSIDERATIONS

Brady and Roberts (1995) state, "Any psychopharmacological strategy that is not introduced in the context of psychosocial intervention in this population is doomed to failure" (p. 345). They give a clear review of medications. They state that the use of tricyclic antidepressants (TCAs) in this population shows promise. Doses and blood levels of TCAs remain unclear, and Brady and Roberts recommend TCA plasma level monitoring with this population. They further quote studies showing that selective serotonin reuptake inhibitors (SSRIs) have been implicated in the control of alcohol intake as well as in improvement in depression. Brady and Roberts state,

> SSRIs may be a logical first choice in alcoholic populations. The SSRIs may decrease the desire to drink and help initiate abstinence as well as treat depression. . . . SSRIs have fewer anticholinergic and cardiotoxic side effects, so they will be better tolerated and safer in the population at greater risk for noncompliance and impulsive overdosing. (p. 347)

Klerman and colleagues (1994) found, in a review, that many studies support the value of treatment combining medication and psychotherapy. They conclude, "Medications have a positive effect on psychotherapy in symptom relief, which is more readily produced by psychopharmacology, thus render[ing] the patient more accessible to psychotherapy" (p. 762).

Pre-scientific medicines—folk medicines and folkways of healing— must be assessed, understood, and respected.

COGNITIVE-BEHAVIORAL DIMENSIONS

Coping Skills

Self-Liberation

Aaron has taken responsibility for his cocaine addiction but needs continuous support to maintain compliance with his medication. His current 12-step NA program has helped him to gain control over addictions but sends him confusing messages about his depression. Aaron needs support in balancing the demands and opinions of this group and in taking his medication for depression.

Bea needs support and reminding that she does have some control over her life. She feels hemmed in and limited by her symptoms and disabilities. She needs to recognize that she is in control of her symptoms through medication compliance and abstinence. This is especially true because she relies solely on public medical care and ever changing physicians.

Stimulus Control

Stimulus control in the Prochaska and DiClemente (1986) model means controlling stimuli that trigger unwanted behaviors (e.g., substance abuse, withdrawal, isolation, depression). The challenge for the depressed person is to stay engaged in the community as an antidote for withdrawal while, at the same time, avoiding activities in which substances are involved. This also is a challenge for the single person. Aaron isolates himself through working late shifts and sleeping days. With his family and support group as his primary social outlet, he is avoiding situations that trigger his impulse to use cocaine. On the other hand, he lacks the stimulus of an active social group.

Bea avoids her chaotic family. Her near poverty status puts her in a mode of daily struggle for survival. She chooses to use her small amount of money for occasional bottles of whiskey. Avoiding places where people drink is not an issue for her.

Stimulus control also means controlling thoughts that stimulate negative affects (depression). In addition to relaxation and thought-stopping techniques, a person may plan specific activities to do during a low period of the day or plan to avoid places that might trigger sadness.

PSYCHOEDUCATION

Consciousness Raising

A clear goal of treatment for Aaron is a full understanding and definition of his problem or illness. *Denial* is a common term used to describe a person's inability to accept a problem that seems so obvious to others. *Resistance* describes in more behavioral terms a person's refusal to come to terms with his or her condition. Resistance takes the form of refusing to seek medical attention, to take medication, or even to discuss the illness. Aaron *rationalizes* both his former cocaine addiction (he was a kid, everyone was doing it, and he stopped cold) and his depression (his best friend got killed). With these statements, Aaron also is *minimizing* his problems. As he develops more insight into his condition, he might want to blame one condition on the other, for example, by saying, "I have a few beers at night to help me sleep."

Both Aaron and Bea went through long periods of denial of their chemical dependence. Aaron's recovery from his addiction to cocaine was rather dramatic. However, he was young and must understand that he has a lifetime of avoiding drugs and alcohol. Aaron's denial of depression was reflected in his choosing to stop medication without consulting his physician.

Bea has lived with her diagnosis for many years, yet at times she vacillates between believing that she will magically get well and acting the role of a permanently disabled person. The ever present task for Bea is balancing these views.

Both Aaron and Bea need to become aware of (a) the impact of their substance abuse on their mental illness and (b) the realities of their mental illness, specifically, how they can live with depression. Psychoeducation is a tool to be used here with both Aaron and Bea. Aaron's education about depression is very basic. With Bea, the struggle will be to help her see her illness as a manageable part of her life.

Self-Reevaluation

Persons with dual diagnoses must come to terms with a definition of self that includes the dual illnesses. Through psychoeducation, they not only come to understand something of the brain chemistry in depression and addiction but also come to see the role that learning and conditioning play in this process (Wallace, 1993). Understanding the possible genetic influence in both addiction and depression should not render persons with these conditions hopeless. Counter to the genetic influences are the social environment influences that may be seen as possibilities rather than as liabilities. Thus, a biopsychosocial approach to the illness expands and enriches the notion of either illness being "just a disease."

Part of the recovery process for many persons is learning to identify and appropriately manage feelings such as shame, guilt, and anger. Cognitive behavioral therapy is useful in decreasing depressive feelings and changing the faulty thinking that is common among many depressed and chemically dependent individuals. Developing skills in modifying maladaptive feelings, thoughts, and beliefs can be empowering. The person develops an image of someone who can cope. Similarly, identifying and handling urges and cravings for substances is important in recovery. Using strategies such as talking with others, redirecting activities, changing thoughts, and avoiding threatening situations can be learned (Rubinstein et al., 1990).

Aaron and Bea are very different, both in terms of outlook and in terms of practical possibilities for their lives. If Aaron can continue to manage his illness and stay free of alcohol and drugs, then he is capable of earning a good living. He can see the possibility of having his own family. His biggest issue is reaching out and risking himself in relationships. He remains tied to his deceased friend's family members, who have moved on with their lives. Finding networks for meeting young women and dating in this new community are difficult. "Setting goals is one thing," Aaron says, "but getting out there is another."

Bea has had a long and tough struggle with her illness and addiction. She is hardened against all new possibilities for herself. She sees her life as a daily struggle for survival. The fact that she gets out every day for some activity related to taking care of herself is a tribute to her desire to survive, yet she takes no comfort in these abilities. Attaining independent living will be a feat for which she might acknowledge her own strengths in taking care of herself. Bea lives daily with double stigmas: mental illness and poverty. No matter what she does for herself, she finds it difficult to give herself credit for it (e.g., "The government paid for it, not me").

Interpersonal Skills

Environmental Reevaluation

Staying clean is a major goal for Aaron. The impact of his drug abuse on the self and a loved one was dramatically demonstrated with the death of his friend. The resultant pain of grief and depression was difficult for him to manage especially among his old friends. His reaction of relocating helped him to avoid old friends and suppliers but exacerbated his depression. He now struggles less with a need for a fix than with his tendency to bury himself in depression and guilt.

Bea was living with a relative who was addicted to drugs and alcohol and who was abusive to her. Bea protected herself by isolating herself in her room and watching television or playing games. Eventually, she found the strength to explore independent living and endure waiting lists, and she finally freed herself from that environment. It took years and several therapists for Bea to find the hope for a better life and then the strength to move.

Counterconditioning

Aaron has progressed to concern about his health and conditioning. He has gained weight, and his negative self-image feeds his depression. In a small study, Hutchinson, Shrinar, and Cross (1999) discovered that people with differing diagnoses of severe mental illness who exercise regularly experience improvement in self-esteem and mood as well as in overall fitness. Aaron cognitively recognizes the value of exercise and has begun weight training. Presently, he works out sporadically in his workplace gym at the end of his late night shift. Moving to a gym where he could interact with other people is a goal.

Bea has fewer financial resources, and she uses her physical disability as an excuse for not getting any exercise. Her primary outlet is playing video games, watching television, and renting movies. Although such games distract her thoughts about her illness and help to maintain her sobriety, they are addictive and socially isolating. Bea can recall that she was taught certain exercises in rehabilitation, but she has not continued them. She can be helped to investigate exercise possibilities at the local YWCA, where fees might be reduced.

FAMILY RELATIONSHIPS

Family education (psychoeducation) is an important aspect of treatment. The goal for family work is to reduce tension and improve communication, specifically expressed emotion (Jordan, Barrett, Vandiver, & Lewellen, 1999). Living with a person with depression is difficult. The person has feelings of low self-esteem, and many times any intervention by relatives is perceived as a put-down that confirms the low opinion the person holds for himself or herself. Families can increase their skill in getting feedback to ill family members. In conjunction with the person with the illness, families increase their understanding and acceptance of the illness and assist in problem solving.

Families' ethnicities have an impact on their views of mental illness. In fact, some cultures dislike the term *mental illness* (Solomon, 1998). Ethnicity also may affect how families view and participate in family intervention. Clinicians must be sensitive to cultural variations in planning work with families. Families might need information and support but not need formal intervention. For many families, acceptance by the worker and availability of the worker are sufficient (Solomon, 1998).

Neither Bea's nor Aaron's family has been involved in family education. Bea is isolated from her family. She maintains distance from her relatives, and her children distance themselves from her. Both of her children have escaped the abusive family that Bea describes as hers. Her son has made a career as an army noncommissioned officer now stationed in Europe. Her daughter, son-in-law, and grandchild live far enough away to be uninvolved but close enough for a reasonable amount of contact. A goal for Bea would be to establish closer ties to her children, involving them in family education in their area or during visits.

Aaron says that his family knows of his illness from the family doctor. As Aaron understands his illness more, he may be helpful in educating his parents about his depression. With the expectation of future love relationships, Aaron needs to think about and plan for discussing his illness and addiction with friends.

Contingency Management

Twelve-step programs, friends, and sponsors are important adjuncts in managing the environment. Twelve-step self-help groups are a well-accepted adjunct to treatment for the chemically dependent person. Such programs might pose problems for the dually diagnosed. Alcoholics Anonymous has addressed the issue of the need for members to take prescribed medications. However, not all groups have accepted this. Some groups actively oppose taking any medications. Thus, dually diagnosed persons must find a group that accepts the treatment for their depression or a specific group such as Double Trouble. Also, support groups exist for people with depression. A sponsor can be particularly helpful in contingency management provided that the sponsor is sensitive to and accepting of the dual problems.

With addictions and substance abuse under control, the biggest problem for Aaron and Bea is preventing relapse into life-threatening depression. Families and friends have moved from rescuing them from the effects of their addictions to responding to threats of suicide or worrying about suicide.

For both Aaron and Bea, staying clean and dry was in constant contradiction to medicating depression. Contingency management for this population means managing psychotropic drugs and avoiding illegal unprescribed substances and alcohol.

Both Aaron and Bea have been through several relapse episodes. Bea has been ill so long that she now accepts the chronicity of her depression and disabilities. Aaron still is young and holds out hope that someday he will be "normal."

ENVIRONMENTAL INTERVENTION

Social Liberation

Aaron now is living independently and alone. He works a night shift, and this further isolates him. Aaron participates in a 12-step program that is his main social outlet. He makes weekly trips home to see his parents. Aaron wants more relationships, particularly dating relationships. He is concerned about a recent weight gain and being or feeling unattractive. He works out at the gym at work during the early hours of the morning.

For Aaron, social liberation means developing broader social networks rather than continuing to rely solely on his NA group and his parents. As a young man, he desperately wants relationships. Aaron might consider finding a roommate and moving to an apartment complex that has social activities. A good move for Aaron would be to join a gym, where he would be with other people for this activity, and to find other groups to join—church groups, singles groups, and groups performing volunteer work.

AFFECTIVE DIMENSIONS

Dramatic Relief

With depressed persons, the surfacing and expression of anger and frustration is important. Such expression externalizes the feelings rather than turning them inward. With Aaron's dealing with the recent death of a close friend, the therapist helps Aaron to balance grief with the morbid self-loathing that feeds his depression.

Similarly, with Bea, grief over the loss of loved ones can get out of control. She anticipates anniversaries of loved ones' deaths, knowing that she will become depressed and have a "terrible time of it." She turns such occasions into a litany of all of life's losses. In both Aaron's and Bea's cases, grief must be confronted and balanced with the expectation that one recovers from loss.

SUPPORT GROUPS

Both Aaron and Bea are active in support groups. A Double Trouble group (Vogel, Knight, Laudet, & Magura, 1998) might better serve Aaron than does his current NA group. For now, he is managing the pressure to be drug free (except for his Prozac). His relationship with his sponsor and mentor is of critical importance to him; he is educating his sponsor about his mental illness. He also might benefit from a depression support group.

Bea has found, much to her surprise, that her depression support group has been very helpful. All of the group members pitched in to help her move. She was so touched by this display of caring that she has begun to return favors. From that positive experience, she has begun a relationship with the Alliance for Mentally Ill in her community. She needs the support of an advocacy group, but she also has contributions to make because she knows the system so well.

◼ *QUESTIONS FOR DISCUSSION*

1. Aaron and Bea appear to have unlimited treatment resources. Within this context, what are the social work ethical concerns in treating clients with efficiency as well as effectiveness? Do we have an ethical obligation to use the most efficient treatment available?

2. Suppose that Aaron's parents or employer wants to know about his progress or that Bea's children want to know about her progress. How would the social worker involve others in treatment?

6

Bipolar Disorders

Sherlock Holmes is the quintessential example of bipolar illness with substance abuse. Depicted as severely depressed between cases, he uses cocaine to lift his moods. When captivated by a case, he stays up night and day obsessing over clues, riddles, and the search for an answer he knows rests in his memory. This behavior elicits the concern of his friend, Dr. Watson, and his landlady, who try to protect him. Eventually, he crashes. Bipolar disorders are part of the mood disorders. The choice was made to separate bipolar disorders from other depressive disorders because of the special features of this disorder and how it interacts with substances.

DEFINITIONS

Approximately 25% of all mood disorder patients experience a manic or hypomanic episode. Nearly all of these patients will have episodes of depression. Although this nomenclature has been in use for only about 20 years, the illness has been recognized for more than a century (Morrison, 1995). This group of disorders was referred to as *manic depression*. About 1% of the general population, men and women alike, are affected. Bipolar disorder is strongly hereditary.

- ♦ *Bipolar I disorder:* There must be at least one manic episode. Most Bipolar I patients also have at least one major depressive episode (American Psychiatric Association [APA], 1994).

- ♦ *Bipolar II disorder:* A Bipolar II diagnosis requires at least one hypomanic episode plus at least one major depressive episode (APA, 1994).

- ♦ *Cyclothymic disorder:* Cyclothymic patients have had repeated mood swings, but none severe enough to be called major depressive episodes or manic episodes (APA, 1994).

82

Bipolar I disorder is any cyclic mood disorder that includes at least one manic episode. Criteria for a manic episode are that, for at least 1 week, the person's mood is abnormally high, irritable, and expansive and that the person has three or more of the following: grandiose self-esteem, reduced need for sleep, increased talkativeness, flight of ideas, easy distractibility, speeded-up psychomotor activity, and goal-directed activity. The symptoms are severe enough so that at least one of the following are met: psychotic features; required hospitalization; and impaired work, social, or personal functioning. A bipolar mixed episode requires that the person have both major depression and a manic episode nearly every day for a week or more (APA, 1994).

Bipolar II disorder is distinguished by the degree of disability and discomfort imposed by the high phase, hypomania, which never leads to psychosis and hospitalization. Criteria for hypomania are the same as for manic episode except in severity; that is, the episode is not psychotic; does not require hospitalization; and does not impair work, social, or personal functioning (APA, 1994).

Other bipolar types include rapid recycling, seasonal patterns, and postpartum onset. Rapid recycling occurs in 10% to 20% of bipolar patients with poor lithium response and is more common in women, especially postpartum and postmenopausal women. It is defined as at least four episodes of mania, hypomania, or major depression during the previous 12 months. In the seasonal pattern, symptoms occur at specific times of the year. Onset for postpartum must be within 4 weeks of delivery.

Medical conditions associated with bipolar disorder include the following:

♦ Central nervous system trauma (e.g., poststroke)

♦ Metabolic disorders (e.g., hyperthyroidism)

♦ Infectious diseases (e.g., encephalitis)

♦ Seizure disorders

♦ Central nervous system tumor (Preston, O'Neal, & Talaga, 1997, p. 75)

UNIQUE PROBLEMS

According to the Epidemiological Catchment Area study (Regier et al., 1990), about 60% of persons who are bipolar also meet the criteria for alcoholism or other substance abuse. The ratio for alcoholism in bipolar illness is 6 to 2. Bipolar is the most frequent non-substance abuse Axis I diagnosis in patients with alcohol or substance abuse disorders (Sonne, Brady, & Morton, 1994). Keller and colleagues (1986) found that a higher percentage (13%) of mixed or cycling patients also were alcoholics. Substance abuse and affective disorders may start out as separate illnesses, but they appear to be related for two reasons: "(1) predisposition to substance abuse in bipolar disorder because of subjective effects of drugs [and] (2) diagnostic confusion because the effects of abused drugs resemble manifestations of affective disorders" (Swann, 1997, p. 507).

Drugs can mimic or exacerbate affective symptoms, specifically the highs and lows. For example, opiates may calm a person who seeks to feel "normal," mellow, and soothed, and they may dull sensations of physical and psychic pain. Alcohol gives a false sense of control and, while calming and providing a release from anxiety, also reduces inhibitions and suppressed feelings. Stimulants produce a greater stimulation for extroverts (which helps prolong high moods) and, for those suffering from depression, provide relief from fatigue and depletion (Cohen & Levy, 1992).

Swann (1997) concludes from his review that an underlying mechanism might be operating as either a reward or impulse control. Persons use drugs to adjust their moods so as to resemble their high moods. This is similar to the findings of Nunes, Deliyannides, Donovan, and McGrath (1996). They state that substance abusers are seeking a lift or memories of the lift. This fits the idea of self-medication. Drugs or alcohol may reduce symptoms of depression, and cocaine may either treat depression or produce mania.

Persons with this dual diagnosis (a) have stronger family histories of bipolar disorder (Winokur et al., 1995), (b) have earlier onsets and more frequent episodes in hospital-based studies (Sonne et al., 1994), and (c) seem to have more "revolving door" hospitalizations (Haywood et al., 1995). Swann (1997) concludes,

> Among individuals with substance abuse and bipolar disorder, those whose bipolar disorder started first have more severe bipolar disorder but have a course of substance abuse that is tied to their bipolar disorder and remits when affective symptoms do. Individuals whose substance abuse started first have fewer episodes of bipolar disorder but a more chronic course of substance abuse. (p. 509)

The presence of substance abuse may decrease the effectiveness of the use of lithium, the most common treatment of bipolar illness. Swann (1997) writes that the adage of "speed kills" applies to bipolar disorder, where the addition of substance abuse increases the risk of suicide. He continues that there are two groups with this dual disorder:

1. Substance abuse is associated with a severe form of bipolar disorder characterized by strongly positive family history, early onset, and frequent episodes. This group may be overrepresented in patients hospitalized for bipolar disorder.

2. [The second group is] . . . characterized by relatively mild bipolar disorder *per se*, perhaps requiring the neurochemical or environmental stress of substance abuse to trigger the onset of bipolar disorder. (p. 509)

In both cases, there is a predisposition to increased sensitivity to the rewarding aspects of the abused drugs and cross-conditioning between drug effects and affective episodes. Thus, treatment is complicated.

Leibenluft (1996) found that rapid cycling is more common among bipolar women and that bipolar women have more depressive episodes and may be more likely to suffer from mixed mania compared to bipolar men.

Gitlin, Swendsen, Heller, and Hammen (1995) followed 82 bipolar outpatients for an average of 4 years and 3 months. They found that, despite maintenance treatment, survival analysis indicated a 5-year risk of relapse for 78% of the outpatients and that many had multiple relapses. "Poor psychosocial functioning, especially occupational functioning, predicted shorter time to relapse. . . . Number of depressions was more associated with family and social disruptions than [with] mania" (p. 1639). They found significant psychosocial disability among their sample participants. Furthermore, family and social outcomes were more associated with depressive episodes than with manic episodes.

Goldberg, Harrow, and Grossman (1995) reported on a longitudinal follow-up study of 51 bipolar patients. They found that 21 had overall good outcomes and that half were rehospitalized at least once during the 4½-year period. They state that many factors contribute to the poor clinical course of these persons including previous history of treatment failure, medication noncompliance, rapid recycling, and poor work and social supports. They found that these persons achieve remission of symptoms but have difficulty in resuming previous psychosocial functioning after major episodes of the illness.

Winokur and colleagues (1995) conducted a 5-year study to explore alcoholism in persons with bipolar illness. They found alcoholism to be more common in persons with this disorder than in comparison participants. The alcoholism in this group could not be explained by family histories of alcoholism. They conclude that alcoholism in persons with this bipolar disorder often is a secondary complication. Feinman and Dunner (1996) found a connection between early onset of bipolar disorder and subsequent drug abuse. They conclude that "early bipolar illness might predispose one to substance abuse, [perhaps for social or emotional reasons]" (p. 47).

Miklowitz and Goldstein (1997) state that they often have marveled at the intensity with which bipolar persons experience life and that their creativity and artistic contributions have been documented in the literature. Despite these strengths, they say, the severe suffering of these persons and their family members is overlooked. "Despite medication, these persons experience intense pain in the form of ruined family relationships, financial problems and ruin, or lost hopes and dreams" (p. xi).

Episodes of bipolar disorder are associated with severe impairment in interpersonal relationships and work functioning. This, coupled with the recurring nature of this illness, may account for this phenomenon. Miklowitz and Goldstein (1997) say that, even in the absence of symptoms, bipolar persons describe an "apathetic, anergic state in which they feel unmotivated to resume work [and] school social activities" (p. 22). They conclude that bipolar disorder, like schizophrenia, is associated with severe psychosocial deficits.

CASE EXAMPLES

Dennis was 30 years old when he had his first manic episode, which seemed to interrupt his grieving over his mother, who recently had died of cancer. Dennis's mother had been dead for about 4 months. As the second child, he had been particularly attached to his mother and had participated in her care more than his older sister, who had been busy managing a career in banking and caring for three young children. At a point when the family became concerned about Dennis's depression, he threw himself into work with a vengeance. A landscape architect, he returned with renewed vigor to several projects, soon working 18 hours a day, 7 days a week. He ignored his family and became argumentative with his colleagues. Occasionally, he would crash and sleep for a time, and when awoke he would be angry that he had wasted time. At those times, he would use some of his mother's pain pills, combined with vodka on the rocks, to lull himself to sleep. His crisis came after a three-martini lunch when he insulted a client, and his partners decided to hospitalize him. He was released within 24 hours with a diagnosis of Bipolar I disorder and suspected substance abuse. Within 4 months, his wife brought him to outpatient treatment, with both Dennis and his wife minimizing both disorders and attributing his depression to his mother's death and attributing his work behavior to his desire to get ahead.

Eleanor Jane (E. J. for short) presented as recently relapsed from Bipolar I disorder and substance abuse disorder. E. J. is 28 years old and has been diagnosed for 5 years. She is an African American who left home when she was 16 years old to travel with a rock band for which she was the lead singer. The group was heavily into drugs and would play all night, get high toward the morning, and sleep most days. E. J. recalled that it had become more and more difficult for her to get the rest she needed, and she often would go for days without sleep. When she finally would crash, she would experience depression.

During one of these downs, E. J. overdosed. Hospitalized for 2 weeks, she was diagnosed as Bipolar I with substance abuse. She returned to her family for her recovery, but that was short-lived. She soon was back on the road and back to her old ways. She continued this cycle for several years until the band dissolved and she was home for good. She had a long rehabilitation ahead of her. She experienced her drug program as most critical, immersed herself in 12-step programs, and convinced herself to get rid of all her drugs. Her recovery was compounded by the reappearance of her former lover with whom she used to go barhopping. She did not seem to understand that alcohol also was a dangerous drug for her. Her parents insisted that she receive treatment this time.

Biopsychosocial problems for Both Dennis and E. J. include problems with sleep and wakefulness. Neither of them has ever required much sleep, and their work experience has tended to support erratic sleep patterns. As teenagers, each began the pattern of working late into the night and crashing during the day.

Dennis, an excellent student, states that he would just "get going good at the books" when everyone else was going to bed. He also reports that he could hit the books after a big fraternity party when everyone else was passing out. He claims that he drank. He says that his girlfriend (now his wife) "kept pretty close tabs on me to be sure I could always drive." This work-sleep pattern continued to become his work pattern.

E. J. still calls herself a night owl and has trouble keeping a job because "I can't get up in the morning." E. J. is a beautiful woman who is rail thin, insisting that she cannot gain weight.

Both E. J. and Dennis have grief and loss issues. E. J. still talks about her long-term (nearly 10-year) relationship with Frankie. She still wants him to tell her why he left her for someone else.

Both Dennis and E. J. have families who are active in their lives and available for work with professionals. Dennis has a career that offers him a great deal of flexibility, but he has deadlines to meet and is very competitive. E. J. has only worked in the entertainment industry, and even then, at the initiative of others. She did not finish high school and never has completed her general equivalency diploma.

Regarding gender issues, Breakey, Calabrese, Rosenblatt, and Crum (1998) found a low recognition by professionals of women's alcohol use disorders. They opine that therapists expect women's rates to be lower and, therefore, ask fewer questions. Another explanation might be that because men are known to drink more heavily and have conspicuous drinking habits, women might not seem to have problems by male drinking standards.

Feinman and Dunner (1996), in their study of bipolar disordered persons, report that 35% of women and 55% of men had histories of substance abuse. They conclude that women develop alcoholism with a later onset than do men. Bipolar disorder with comorbid substance abuse is greater in men than in women (Winokur et al., 1995).

ASSESSMENT CONSIDERATIONS

Defining the Problem

As with all depressive disorders, suicide is a threat and must be assessed early and at subsequent times when the person is in an acute phase. Substance abuse seems to be severely underdiagnosed and undertreated in patients with bipolar disorder (Miller, Faulkner, & Craig, 1994). Bipolar illness is inherently difficult to diagnose in the presence of substance abuse because of the effects of the drugs on the illness (Brady & Sonne, 1995). With chronic use, drugs can mimic a psychiatric disorder. "Stimulant intoxication can produce a syndrome indistinguishable from mania or hypomania, and substantial depressive symptomatology can emerge during stimulant withdrawal" (Brady & Sonne, 1995, p. 21). Diagnosis should be postponed unless the mood swings began before the substance abuse or they persist during long periods of abstinence.

Substance-induced symptoms of depression may abate within 2 to 4 weeks (Dorus, Kennedy, & Gibbons, 1987), and treatment may wait until an accurate diagnosis is made. With bipolar illness, the manic phase may last as few as 3 days; therefore, a shorter period of abstinence is required (Brady & Sonne, 1995). Hospitalization might be needed to attain the necessary abstinence for the purposes of diagnostic clarity. Brady and Sonne (1995) write, "The recent addition of bipolar spectrum disorders, including cyclothymia, to the diagnostic interview schema used in alcohol abuse studies significantly increases the reported percentage of patients with mood disorders" (p. 21).

Brady and Sonne (1995) add that differentiating the subtle mood disorders from mood-altering substances is difficult but important. When mood disturbance contributes to substance abuse, treatment of these conditions takes on greater importance.

"Substance use problems can easily be overlooked in someone with a major mental illness" (Lehman, 1996, p. 34). Breakey and colleagues (1998) state that the ideal evaluation of a patient would include an evaluation of all the *Diagnostic and Statistical Manual of Mental Disorders* (*DSM-IV*) criteria for substance abuse and dependence (APA, 1994) as well as the lifetime use. They continue that quantity and frequency of use is not sufficient. The personal and social consequences of use and abuse need to be assessed. These consequences may be greater than the amount consumed. The authors add that the use of both the CAGE (Mayfield, McLeod, & Hall, 1974) and the Michigan Alcoholism Screening Test (MAST) enhance practitioners' evaluations.

Who Is Involved in the Problem Situation?

Families are important sources of information about people and the course of their illnesses. Family members may recall prior episodes that people have forgotten and may be able to describe the behaviors more accurately. Families also can help to report family histories of illnesses. Families are a source of support to ill family members. They also have the potential to subvert treatment.

Understanding ill people's family context is important in assessment, both to discover the stress and strain that emanate from families and to assess the manner and degree of support that can be brought to bear on people as they cope with their illnesses. Persons are best understood within the context of their families, and families are best understood within the context of culture (both their own and their culture within a culture). Views of mental health and attitudes toward mental health services, interventions, and medication may be culturally determined. In assessment, a determination is made as to who the family is and may include immediate relatives as well as fictive kin.

Culture influences the manner in which people present themselves and their issues. Some families may be more expressive and others more closed. Families differ in problem-solving styles and in conflict resolution. Roles and role structures differ in flexibility as well as in how roles are assumed inside families and how they are presented in public. Different ethnic groups view illnesses differently, seeing a greater connection among physical, emotional, and behavioral aspects. Embedded within cultures and families are sources of strength that are useful for recovery (Finley, 1998).

The Person With the Problem

Rapp (1998) states that "[our] purpose is to assist another human being, not to treat a patient" (p. 44). The work should focus on what the person has achieved, what resources currently are available to the person, what the person knows, and what aspirations and dreams the person holds. This strengths perspective attends not only to the person with the illness but also to the surrounding environment. In such an assessment, the person's personal and environmental assets are identified. These assets are in six domains of life: daily living, financial, vocational/educational, social and spiritual supports, health, and leisure/recreational.

Furthermore, Rapp (1998) continues to state that each life domain is divided into three categories: current status, desires and aspirations, and history. History focuses on how the person has coped rather than on a lengthy reiteration of the illness. The focus is on the here and now.

The culture of the person also is considered for the assessment. Dennis is Caucasian, and E. J. is African American. Dennis is from an upper-middle-class family and is maintaining that status in his current family. E. J.'s family also is upper middle class. Her parents are professional people, and E. J. is their only child who did not attend college. The model of ethnic reality provides a framework for assessing E. J. and her family.

Devore and Schlesinger (1996) first proposed in 1981 that ethnic reality is best understood by using a combination of general knowledge of human behavior, ethnic group norms, and social class. This model assumes that because social class includes occupation, education, and income, social class along with culture will provide useful information about personal values, beliefs, and lifestyles. Social class is used to describe people in terms of opportunities available because of the occupations and positions that people hold in the marketplace. Income and education are interwoven because they lead to positions and occupations that are powerful and prestigious.

The assumption of ethnic reality is that people who occupy similar positions of power, influence, and prestige may share more common values than those of similar cultures and ethnic groups. Although social class is not a community in the sense that an ethnic group may be, people of similar social class do tend to share beliefs and location. Middle and upper class ethnicities are integrated into middle and upper class neighborhoods and take on or share the dominant culture's values and behaviors. Understanding a family's ethnic reality and the values implied is important in assessing and understanding a family's attitudes, beliefs, and behaviors toward a mentally ill person. Such beliefs and attitudes will shape their help-seeking behavior and their expectations of and ways of relating to the professional helpers (Jordan, Barrett, Vandiver, & Lewellen, 1999).

TREATMENT GOALS

Considerations for treatment are as follows:

1. The presence of substance abuse modifies treatment in bipolar disease, apparently reducing the effects of lithium.

2. Both hypomania and abused drugs are powerful reinforcers with the possibility of strong conditioning and cross-conditioning.

3. Withdrawal from substances is aversive and may resemble depression and the effects of some psychotropic drugs. . . . Both must be treated vigorously, and the notion that the treatment of one will resolve the other is generally wishful thinking. (Swann, 1997, p. 510)

Swann (1997) continues,

The idea that individuals with both an affective disorder and substance abuse should strive to be "chemically" free is pernicious and would never be entertained if the "chemicals" in question were needed for the treatment of essential hypertension or diabetes mellitus. (p. 510)

Swann (1997) further states that someday we will understand the underlying "diathesis"—the rewarding effects of both the illness and the substance—and will be able to treat them better. "Meanwhile, we must assume that the person has two lifelong but episodic and variable diseases and treat both" (p. 510).

Lehman (1996) states that appropriate treatment for persons with co-occurring disorders is an integrated treatment for both problems. He concludes that "failure to address both problems may render treatment for either ineffective" (p. 34).

TREATMENT MODEL

The transtheoretical model (Prochaska & DiClemente, 1986), a three-dimensional model described in Chapter 1, provides tools for assessment (readiness for change), areas for focus in treatment (processes of change), and the context for therapeutic work (levels of change). Within this model, both psychopharmacology and psychotherapy are important. Pies (1993) writes that, despite the biological substratum of this disorder, "a psychological approach to the patient is essential and may critically affect compliance with lithium" (p. 95). Furthermore, specific issues of concern to bipolar persons need to be dealt with in a psychotherapeutic way. Some of these are fear of recurring mood swings, difficulty in discriminating between normal and pathological mood swings, problems arising from interpersonal relationships, developmental stages of the illness, and concerns about passing illness on to children.

Interpersonal psychotherapy and cognitive behavioral therapy, shown to be efficacious in the treatment of depression (Elkin, 1994), may be used within the transtheoretical model to deal with problems associated with bipolar disorder and substance abuse.

READINESS FOR CHANGE

Assessment of readiness for change is essential to treatment planning and implementation. Writing about depression and substance abuse, Schutte, Hearst, and Moos (1997) urge that the practitioner consider what stage of change the person is in when evaluating the effects of the illness on drinking behavior (p. 401). This is true for planning treatment given that the practitioner and person should be working on the same area. Writing only about alcoholism, Barber (1994) suggests that the target of intervention would differ considering the stage of change.

During the precontemplative stage, the target would be the microsystem, specifically the family members or partner intervention. When the person moves into contemplation, the focus still is on small systems, and the objective is supporting motivation for change. During the action stage, the target becomes the individual and the systems with which the person interacts, and the objective is both behavioral and lifestyle changes. During the maintenance stage, the focus is on all systems adding environmental contingencies and social supports (Barber, 1994). Rollnick, Heather, Gold, and Hall (1992) developed a short instrument to assess these specific stages of change for alcoholics.

Dennis is working on coming to grips with his illness. This puts him in the precontemplative stage. Both he and his wife, Gretchen, voice acceptance of the doctor's diagnosis. At the same time, they see Dennis's episode as situational. They go along with whatever the professionals say, but in the backs of their minds, they seem to believe that time and distance from the event will demonstrate that the episode was a one-time occurrence.

So far as his drinking is concerned, Dennis and his wife view him as a controlled drinker who has lapsed because of the pressure of his project. Gretchen recalls that when the two were dating (and partying), Dennis drank too much. She would tell him to stop and he would. They agree that noontime drinking is strictly forbidden, and he complies. By Gretchen's report, "Other than that, he drinks a few beers when he plays golf or watches games . . . and of course we have wine with dinner." Their denial is related to their plans to have children. When the episode occurred, they were planning to start a family right away. They want to be reassured that this will not be transmitted to their children or, better still, that he is not ill but merely misdiagnosed.

E. J. could be considered to be in the maintenance stage, with occasional lapses, relapses, or perhaps recurrences. She can articulate her problems and uses 12-step problems to stay clean. The only time that she gets into trouble is when Frankie comes around.

HELPING RELATIONSHIP

The therapeutic relationship is an important ingredient in treatment and outcome. An APA (1993) task force reported that some studies estimate that at least 40% of the variance of all forms of psychotherapy can be accounted for by the strength and quality of the relationship. This relationship is developed through imparting respect for and interest in the person and a hopeful stance about recovery.

Basco and Rush (1996), addressing the therapeutic alliance when working with bipolar persons, discuss the importance of commitment on the part of the caregiver. Treatment for these persons is long-term, and they need to believe that the clinician will be with them for the long term. These authors continue that cognitive behavioral therapy for bipolar disorder hinges on a strong collaborative relationship in which the person's opinions and wishes are invited and explored. Sometimes, the client will make the wrong choice in the short run. However, Basco and Rush (1996) add that "in the long run . . . , clinicians' respect for their patients' opinions and willingness to give patients' ideas the benefit of the doubt will build trust" (p. 14).

Rapp (1998) describes the relationship with a chronically mentally ill person as purposeful, reciprocal, friendly, trusting, and empowering. The foundation of the relationship is built on the Rogerian principles of empathy (Rogers, 1951)—genuineness and unconditional positive regard. Rapp (1998) asserts that practitioners "use themselves . . . as a countervailing mirror . . . , highly sensitive to the abilities and talents of clients . . . [and] sensitive to [their] courage and resilience and to their achievements" (p. 65).

The development of the relationship is partially dependent on the availability of the practitioner to the person with the illness. This might mean finding and making accommodations for the person to meet with the practitioner such as transportation, child care, evening appointments, and accessibility through scheduling of additional appointments and arranging for emergencies.

PSYCHOPHARMACOLOGICAL CONSIDERATIONS

"The most commonly used and best studied antimanic medication is lithium" (Basco & Rush, 1996, p. 46). This medication is used for all phases of bipolar illness. Treatment of acute mania has been well established by numerous controlled trials in which both lithium and neuroleptics have demonstrated efficacy. Two anticonvulsant drugs, carbamazepine (Tegretol) and valproic acid (Depakote), have been used for lithium-resistant persons. Lithium also has proved to be efficacious in preventing recurrences of both depressive and manic episodes. Brady and Sonne (1995) report that persons with mixed mania might require mood-stabilizing medications other than lithium. Divalproex (Depakote) and carbamazepine have been shown to be effective mood stabilizers in bipolar disorders as well as useful in alcohol withdrawal (Brady & Roberts, 1995; Brady & Sonne, 1995). Cyclothymia also is treated with lithium (Klerman et al., 1994). By contrast, O'Connell, Mayo, Flatow, Cuthbertson, and O'Brien (1991) report that in their study, 36% of poor lithium responders had histories of alcohol abuse. Lin and Cheung (1999) report that Asian patients often respond to lower doses of psychotropics, particularly "in the range of serum lithium concentrations regarded as therapeutic" (p. 778).

Drug noncompliance is a serious problem in bipolar patients (Miklowitz & Goldstein, 1997). Most persons experiment with discontinuance at some point (Goldstein & Miklowitz, 1990). In one follow-up study of first- and second-episode persons, 70% showed noncompliance either in stopping altogether or in skipping medications (Miklowitz, Goldstein, Nuechterlein, Snyder, & Mintz, 1988).

COGNITIVE-BEHAVIORAL DIMENSIONS

Coping Skills

Self-Liberation

For the bipolar patient, when a manic episode takes on expansive proportions, the person might believe that he or she can do anything and everything. Self-liberation means maintaining a balance between realistic and unrealistic expectations of self. This means managing the illness. Symptom monitoring is an important step in managing illness. Rapp (1998) speaks of helping the person to identify, secure, and sustain resources that he or she needs including social relations, aspirations, and competencies. A strengths perspective enhances individualization of the ill person, enhances motivation, and is empowering.

The Basco and Rush (1996) book on bipolar illness actually is a treatment manual that outlines the cognitive behavioral dimensions of this illness. In differentiating manic and depressive episodes, these authors discuss cognitive changes common to each episode. Suggestions for tracking the changes and altering cognition are clearly given.

E. J. uses several Alcoholics Anonymous (AA) groups to help her manage her addiction. She uses a family vehicle to get where she needs to be. She also works sporadically. Having her own money is very important to her. As generous as her family is, she prefers to pay her own way. E. J. never has found a way in which to use her talents to support herself. To her, help in this area would be development of a plan to be able to sing publicly.

Dennis's challenge with self-liberation will be to fully accept that he has two illnesses that he must manage. Dennis also will feel freer to know that his illness will not invade his future family.

Stimulus Control

For this dual diagnosis, stimulus control means avoiding stimulus for drinking and drug abuse as well as understanding and avoiding the triggers for the illness. The task for the practitioner and persons with the illness is to identify stressors and to learn the interaction between their illnesses and their stressors.

Stressors include both internal and external events. Perceptions (cognitions) of stressors as good, bad, or indifferent are a key mood (or emotion) inducer. Depressed persons have a general negative view of self and the world. The improved mood associated with mania promotes energy, excitement, optimism, irritability, agitation, or a mix between good humor and extreme thoughts (Basco & Rush, 1996). Thus, stimulus control involves identifying thoughts (cognitions) and feelings (affects).

Dealing with craving needs to be discussed and planned for in advance. Triggers involve people, places, and things. These are to be identified, and substitutions are to be suggested. When a person is substance free, the person must learn to cope with the symptoms of his or her mental illness. Specifically, the person needs to be able to identify any signs of the illness returning. He or she needs to be able to cope with some down feelings and some painful feelings that are part of normal human existence.

Dennis and Gretchen have established parameters for him in terms of drinking. They are not considering abstinence but have agreed to "only wine with dinner" for both of them. They are quite sure that he will not drink at office functions or at sports events with friends. So far, this has worked. They have set parameters for his work behavior. Dennis is trying to moderate his schedule by setting reasonable goals and working steadily toward deadlines. Thus, these behavioral changes modify the circumstances that trigger negative emotions. Both Dennis and Gretchen deal with issues cognitively and are depending on Dennis's willpower and Gretchen's support to see them through. Stressors for him, they believe, are deadlines. Other triggers are family gatherings and visiting his mom's grave. He has decided against grave visiting for now, and the next holiday gathering will be at his house, not at "Mom's house." Dennis understands, cognitively, that his father must move on, but Dennis does not want to deal with that now.

E. J. can avoid substances when she avoids the club scene and avoids hanging out with her old friends. Frankie's voice is her biggest trigger, as is ruminating about the relationship. Further stimulus control would include gaining a greater understanding between her automatic thoughts and her subsequent mood shifts. Keeping a journal of feelings, thoughts, and behaviors is a step toward controlling events that stimulate negative emotions.

PSYCHOEDUCATION

Consciousness Raising

Education focuses on understanding both illnesses and the interaction between them. Furthermore, psychoeducation includes teaching the person about the course of the illnesses and treatment including the role of medication in treatment and the signs and symptoms leading to relapse. A person with bipolar disorder needs to understand the signs and symptoms of both depression and mania. Consciousness raising helps the person to connect the roles of stress and life events to the illnesses as well as the vulnerability-stress connection. Acceptance of the reality of the illnesses is part of consciousness raising, and denial and resistance are mechanisms that exist for both disorders.

Maintaining a mood graph (Basco & Rush, 1996) is a useful mechanism for raising consciousness and managing illness. A mood graph starts with a baseline of what the person considers a normal mood. Normal mood is scored zero (0), manic is scored +5, and depression is scored –5. Basco and Rush (1996) recommend that a ±3 is an indicator for treatment.

Dennis and Gretchen want to know everything they can about this illness. Some people use the facts to help them deny the illness or minimize its course and consequences. This seems to fit Dennis and Gretchen. One aspect of consciousness raising is to help the person and family identify each symptom as it occurred in the last (or first) episode. The feedback that Gretchen can give Dennis about his behavior will help him to come to terms with the diagnosis.

E. J. understands a great deal about her illness but has not quite put together her vulnerability to the stressor of Frankie and his milieu. She does not see that her obsessing about him is part of her illness. E. J. needs to keep a record of her automatic thoughts, and the work of the practitioner is to help E. J. to change these cognitions. She also needs to be attuned to these thoughts as a signal of an oncoming mood shift.

Self-Reevaluation

Daley and Thase (1994) state that during early recovery, the person learns nonchemical ways of coping with the people, situations, and feelings that led him or her to use chemicals. As the person makes internal changes, the "sober" side becomes stronger. The person begins to see the self as someone who can cope with dual illness. The practitioner aids in self-reevaluation by helping the person to identify new thoughts (cognitions) and feelings (affects) that accompany growing mastery. The person can change from thinking "I'm sick and helpless" to thinking "I have an illness and I can take care of myself."

E. J. has incorporated her illness into her definition of self. What she has not yet done is to see herself as an able person who can cope with illness and find a better life for herself.

Dennis has not progressed to the point of identifying himself with this illness. Miklowitz and Goldstein (1997) state that, with first break persons, it is best "to paint a cautious but optimistic view of the future . . . [that although bipolar is a recurrent illness,] in reality we don't know what the future holds" (p. 114). A key notion to communicate is the importance of minimizing expectations for the person making an immediate return to "normal."

INTERPERSONAL SKILLS

Environmental Reevaluation

The environmental assessment points to the need to assist the person in evaluating those aspects of his or her environment that support the addiction and emotional extremes. The persons, places, and things that serve as triggers are identified as stimulus control. This strategy helps the person to develop a supportive nontoxic environment. Changing the interpersonal environment may include both values clarification and cognitive restructuring.

Dennis has made decisions to lessen the areas in which his drinking occurs. His wife is supportive of this plan and actually monitors him (with his approval). He is on his own at work but has voiced a commitment to change his habits of procrastination and then pushing himself to get his work finished. They have talked about some lifestyle changes that would include lowering their standard of living to accommodate his going into business by himself. They seem to understand that this will bring added pressure that might not counterbalance the freedom that comes with self-employment. They are moving slowly in this area.

E. J. wants to live alone, something that she has never done. On closer inspection, she just wants to be out of her parents' house. She worries that she is too comfortable there and too old to live at home. Independence is an important goal for people whose illnesses have made them dependent. Her goal should be considered carefully and accepted as a long-range goal, with help focused on the short-term goals that could affect that larger goal.

Counterconditioning

Related closely to environmental reevaluation, Dennis and E. J. both must find new ways of coping with the stress that prevailed with the onset of their illness and find new ways of doing things. To make behavioral changes, Dennis and E. J. must make cognitive changes, specifically the reinterpretation of life events.

Dennis is going to continue his old way of life, eliminating (or slowing) his drinking with his friends at sports events and slowing down at work. E. J. has been shut out of her old life; she uses self-help groups to fill her time while they offer the support she needs to stay "clean." These activities keep her mired in her illness and offer little in the way of renewal. Both persons might benefit from programs that focus on relaxation and meditation so that they can learn how to slow down.

Following a careful planning process to reach her long-term goals, E. J. might find classes or training programs that could help her with occupational goals necessary for her to achieve self-sufficiency.

FAMILY RELATIONSHIPS

Miklowitz and Goldstein (1997) see bipolar disorder as a family problem. For many families, bipolar episodes represent a major disaster. These authors write about the important impact that bipolar illness has on family relation-ships. All of the psychosocial problems related to the illness negatively affect families. Some families may react with criticism, hostility, or overinvolve-ment (known as *expressed emotion*). Other families may be characterized by negative, conflictual interactional styles (known as *negative affective* style).

To assist both ill persons and their families, Miklowitz and Goldstein (1997) designed a 9-month program for families of persons with bipolar ill-ness. This is similar to other family psychoeducation programs that focus on education about the illness, development of communication skills, problem solving, and crisis intervention (Jordan et al., 1999). The program aims to promote health and prevent relapse. Miklowitz and Goldstein (1997) state that their program helps family members to recognize the early warning signs of new episodes and to make plans for intervening:

> We also teach patients and family members to recognize the risks associ-ated with biological and social factors [e.g., drug abuse]. Once family members are able to integrate and understand their and the patient's experiences with the illness, and develop better ways to cope, their level of caretaking burden correspondingly decreases. (p. 23)

Finley (1998) writes that all families bring unique sociocultural histories. Although not all ethnic families are trapped in a victim system, those that are bring a different worldview in which the environment and its institutions are seen as hostile, dangerous, and unpredictable. Mirowsky (1985) calls this "cultural paranoia," which is a protective survival mechanism. These families may be wary of outsiders' help. They may mistrust the diagnosis and its implications, preferring to use resources within their own community. Lefley (1990) writes that members of different ethnic groups may assign different names to symptoms and illness that are acceptable within their groups. This may have the effect of keeping ill members connected to these groups. An example of this, noted in Chapter 5, was the meaning that Asians give to depression and its acceptability within Asian cultures.

Wright and Anderson (1998) state that, in working with urban African American families (e.g., E. J.'s family), approaches that incorporate an under-standing of strengths and competencies are important. Such approaches engage families in therapeutic processes and create a context for concepts of competence, attachment, process, reconceptualization, manageability, and the use of self.

Baxter and Diehl (1998) report on a conceptual model, Stages of Emotional Responses Among Family Members, developed by Burland (1995) and used in the Journey of Hope. These stages assist in designing family education to fit the state of the family's acceptance of the illness.

Jordan and colleagues (1999; see also Jordan, Barrett, & Lewellen, 1997; Jordan, Lewellen, Vandiver, & Barrett, 1997) offer suggestions for adapting family psychoeducation models to other cultures.

Contingency Management

Families play an important role in contingency management, both in the ways that they respond to the ill persons and in the planning they do to prevent and manage relapse. The ill person also develops his or her own plans. Montrose and Daley (1995) recommend contingency cards. These cards help the person in emergencies and difficult situations such as friends offering substances, flaring up of symptoms, anniversaries, and negative or unpleasant feelings (e.g., depression, boredom, anger). Cards may be lists of phone numbers to call for specific issues or action strategies such as thought stopping, reframing, and redirecting activities. For people in support groups, a sponsor's phone number is important. Other desirable phone numbers would include those of physicians, therapists, and treatment centers. If E. J. gets stranded at work, at AA meetings, or at treatment centers, she needs reminders of whom to call for transportation.

Environmental Intervention

Social Liberation

Social liberation gives consideration to the person's housing, work, education, and recreational opportunities. Assessments of strengths in these areas guide the practitioner in work with the person, as do the aspirations of the person and the provisions within the physical and social environment for goal attainment. The practitioner helps the person to set short- and long-term goals. Rapp (1998) states that short-term goals are means to an end, whereas long-term goals are an end in themselves. "They are task *and* goals" (p. 105, italics in original).

For example, E. J. wants to live on her own again. She understands that she must have a consistent income for some time to make deposits, pay rent, and pay monthly bills. In preparation for employment, E. J.'s short-term goals would be to prepare for employment by adjusting her waking-sleeping cycles to conform with employment and with her parents' schedules to provide her transportation. This requires careful adherence to her medication schedule and monitoring by her physician. Another part of the preparation could be a short-term goal to increase her stamina through proper nutrition and exercise. Could E. J. cook one meal a day for her family, feeding family members as well as herself? An exercise video might be a start for her, with the plan to move into group exercise at some point to counter her social isolation.

Dennis's goal is to liberate himself from work pressures and activities with friends that involve heavy drinking. At present, he vacillates between the precontemplative and contemplative stages. That is, he sees things as not being a problem ("I can handle it"), on the one hand, and wonders whether he should make some lifestyle changes, on the other. Making lifestyle changes requires reassessment of values, hopes, expectations, and cognitions that go along with these changes.

AFFECTIVE DIMENSIONS

Dramatic Relief

Development of insight into problems and actions can result in a range of emotions from a mild "aha" through an emotional catharsis. Such insight development can be useful to most ordinary people. For those with a disorder given to manic phases, caution should be used in fostering dramatic displays of feeling. Nevertheless, both positive and negative feelings about themselves, their losses, and their illness need to be surfaced and explored. Such persons need to maintain a healthy balance among dealing with losses, with the accompanying sad feelings, and with any negative feelings about self that result. Negative affects play a significant role in development of depression. Grandiose thinking and affects figure importantly in manic episodes.

Both E. J. and Dennis tend to obsess over their losses. Such obsessions are part of the grief process but also are a part of their illness. Thus, goals and a behavioral plan may be established for them to limit the time that they think about loved ones.

SUPPORT GROUPS

Persons with this bipolar disorder and substance-related abuse benefit from support groups. Care should be taken to identify groups that support use of psychotropic drugs for treatment while offering support for abstinence from other substances. Various combined groups are emerging. For example, members of the Double Trouble group report that the group is a setting in which members can feel comfortable and safe in discussing both of their "disabilities" (Vogel, Knight, Laudet, & Magura, 1998). DiNitto and Webb (1998) present two studies that demonstrate the effectiveness of Good Chemistry groups for the members involved.

Support Together for Emotional and Mental Serenity and Sobriety is a self-help group that recognizes coexistence of mental illness and substance abuse. The model includes recognition that mental illness requires medical management. The group acknowledges the need to be alcohol and drug free (excluding prescription medicines from that definition). Group family psycho-education programs can be very helpful to ill persons and their family members.

▮ QUESTIONS FOR DISCUSSION

1. Neither Dennis nor E. J. has had a manic or depressive episode so extreme that suicide was threatened. However, suicide ideation is part of both cycles. What is the practitioner's responsibility to the person with the illness and family members in discussing the potential of suicide ideation and risky behaviors seen in a manic phase?

2. In the section on contingency management, it was suggested that ill persons carry emergency phone numbers. What numbers should they have, and how can the practitioner maintain boundaries and be available to clients/patients?

Severe Personality Disorders

Treatment personnel generally consider clients who have personality disorders in addition to substance abuse problems to be the most troublesome in treatment programs in either mental health or substance abuse treatment settings. These clients also tend to have a poor prognosis. Some research findings support this negative view (Seivewright & Daly, 1997). Fully 42% of persons with antisocial personality disorders have or have had a drug use disorder (Onken, Blaine, Genser, & Horton, 1997). Substance abusers with personality disorders are more likely than non-personality disordered clients to use illegal drugs, to have more severe psychopathology, to have lower levels of life satisfaction, and to be depressed (Nace, Davis, & Gaspari, 1997). On the other hand, some researchers have found this client population to be indistinguishable from others in treatment outcomes (Clopton, Weddige, Contreras, Fliszar, & Arredondo, 1993; Marlowe, Kirby, Festinger, Husband, & Platt, 1997).

There are several factors that may contribute to the negative perception by professionals of this client population. Unlike severely and persistently mentally ill persons, those with personality disorders do not look ill and, therefore, are less likely to elicit empathy from personnel. In fact, they might seem to be competent and self-assured. Consequently, when they are not in compliance with treatment recommendations, they appear to be deliberately resistant, raising countertransference issues with treatment personnel. In addition, the large variance in the manner in which personality disorders manifest themselves makes them difficult to recognize and leads to few generalizations about how they should be treated. Personnel see little applicability of their hard-won understanding of antisocial personality disorders to clients with dependent personality disorders. Also, personality disorders are, by definition, resistant to change. Therefore, treatment personnel do not get the reinforcing feedback they seek from these clients' rapid recovery. It is appropriate to begin this chapter with a discussion of the nature of personality disorders.

103

DEFINITION

A *personality disorder* is an inflexible and maladaptive personality that results in substantial subjective distress or functional impairment affecting a variety of situations and dimensions of the person's life. Personality traits are defined in the *Diagnostic and Statistical Manual of Mental Disorders* (*DSM-IV*) as "enduring patterns of perceiving, relating to, and thinking about the environment and oneself that are exhibited in a wide range of social and personal contexts" (American Psychiatric Association [APA], 1994, p. 630). "People with personality disorders have deeply embedded pathological patterns of thinking, feeling, behaving, and relating to others that are largely unconscious" (p. 3).

Contemporary perspectives on personality disorders emphasize the complex interaction of physiological, psychological, and sociocultural factors that contribute to the development of the disorders. Temperament and neurotransmitters are believed to greatly influence the development and functioning of the personality. Cloninger, Svrakic, and Przybeck (1993) identify innate, genetic, and constitutional factors that create temperament. Learned psychosocial influences described as character, added to temperament, create personality.

Personality disorders reflect problems in character relating to degrees of self-directedness, cooperativeness, and self-transcendence (Sperry, 1995). It is important for the purposes of this chapter that personality functioning and dysfunction be recognized as a continuum, ranging from healthy individuality, to an exaggeration of personal style, to the point where it is maladaptive and destructive, characterizing specific *DSM-IV* criteria (Sperry, 1995). The rate of coexistence of Axis I disorders such as panic disorder, anxiety, and depression with personality disorders is estimated at 40%.

The interaction of alcohol and other psychotropic drugs with personality disorders greatly complicates the assessment and treatment of both the mental illness and substance abuse problems. Some authorities estimate that two thirds of substance abusers in treatment have personality disorders, most commonly antisocial personality disorder (Seivewright & Daly, 1997).

Whereas "each personality disorder is characterized by a circumscribed pattern of defenses, interpersonal expectancies, and core conflicts" (Magnavita, 1997, p. 4), the 10 personality disorders recognized in the *DSM-IV* have been grouped into three clusters based on descriptive similarities. Cluster A consists of paranoid, schizoid, and schizotypal personality disorders, all of which are characterized by a basic flaw in self-other relations, believed by some to result from faulty identification with a healthy caregiver in infancy (Magnavita, 1997). Cluster B includes the antisocial, borderline, histrionic, and narcissistic personality disorders, all of which display dramatic, emotional, or erratic behavior. Cluster C consists of the avoidant, dependent, and obsessive-compulsive personality disorders, displaying anxious or fearful appearance (APA, 1994). Each of these clusters, when combined with the use of psychotropic drugs, presents unique problems in assessment and treatment. Therefore, the clusters are discussed separately in the remainder of this chapter. Because of the prevalence of Cluster B disorders within the substance-abusing population, with antisocial personality disorder being the most commonly coexisting psychiatric illness among substance abusers (National Institute on Drug Abuse, 1991), major attention is focused on Cluster B clients and less attention on persons with Cluster A and Cluster C disorders.

CASE STUDY

Joe is a 32-year-old Caucasian male, married, with three children. His wife sought help from a family counseling agency because she was "fed up" with his destructive behavior, which included drug use and sales, property damage, theft, assaults, homosexual prostitution, and numerous angry confrontations with a broad array of people. His behavior had resulted in multiple evictions, chronic financial problems, frequent stints in jail, and constant harassment by creditors and other persons with whom Joe was in conflict.

Joe agreed to see the counselor because he did not want his wife to leave him. During several brief separations, he had found that other women "did not understand" him, did not appreciate his good looks and talents as much as his wife did, and generally did not provide the comfortable home life on which he depended. Joe acknowledged using a variety of drugs, his favorite of which was cocaine. Most of his destructive behavior was committed either when getting money for drugs or when under the influence of cocaine or amphetamines. He was charming and cocky during his first interview with the counselor, whom he unabashedly asked to help him figure out how to keep his wife from leaving. The counselor identified an antisocial personality disorder with some coexisting narcissistic traits, mild depression, and substance use disorder.

UNIQUE PROBLEMS

Cluster A: Paranoid, Schizoid, and Schizotypal Personality Disorders

The greatest challenge presented to therapists of persons having Cluster A disorders is in developing a helping relationship. Never having developed a satisfactory attachment early in life, these clients are severely restricted in their ability to trust the therapist sufficiently to establish a thera-peutic bond.

Cluster B: Antisocial, Borderline, Histrionic, and Narcissistic Personality Disorders

People with Cluster B personality disorders have the highest incidence of substance abuse disorders (Nace, 1990; Toner, Gillies, Prendergast, Cote, & Browne, 1992), and the impulsivity of this population, especially border-line and antisocial personality disorders, correlates with multiple-drug de-pendency (McCown, 1988; O'Boyle, 1993). Numerous research studies report relatively poor clinical courses and outcomes for Cluster B substance abusers (Cacciola, Rutherford, Alterman, McKay, & Snyder, 1996; el-Guebaly, 1995). Evans and Sullivan's (1990) statement about antisocial per-sonality disorders is applicable to this entire cluster. "These disorders fre-quently coexist with chemical dependency, and they are ones that present the greatest challenge to service providers because individuals with these dis-orders use 'acting out' defenses" (p. 95). The thoughts and behavior of per-sons with these disorders are self-centered to the extent that the individuals have difficulty in sustaining relationships of mutuality and honesty. Often, their need to control others for their own ends leads to elaborate attempts to manipulate the therapist, raising the risk of countertransference reactions. This manipulativeness and the impulsivity of their behavior are particularly troublesome to personnel in substance abuse treatment programs who might not have a clinical understanding of the defensive purposes of the behavior.

The use of alcohol and other drugs is a result of both the psychic pain and the general impulsivity of the client. It also lowers the already weak impulse control and inhibitions of the client, thereby exaggerating the inherent tendency to act out emotions in irresponsible and destructive ways including further substance abuse.

Cluster C: Avoidant, Dependent, and Obsessive-Compulsive Personality Disorders

Persons with Cluster C personality disorders (sometimes referred to as the neurotic character disorders [Magnavita, 1997]), generally are easier to work with in clinical settings, have a better prognosis, and do not generate countertransference reactions as compared to other personality disordered clients. Professional literature, as well as self-help literature, historically has characterized the addictive personality as having the traits of social insecurity, dependence, and compulsivity, all central to the diagnostic criteria of this cluster of disorders. Therefore, these clients present as typical substance-abusing clients. A major issue in their treatment is that they often are undiagnosed, with the result that the persistence of their symptomatic behavior is unanticipated. Treatment results are slower than expected because the behaviors are characterological (deeply ingrained in the basic personality structure) rather than neurotic (more superficial), often leading to their being labeled as resistant clients.

ASSESSMENT CONSIDERATIONS

Because many clients with personality disorders also have problems with substance abuse and other Axis I disorders such as anxiety and depression, assessment must be broad and multifaceted. Three sources of information are valuable in assessment: psychological testing (including self-report inventories), the clinical interview, and collateral contacts. Psychological tests that have proved useful in identifying personality disorders include the Minnesota Multiphasic Personality Inventory, the Millon Clinical Multiaxial Inventory, Cloniger's Temperament Character Inventory, the Personality Disorder Inventory, and the Personality Disorders Questionnaire–Revised (Magnavita, 1997; Sperry, 1995).

Whereas the use of psychological tests in identifying personality disorders is highly desirable, the skillful clinical interview is essential. Researchers recommend the use of formalized structured interviews such as the Diagnostic Interview Schedule or the more specific Structured Clinical Interview for *DSM-IV* personality disorders. Research reports relatively little consistency in findings among these structured assessments (Butler, Gaulier, & Haller, 1991), thereby reinforcing the importance of multifaceted assessments. In clinical practice, less formalized interviews are common. The assessment-focused clinical interview usually follows the behavioral assessment funnel model (Cone & Hawkins, 1977), which begins with general questions to identify the broad problem area(s) and proceeds with more specificity so as to pinpoint problem areas and assess the client's amenability to therapeutic intervention.

Characteristics that suggest the presence of a personality disorder include a lifelong history of problems in establishing or maintaining relationships, long-term and inflexible maladaptive behavioral patterns that have resulted in significant impairment in functioning or subjective distress, and unstable or unrealistic perceptions of self or others. Once the presence of a personality disorder is established, the clinician needs to assess the client's ability to experience and be aware of a wide range of feelings. Does the client have the ability to see the connection between one's own behavior and the consequences of that behavior? Does the client have the ability to relate to the therapist? What is the client's reaction to stress within the interview? What are the extent and consequences of substance abuse in the client's life and the source and severity of the client's subjective distress (i.e., level of motivation)? These aspects of assessment are dependent not only on the content of the client's verbalization but also on the clinician's observations of affective and nonverbal reactions.

> The clinician, when processing the complex stimuli presented by the personality disordered patient, faces a daunting task indeed. . . . Non-verbal communications, symptom constellations, character defenses, countertransference reactions, and verbal content are all expressed simultaneously, so that even highly experienced clinicians sometimes feel overwhelmed. (Magnavita, 1997, p. 30)

The personality disordered client often is most vulnerable and least defended during the first interview, thereby making this the ideal time to get a clear picture of the client's personality disorder (Magnavita, 1997). This fits well with current trends toward shorter periods of treatment that necessitate abbreviated assessments. Effective assessment is dependent on competence in the assessor, so that this responsibility should be reserved for senior and well-trained professional staff.

The use of collateral sources of information such as family members increases the speed and accuracy of assessments. Substance abusers tend to understate the extent of their substance use. Clients with personality disorders might have cognitive distortions and generally are unaware of the extent to which their behavior disrupts the lives of those around them. Therefore, they tend to understate their problems, especially if their disorders are characterized by ego-syntonic behavior. "When you add the denial and control issues normally associated with chemical dependency to those same characteristics found in the personality disordered client, you have double denial" (Evans & Sullivan, 1990, p. 96). Therefore, information from other persons who are affected by such a client often presents a far more complete picture of the problem. Particular attention is needed to distinguish between problematic behavior (which represents a personality disorder) and anger, destructive behavior, and feelings of worthlessness and hopelessness. These are understandable results of the psychologically assaultive societal attitudes and policies toward oppressed groups (e.g., racial minorities, women, gays, lesbians) (Goldstein, 1993).

Each of these three sources of information—standardized measurement instruments, the clinical interview with the client, and interviews with collaterals—is fallible alone, but in combination, they can provide sufficient data for a tentative working plan for the beginning of the treatment phase. Often, the clinical interview has begun the development of rapport between the client and the therapist, based on the clinician's focused attention to the client and the understanding and acceptance that have been demonstrated by the skilled clinician.

Assessment always is an ongoing process, subject to modification with each progressive contact with the client. With the population in question, there also is an element of uncertainty concerning how much of the client's problem is a result of the substance abuse and how much is due to the preexisting personality disorder. Only a period free from the use of psychotropic drugs will clarify this matter, although some research suggests that diagnoses of personality disorders in drug dependent clients remain relatively stable regardless of clients' current drug use patterns (Weiss, Mirin, Griffin, Gunderson, & Hufford, 1993).

Within the broad category of personality disorders, there is a considerable variation in the sex ratio of the population diagnosed with the various disorders.

> Although these differences in prevalence probably reflect real gender differences in the presence of such patterns, clinicians must be cautious not to overdiagnose or underdiagnose certain personality disorders in females or in males because of social stereotypes about typical gender roles and behavior. (APA, 1994, p. 632)

TREATMENT GOALS

By definition, a personality disorder is highly resistant to change. Consequently, it is important to set goals that are realistic in view of the high level of defensiveness inherent in the disorder. Kantor (1992) speaks of three ranges on the continuum of personality disorderedness: normal, seminormal, and abnormal. The normal may antagonize others through inconsiderate behavior but is not perceived as pathological. The seminormal is overreliant on defensive character mechanisms to deflect anxiety, but the seminormal's symptoms are more fluid and more multicategorical than those fitting the profile of a specific character disorder, and they are less driven and more intermittent than those of the abnormal. Symptomatic behavior of the abnormal is more pervasive, chronic, unremitting, and troublesome. Realism in goal setting may mean helping the client to move from the abnormal to the seminormal as opposed to expectations that the client will become normal. Sperry (1995) refers to this movement as being from personality disordered functioning to a personality style functioning. It is unlikely that the client ever will lose the flavor of the disorder, but its severity can be reduced so that the client can function more acceptably in the social world. Any reduction in the use of alcohol and other drugs will move the client away from the abnormal extreme of the continuum. Lessening the client's defensiveness (in the psychodynamic sense) and teaching new social skills will further move the client toward a more prosocial adjustment. The general professional pessimism about treatment of persons with personality disorders is less justified if one accepts goals that are less than that of a total cure.

In the case of the Cluster A client with concurrent substance abuse disorder, the long-range goal is the ability to function in the social world in spite of severe deficits in relationship abilities. Providing a structure that enables the client to remove the added complication of alcohol and other drugs from his or her life is a major step. This is difficult to achieve, however, because of the client's indifference to interpersonal relationship-related motivations. The therapist must identify the areas of client discomfort, which can be used as motivation for change. The development of a therapeutic alliance, although difficult, eventually can become a first step in the client's ability to relate to others in his or her environment.

Treatment goals for Cluster B clients include development of a structure that contains the client's acting out behavior enough to engage in cognitive-behavioral substance abuse treatment with abstinence as a long-term goal. The therapeutic bond may be developed with relative ease through addressing the client's narcissistic need for empathy but is difficult to sustain through periods of confrontation. Tolerance for repeated relationship testing and numerous relapses is needed.

Cluster C clients often are considered easier to treat than others within the personality disorder category because they exhibit more neurotic ego-dystonic features with severe discomfort, thereby providing motivation for change. An initial therapeutic goal is to engender hope and to nurture growth through meeting client needs for security in the therapeutic relationship. Structure that enables the client to stop the use of psychotropic substances will contribute to his or her emerging sense of adequacy.

TREATMENT MODEL

Single-method treatment of clients with personality disorders and substance abuse problems has been notably ineffective, adding to the poor prognosis often attributed to this client group. Effective treatment is dependent on an eclectic approach combining supportive therapy that fosters the therapeutic relationship, that is, insight-oriented methods that erode negative transferences and cognitive-behavioral interventions that, in turn, aid in the development of new attitudes and habits and are essential to changing substance abuse behaviors. In some cases, medication (directed at symptom relief) and self-help groups may increase treatment effectiveness. Eclecticism facilitates the tailoring of treatment to the specific needs of a particular client.

Because of the unique characteristics of persons with coexistent substance abuse and personality disorders, major foci of treatment are (a) the development and maximization of motivation for change, (b) the establishment of a meaningful treatment relationship that gives leverage in the change effort, and (c) the application of cognitive and behavioral methods to bring about change. These elements are covered in the following sections.

READINESS FOR CHANGE

Resistance to treatment is common in both substance abusers and persons with personality disorders, and it is particularly evident in persons having both disorders (O'Malley, Kosten, & Renner, 1990). The first major obstacle in treatment of these clients is the client's apparent low level of motivation for change. Motivation can be conceptualized as awareness of discomfort with one's present condition and a hope that one's condition can be improved through work with the therapist. The motivating discomfort may come from unhappiness with oneself such as in the case of anxiety-ridden Cluster C disordered clients. These clients have negative or hostile relationships with others, as in the case of Cluster A disordered clients. The motivating discomfort also may come from trouble with external forces (e.g., the legal system, threats to marital status, difficulty in maintaining employment) often found among Cluster B clients with any combination of these factors.

Personality disordered substance-abusing clients seldom seek therapy for its own sake. They are in the precontemplative stage of change as described by Prochaska and DiClemente (1986). Clients are in crises that involve unpleasant consequences of their own behavior and are seeking symptomatic relief. The temporary disequilibrium caused by the crises provides a unique window of opportunity for therapeutic intervention. The problems generally are viewed by these clients to be caused by people other than themselves. They seldom are aware of the extent of suffering they bring on themselves and others. Nevertheless, the combination of discomfort and the hope that the therapist can do something to stop it provide sufficient opportunity for the therapist to get a foot in the door in intervention. It frequently is reported that this population tends not to follow through on a long-term basis with treatment, so it is imperative that the clinician hook the client's interest quickly. Even very short-term treatment can disrupt the client's dysfunctional reactive behavior enough to bring modest long-term improvement. Prochaska and DiClemente report that few of their processes of change are operative in the precontemplative stage of change.

The most effective means of engaging the client in the treatment is the development of a helping relationship initially based on empathic responses to the client's expressions of unhappiness with the state of his or her life at this crisis point. This empathic and nonjudgmental approach reduces the wariness of a Cluster A client, meets the narcissistic demands of a Cluster B client, and bolsters the self-confidence of an anxious Cluster C client, thereby providing a psychologically rewarding relationship for the client and increasing readiness for change.

Having established a tentative relationship, the clinician can begin to judiciously confront the client with the connectedness of the client's dilemma with concrete behaviors that have brought him or her to this point. This confrontation must be clearly prioritized and provided in small enough steps that, alternated with supportive empathy, it does not antagonize or overwhelm the client sufficiently to cause a retreat from treatment. Because therapeutic engagement is tentative, each contact with the client must be conducted as if it might be the final one. The client generally is less threatened by cognitive issues than by emotional ones, so initial confrontations should be presented in a nonemotional factual style such as the following: "Have you noticed that each time you have gotten arrested, you were under the influence of drugs?" "Are you perhaps not as much in control of yourself when on drugs?" Not feeling attacked or crowded, the client is more likely to begin to make cognitive connections that can lead to the decision to begin behavioral change, thereby enhancing his or her sense of being in control and minimizing resistance. Each time that resistance becomes apparent, more empathic support is needed. In residential settings or when group sessions augment individual treatment, the character disordered client generally will receive more aggressive confrontation from other clients. This allows the clinician to provide a more supportive relationship in which the client can process the negative group feedback in a nonthreatening setting, thereby enabling him or her to accept it in manageable doses.

This obviously is a slow process, with disengagement a constant threat. The client should be asked to contract for a specific number of sessions (even as few as four) so as to reduce the likelihood of abrupt withdrawal from treatment. It is important to deal early on with issues that are most likely to bring meaningful behavioral change. The connection of substance abuse to the client's felt problems is the most central to the problems of the person with coexisting substance abuse and personality disorders. These, therefore, should be brought to the fore early in treatment. Any degree of success in reducing the client's use of nonprescribed psychotropic substances will improve impulse control and the ability to make more deliberate choices, thereby raising the client's hope for further improvement in handling problems in living.

Clients can make constructive changes while still not consciously considering having real problems, but positive consequences of the changes may bring some awareness of clients' role in their difficulties, moving them into the contemplative and (eventually) action stages of change. There is likely to be vacillation from stage to stage, maintaining a highly tentative commitment to the treatment process.

It is not unusual to see personality disordered former substance abusers who have achieved a drug-free status for about a year (and, therefore, are in the relapse prevention stage of change) seek treatment for the emotional pain that no longer is being dulled by substance abuse. "Their character defenses are cracking, they enter treatment in severe emotional distress . . . , [having] long been suffering from dependent, avoidant, narcissistic, passive-aggressive personality disorders or, more commonly, mixed types that have long been untreated" (Magnavita, 1997, p. 54). They are returning to an active stage of change, addressing problems of mental status that were not addressed during their earlier work on their substance abuse.

HELPING RELATIONSHIP

With a personality disordered client, "the most important predictor of treatment success is the ability to form a therapeutic alliance" (Sperry, 1995, p. 28). The helping relationship is the key link between the client's discomfort with the status quo and engagement in the treatment process. It should be collaborative in nature and based on the clinician's understanding of the client's attachment, oedipal, and control issues (Magnavita, 1997). "When you add the denial and control issues normally associated with chemical dependency to those same characteristics found in the personality disordered, you have double denial" (Evans & Sullivan, 1990, p. 96). The steady, nonjudgmental, empathic, but reality-based relationship between the clinician and client lessens the personality disordered client's paranoia, aloofness, volatility, impulsiveness, anxiety, and excessive dependency.

The relationship between the clinician and the client with borderline personality disorder is particularly vulnerable. Goldstein (1993) states,

"Borderline individuals generally are angry, volatile, impulsive, and self-destructive. Highly contradictory in their feelings and behavior, they show severe identity disturbances and may develop brief psychotic episodes. They are plagued by fears of abandonment and become panicked when separated from those upon whom they are dependent" (p. 270). Highly confrontive or blatantly interpretive approaches frighten away these clients, whose frequent histories of physical and sexual abuse have left them too fragile for such emotional attacks. A delicate balance of empathic support and comfortable distance, with flexibility to ride out the storms of client emotional extremes, is needed to stabilize these clients.

Clients having personality disorders and substance abuse problems engender powerful countertransference feelings in treatment staff. Depending on the nature of the personality disorder, the clinician may experience rescue fantasies, defensiveness against the client's hostility, power struggles against the manipulations or threats of the antisocial client, or anger at the client's lack of compliance with treatment expectations. Each of these reactions interferes with therapeutic objectivity and ability of the therapist to remain stable, persistent, and thoroughly incorruptible (Sperry, 1995).

PSYCHOPHARMACOLOGICAL CONSIDERATIONS

Although not usually a major part of treatment of personality disorders, pharmacological intervention may be considered in three different contexts in treatment of persons with coexisting personality and substance abuse disorders:

1. As an aid in reducing or eliminating alcohol and drug abuse

2. To address basic elements of the personality disorder

3. To provide symptomatic relief due to Axis I elements that are complicating the personality disorder

For several decades, substance abuse treatment frequently has included the use of medication as a part of contingency management (e.g., the use of Antabuse to discourage alcohol intake). Medication also has been used to reduce the symptoms of withdrawal or as a replacement for a more dangerous or illegal substance (e.g., methadone maintenance for heroin addicts).

The use of medication for treatment of personality disorders is controversial. "The controversy over the use of psychoactive drugs ranges between the extreme positions of those who view them as a panacea and those who consider them a crutch" (Magnavita, 1997, p. 284). During recent years, psychopharmacological treatment directed at basic dimensions of personality have shown promise with personality disordered clients. Low-dose antipsychotics have been suggested for addressing cognitive/perceptual difficulties in schizotypal and passive disorders: (a) serotonin blockers to reduce impulsivity and aggression in borderline and antisocial personalities, (b) tricyclic and tetracyclic antidepressants or serotonin blockers for the affective instability in borderline and histrionic personalities, and (c) serotonin blockers and monoamine oxidase inhibitor agents for the anxiety and inhibition of the avoidant personality disorder. Although lithium carbonate has shown some success with impulsive, violent, explosive traits or mood swings in antisocial patients, such patients often are unwilling to tolerate its side effects or to comply with the required regimens (Sperry, 1995).

Considerable research has addressed pharmacological treatment of borderline personality disorder. Low doses of neuroleptics (antipsychotic medications) have been shown to be effective in stabilizing reality testing; diminishing cognitive dysfunction; and alleviating impulsivity, depression, and hypersensitivity to rejection. "Individuals characterized by anger, hostility, paranoid or schizotypal features, and impulsivity may be particularly helped by neuroleptic treatment, though noncompliance is a frequent problem" (Ellison & Adler, 1990, p. 46). Depression often accompanies substance abuse and borderline personality disorder. In some cases, the use of monoamine oxidase inhibitors has proved helpful. Some authorities are cautious about pharmacological treatment of personality disorders. "Except in alleviating depression where there is an affective disorder or mild disorganization, neuroleptics usually are contraindicated in the treatment of borderline individuals and do not alter their characteristic difficulties in any case" (Goldstein, 1993, p. 274).

Ellison and Adler (1990) state, based on a review of research on pharmacological treatment of personality disorders, that there is not yet a specific medication that can be recommended for any specific personality disorder. They conclude, "One solution to this dilemma is to put aside diagnostic categories and instead concentrate on profiling target symptoms amenable to pharmacotherapeutic intervention" (p. 48).

In view of the mounting evidence of biological factors in the development of personality disorders, it is likely that further research will greatly enhance current knowledge of psychopharmacological intervention with this population. However, until there is reasonable assurance that the personality disordered client will remain free of nonprescribed drugs and alcohol, there is high risk in prescribing drugs that are likely to interact dangerously with the illicit ones.

COGNITIVE-BEHAVIORAL
DIMENSIONS

In general, personality disordered clients have little understanding of the connection between their thoughts and behavior or between their behavior and its social and interpersonal consequences. Nevertheless, these noninsightful clients are more amenable to cognitive channels of feedback than to affective ones, and behavioral consequences that are reinforced by intellectual (cognitive) explanations (confrontations) make an impact on such clients.

Once the client has been led to see the connection between substance use and acting out behavior with its negative consequences, the client can be engaged in a joint effort at identifying situations, thoughts, or emotional states that tend to trigger substance use. Collaborative brainstorming then can produce strategies for either avoiding the potential triggers (stimulus control) or substituting less destructive responses to the triggers (counter-conditioning). It is important to (a) keep the focus on concrete benefits to the client that will result from changes in behavior and (b) keep reminding the client of the strategies that he or she has developed because new behavioral and cognitive patterns must become second nature to the impulsive client.

It should be expected that progress will be slow and that old behavioral patterns will reemerge from time to time, in which instances the client should be made to experience again the negative consequences inherent in relapse behavior. Successful efforts at change will be self-rewarding through the lessened difficulties with the social environment.

COPING

One dynamic underlying clients' denial of the extent of their problems is anxiety about their ability to cope with life without the comfort, excitement, or escape they receive from substance abuse. Their acting out behavior sometimes is attributed to a need to escape deep hurts from early-life conditions. In a sense, both the substance abuse and characterological behaviors are attempts to cope. New coping strategies can be taught. These may include techniques of anger control (as in the case of Joe), nondestructive ways of experiencing excitement (Joe became a very competitive player on a community athletic team), and self-nurturing methods (as in the case of a dependent or borderline personality).

PSYCHOEDUCATION

There are two major contributions of psychoeducation for clients with coexisting personality and substance abuse disorders. First, consciousness raising occurs in a minimally threatening context when classes about substance abuse and personality disorders are presented. The impersonal nature of the didactic presentations allows clients to learn about themselves without having to admit or deny their problems. They do not feel attacked and, therefore, are less defensive.

Second, psychoeducation groups for family members give them understanding of the nature of clients' problems, teach them how to avoid being used, and give them encouragement to provide logical and natural negative consequences to clients when destructive behavior occurs. This leads to appropriate contingency management (i.e., replacing the payoff of acting out behavior with unpleasant consequences).

INTERPERSONAL SKILLS

Interpersonal skills are a major deficit of many clients with personality disorders. Their narcissism interferes with their taking the role of others to the extent that cooperative relations demand. Some progress can be made, however, through deliberate social skills training. In some instances, the additional problem of substance dependence seems to have taught these clients to read others so as to manipulate them to facilitate the procurement of drugs. This strength can be built on in teaching these clients interpersonal problem solving and conflict resolution. Motivation for such training is dependent on consistently demonstrating how better social skills will reduce the hassles that clients want to avoid. Thus, learning to better respond to the needs of others is in clients' best interest. Although underlying dynamics might remain unchanged, clients can learn to be less offensive to those with whom they interact. For example, Joe was open to learning how to avoid hostile confrontations with neighbors in his apartment complex so as to contribute to the stability that his wife demanded.

FAMILY RELATIONSHIPS

Family relationships often have been badly damaged or even severed long before the client gets into a treatment program. Members of the client's immediate household can be constructively brought into family therapy, where expectations can be made explicit and behavioral exchange contracts can be negotiated. If the family is a major source of leverage with the client, then a great deal can be accomplished in changing specific behaviors. It should not be assumed that the client will generalize change into areas not specifically addressed in these sessions. Family members might need to be coached not to make threats that they are not willing to carry out, not to enable further destructive behavior such as substance abuse and acting out, and not to expect emotional responsiveness or control beyond what is realistic for the client.

ENVIRONMENTAL INTERVENTION

Insufficient attention to posttreatment community living is a major cause of relapse for clients who have been through treatment programs for substance abuse and mental illness. Assertive case management, community living skills training, and development of community resources have been recommended to combat this problem. Skills training for dually diagnosed clients requires repetition, positive reinforcement, modeling, and practice (Nikkel, 1994). It often is necessary to use the leverage of possible criminal justice system involvement or hospitalization to provide the motivation for postdischarge follow-through with personality disordered clients.

Social skills needed by the client include the recognition of the role of substance use in his or her problems. Although this point is stressed early in treatment, continuous reinforcement as the client reenters the community is needed. Similarly, relationship and communication skills learned at the treatment center must be generalized to interpersonal interactions with family, peers, employers, and other persons in the client's natural community networks. Reinforcement of stimulus control skills (e.g., avoiding situations that present temptations to use drugs or act out again, refusing involvement with substance use or destructive behavior when in high-risk situations) is essential. In addition, assistance is needed in ordering the client's life so as to minimize the chaos that characterized his or her pretreatment lifestyle. This may cover basics such as developing and sticking with a budget; keeping appointments with physicians, treatment personnel, and after-care groups; and developing constructive recreational and leisure time skills.

Unlike the client with chronic schizophrenia or major affective disorders, the personality disordered client is not easily recognized by the general public as being mentally ill. This client is likely to be able to get a job interview or look at a rental apartment without the immediate stigma that other clients encounter. Finalization of procuring the job or signing the lease agreement, however, might be difficult because of the record of instability that becomes evident when references are checked.

AFFECTIVE DIMENSIONS

Most authorities theorize that personality disorders result from unmet emotional or safety needs during childhood. The strong link between early sexual abuse and later borderline personality and substance abuse in females, for example, supports this theory. The pain from these unmet needs has been sealed off through strong defense mechanisms including denial. The client typically vehemently rejects therapeutic attempts to open up those painful feelings. One means of getting to them (at least to a limited degree) is through empathic responses to complaints or emotional outbursts from the client. It is rewarding to the client to feel understood, and within the safety of the therapeutic relationship, emotional defensiveness sometimes diminishes enough to allow the client to ventilate the rage that has long been attached to the early pain (Magnavita, 1997).

SUPPORT GROUPS

Self-help groups, such as Alcoholics Anonymous and Narcotics Anonymous, generally are recommended for persons with coexisting personality disorders and substance abuse disorders. These clients typically resent being referred to such a group and might undermine its effectiveness through their closed attitudes. However, if their situational crises are sufficient, then they might find the group intriguing. They are put at ease by the atmosphere of nonjudgmental acceptance at the group meetings. Although they often have a sense of alienation from others, they can identify with other group members who are struggling with impulse control issues and histories of difficulties with family, peers, and authorities. They can learn from the modeling of more senior members and begin to experience vicarious dramatic relief by listening to the stories of others. Furthermore, the structure of the 12-step program provides a systematic focus for self-improvement for motivated clients. Unlike many persons with whom they have been associated, the 12-step group does not give up on them.

The behavioral traits that characterize personality disordered clients often are found in substance abusers with no premorbid mental disorders, so people with personality disorders do not seem markedly different from many other members of the group. Interpersonal problems that typify these clients' relationships are diluted in the group setting. Members with personality disorders might con their sponsors or other group members from time to time, but successful manipulation usually is short-lived because group members have "seen it all" in themselves and others.

Unlike many persons with mental disorders, clients with personality disorders usually are not being medicated as a part of treatment. Therefore, there is no conflict between the group's push toward total abstinence from psychotropic drugs and the professional treatment regimen.

■ QUESTIONS FOR DISCUSSION

1. What types of compromises must be made in setting treatment goals for the dually diagnosed client who has a personality disorder?

2. What are the common characteristics of personality disorders that justify categorizing them in the same diagnostic category in spite of the vast differences in their symptomology?

3. Does the antisocial personality disorder exist without symptoms of substance abuse? How do we know?

4. Are there special traits or abilities needed for the therapist who works with clients with coexisting personality disorders and substance abuse disorders?

5. Clients with personality disorders often are treated more harshly by the public, and especially by law enforcement officials, than are persons with other psychiatric diagnoses. What could explain this phenomenon, and what can be done to reduce this discrepancy?

6. Can you see overlap between some cultural groups and the descriptions of personality disorders? How can clinicians avoid confusing cultural traits and symptoms of personality disorders?

Anxiety Disorders and Substance- Related Disorders

Anxiety refers to sensations and is associated with strong feelings of apprehension related to a real or perceived threat of danger. When anxiety becomes "intense, excessive . . . , with a strong sense of loss of control and inappropriate attentional focus" (Barlow, 1988, p. 579), it may indicate the presence of one of the clusters of anxiety disorders.

Researchers suggest that chronic anxiety disorders represent a complex process of cognitive-affective, physiological, and behavioral patterns. Events associated with anxiety vary greatly according to individual perceptions. For example, some persons associate public speaking with negative thoughts and images, whereas others fear settings such as closed or locked spaces. Some persons with family histories of extreme sensitivity to the environment develop panic for no apparent outward reason. The key factor associated with chronic anxiety appears to be cognitive. Self-statements such as "I can't stand this" and "I think I am going to die" are common. Accompanying bodily sensations such as heart palpitations, shortness of breath, and other physical symptoms can increase fearful feelings. The feelings most commonly considered to be associated with anxiety are fear, distress, anger, shame, guilt, and excitement. Depression often is present as well (American Psychiatric Association [APA], 1994).

There is a high correlation between persons who are treated for addictions and those who have had prior diagnoses of anxiety disorders, yet the nature of the relationship is unclear. Many substance abusers come from environments in which danger is a daily threat. They have employment problems, the constant threat of poverty, few supportive resources, and little hope for the future (Hudson, 1990). Complicating these psychosocial issues is the physiological effect of substances that persons take to ward off feelings of hopelessness and helplessness. During intoxication or withdrawal from alcohol, marijuana, cocaine, amphetamines, heroin, methadone, and high doses of hallucinogens, persons may experience intense anxiety and panic that often is accompanied by depression. These symptoms may prompt persons to seek more drugs, both prescribed medications and illicit drugs. Some researchers believe that anxiety disorders are substance induced (Anthenelli & Shuckit, 1993). Others suggest that anxiety may have been preexisting (Ross, Glaser, & Germanson, 1988).

This chapter emphasizes the need for treatment providers in addiction, mental health, and other settings to become familiar with issues related to differential diagnosis, immediate and long-term assessment considerations, and treatment goals and strategies. We use the conceptual framework of Prochaska and DiClemente (1986), who emphasize a comprehensive model of change based on 10 transtheoretical processes. In this approach, the client's readiness for change and close alliance with treatment providers are central. Because addictions, as well as mental illnesses, tend to have a chronic course, the framework of rehabilitation works well with dually disordered clients. In rehabilitation assessment and treatment strategies, the emphasis is on client successes in functioning rather than on their failures. Relapse prevention also is a critical component of rehabilitation given that studies still have not demonstrated that treating target anxiety disorders also benefits substance disorders. The following case example is used to demonstrate application of the transtheoretical approach to rehabilitation as well as to relapse prevention.

CASE EXAMPLE

Roberta was driving to work when she began having heart palpitations, dizziness, and uncontrollable trembling. She pulled over to a rest stop and called 911 emergency assistance. When the paramedics arrived, she requested that they take her to the emergency room because she could not breathe. By the time she was evaluated, her breathing had become more regular and she no longer was dizzy. However, she was afraid to drive home alone, so she asked a friend to accompany her and to spend the night.

This single, white, middle-aged woman has been living alone for the past 10 years. She has poor eating habits and smokes up to one and a half packs of cigarettes daily. Although she has a college education, she has been unhappily employed most of her adult life. Two years ago, she asked her physician to prescribe something to help her sleep and to overcome the bad feelings associated with her spells. She described her spells as periods of worry that she could not seem to shake off. During these periods, she also experienced odd physical sensations such as numbness, dizziness, and feelings of extreme agitation. She was given Xanax to take as needed. Recently, she has been taking larger doses than prescribed and has started having frequent panic attacks.

Roberta borrowed pills from friends when she was at work. One of her favorite pills was Valium. She also began drinking three to four tumblers of whiskey every evening after work. One evening, she blacked out and could not remember getting to bed. She did not think that alcohol or drugs was a problem, but she thought that she might be going crazy.

DEFINITIONS

Having anxiety is not a pathological process unless persons meet specific diagnostic features for each disorder. The following anxiety disorders are listed in the *Diagnostic and Statistical Manual of Mental Disorders* (*DSM-IV*) (APA, 1994): (a) panic disorder without agoraphobia, (b) panic disorder with agoraphobia, (c) agoraphobia without history of panic disorder, (d) specific phobia, (e) social phobia, (f) obsessive-compulsive disorder, (g) post-traumatic stress disorder, (h) acute stress disorder, (i) generalized anxiety disorder, (j) anxiety disorder due to a general medical condition, (k) substance-induced anxiety disorder, and (l) anxiety disorder not otherwise specified. The major criteria for anxiety disorders, which separate them from anxiety as a symptom, include the reality of the threat, the length of time that serious concerns persist, the persistence of physiological symptoms, and the degree of impairment. The prevalence of anxiety disorders also is related to cultural background, age, ethnicity, and gender (APA, 1994).

"The substance-related disorders include disorders related to the taking of a drug of abuse (including alcohol), to the side effects of a medication, and to toxin exposure" (APA, 1994, p. 175). Substance use and intoxication can create symptoms that present much the same as do symptoms of anxiety. Also, "high doses of hallucinogens can prompt symptoms of anxiety and panic much like other stimulants" (Ries, 1994, p. 46). Substance withdrawal, which can mimic severe anxiety symptoms, is commonly associated with alcohol withdrawal and also with withdrawal from benzodiazepines.

UNIQUE PROBLEMS

Anxiety disorders are the most prevalent mental disorders in the general population (Kessler et al., 1994). However, because anxiety is a universal emotion, it is easy to confuse anxiety symptoms with diagnoses of Axis I and Axis II mental disorders including mood disorders, anxiety disorders, substance-induced disorders, and personality disorders. For example, in alcohol intoxication and withdrawal, symptoms may mimic clinical depression, an anxiety disorder, schizophrenia, or a personality disorder (Anthenelli, 1994). Anxiety can be caused by any drug of abuse, but biological vulnerability and stress from poor environmental conditions also can be triggers. Genetic inheritance of a hyper-aroused central nervous system or preexisting negative propositions (Beck & Emery, 1985) may be precursors in some individuals who later develop anxiety disorders.

Attempts to differentiate substance-induced anxiety disorders, other mental disorders with associated anxiety, and primary anxiety disorders have yielded mixed findings. For example, persons with Axis I disorders (e.g., schizophrenia) have more expressions of anxiety and depression than do persons with primary substance-related disorders (Tsuang, Cowley, Ries, Dunner, & Roy-Byrne, 1995). On the other hand, in a recent sample of opioid addicts in methadone maintenance programs, 55% had anxiety disorders (Milby et al., 1996). Are persons with primary mental illnesses, including anxiety disorders, self-medicating to alleviate painful symptoms? Do substances themselves have properties that signal the brain to begin a cycle of anxiety that leads to the development of anxiety disorders?

Some researchers use chronology of onset to differentiate between primary and secondary anxiety. For example, if persons meet the criteria for anxiety disorders prior to the onset of a substance-related disorder, then the anxiety is considered primary. However, if the substance-related disorder came first and was followed by anxiety, then anxiety is considered secondary (Goldenberg et al., 1995).

Goldenberg and colleagues' (1995) study found no evidence to support the self-medication hypothesis. However, Anthenelli and Shuckit (1993) believe that there is strong evidence that anxiety disorders are induced or worsened by the use of alcohol and drugs.

DIFFERENTIAL DIAGNOSIS

In the short term, it might not be possible to differentiate among mood disorders, anxiety disorders, primary substance-related disorders, and two or more coexisting disorders. However, Ries (1994) suggests that anxiety symptoms that are substance induced usually dissipate with detoxification and treatment. Symptoms may last for a few days to a few weeks. If they persist, then medical problems should be investigated. For example, serious heart problems, thyroid conditions, brain tumors, and HIV infection may cause prolonged anxiety. Some medications also create anxiety symptoms; examples include cold medicines, digitalis, steroids, antidepressants, and (paradoxically) some anti-anxiety drugs such as benzodiazepines (Ries, 1994).

In alcohol and drug settings, it is not uncommon to have persons with dissociate disorders. Ries (1994) states, "Differentiation between blackouts and dissociation can be extremely complicated" (p. 47). If treatment staff detect glassy eyes and unresponsiveness, then they should refer clients for immediate toxicological screens and inpatient observation.

In the case example, Roberta had experienced spells of anxiety for more than 10 years. However, full-blown panic attacks did not occur until she began abusing alcohol and prescribed drugs. She also might have had a genetic predisposition for anxiety disorders given that she described her mother as a nervous type with frequent apprehensive episodes. Roberta did not improve with Xanax but instead actually became more agitated, seeking relief from smoking, a diet heavy in sugar and carbohydrates, the use of friends' pills (e.g., Valium), and excessive alcohol intake. Roberta appears to have a preexisting primary anxiety disorder that worsened with benzodiazepine treatment and abuse of alcohol and other prescription drugs. She currently has a substance-related disorder accompanying a preexisting anxiety disorder.

ASSESSMENT CONSIDERATIONS

Short-Term Assessment Considerations

Woolf-Reeve (1990) suggests that to identify immediate treatment needs, providers cannot wait for a firm diagnosis. She offers the following suggestions that focus on current symptoms and current treatment concerns:

◆ Is the person intoxicated, overdosed, or in withdrawal? A medical assessment should be completed to determine the extent of medical threat. "Delirium can result from drug overdose, drug or alcohol withdrawal, head trauma, or infections such as HIV encephalitis" (p. 80). Another major concern is delirium tremens during alcohol withdrawal. Some indicators of delirium are elevated pulse rate, rising blood pressure, high temperature, and profuse sweating. Disorientation, which comes and goes, and visual or tactile hallucinations are other danger signals of delirium. Because it is not possible to interview clients effectively when they are intoxicated or in withdrawal distress, every effort should be made to obtain a recent history from family, friends, or acquaintances.

◆ Is there a potential for violence? In medical evaluation settings and many addiction treatment centers, so many clients experience anxiety symptoms during intoxication and withdrawal that treatment providers might no longer pay close attention to symptoms of suicide ideation or violent expressions. It is critical not to release the client from services without providing for physical protection for the client until he or she has become sober. In addition, if threats have been made against family members or acquaintances, then these persons should be given instructions on how to protect themselves and the client if the situation should worsen.

◆ Symptoms indicating that persons are not in control of their behaviors and might need extra protection include anxiety symptoms accompanied by depression, dissociation, extreme agitation, visual and tactile hallucinations, specific plans to commit violent acts, the means to commit violent acts, a prior history of violence, recent painful events or grief, confusion over sexual orientation, and history of mental illness.

◆ Homes in which weapons are kept are unsafe environments for persons who still are intoxicated or in withdrawal. Some type of 24-hour supervision needs to be available in a location with access and transportation to emergency services.

Roberta feared being alone, but with no prior history of suicidal ideation or violence, she was not a high-risk candidate for needing hospitalization or extra protection. However, her extreme agitation, possible family history of mental illness, and anxiety symptoms indicated that she needed a thorough biopsychosocial assessment and plan for long-term treatment. Like most sufferers of anxiety, she was seen by a general physician rather than by a mental health professional.

Long-Term Assessment Considerations

Clients with anxiety disorders, substance-related disorders, and coexisting dual diagnoses often show early improvement and then later encounter setbacks in between periods of progress. For many persons, the dual disorders are chronic. For this reason, it is important that treatment providers focus on increments of progress and client strengths rather than on client setbacks.

Persons with alcoholism and drug addictions may benefit from psychosocial psychiatric rehabilitation approaches targeting anxiety. However, short-term treatment for anxiety disorders with some antidepressants and benzodiazepines might interfere with the long-term success of psychosocial interventions (Brown & Barlow, 1995). Long-term assessment considerations should combine goals for dealing with both alcohol and drug use as well as goals for increasing biopsychosocial functioning.

Ries (1994) reports that treatment providers should focus on here-and-now functioning rather than on the person's internal history. There are many rehabilitation instruments that focus on vocational, psychosocial, and independent living indicators, but it is difficult to find scales that measure both improved functioning regarding a mental illness and improved functioning regarding alcohol- or drug-related problems.

A comprehensive assessment package should include a psychosocial history related to alcohol and drug use. Dinitto and Webb's (1994) structured outline focuses on 10 areas: (a) education; (b) employment; (c) military history; (d) medical history; (e) drinking and drug use history; (f) psychological-psychiatric history; (g) legal involvement; (h) family history; (i) relationship with spouse, children, and other significant individuals; and (j) why the client needs assistance at this particular point in time. They stress that this approach should focus on client strengths and assets as well as on client problems and needs. Examples of questions related to client strengths would be as follows: What is the client's favorite type of work? What work is the client well educated to do? (p. 84).

Kopp and Ruzicka (1993) also urge that self-observation measures provide an empowerment strategy to increase clients' feelings of participation in wellness. Examples are frequency counts, duration of events, severity of experiences, diaries or logs, and rapid assessment instruments such as Spielberger's (1985) State-Trait Anxiety Inventory.

Real environmental threats, such as women's unrealistic role demands, minorities' experiences of victimization, and lack of social supports for single-parent and poor families, have been found in persons with chronic anxiety (Lewellen, 1993). Roberta's status as a single woman, social isolation outside of the work setting, unhappiness with her chosen vocation, and feelings of lack of control over anxiety symptoms increased her vulnerability to both anxiety disorders and substance-related disorders.

TREATMENT GOALS

Treatment goals should maximize clients' focus on areas in which they are functioning well and should minimize expressive therapies that trigger old feelings of anxiety and depression. However, unless abuse and dependence issues also are addressed, clients probably will persist in experiencing both the substance-related disorders and the anxiety disorders.

TREATMENT MODEL

The following treatment model is an adaptation of Prochaska and DiClemente's (1986) 10 processes of change applied to the unique needs of persons with coexisting anxiety disorders and substance-related disorders. They stress that within this model, "the integration of stages and processes of change can serve as an important guide for therapists" (p. 9).

READINESS FOR CHANGE

Prochaska and DiClemente (1986) identify the following stages of clients' readiness for change: precontemplation, contemplation, preparation for action, action, and maintenance. Clients in the first stage, precontemplation, often are termed *treatment resistant* because they appear to have little insight or desire to change. The uncomfortable feelings of anxiety, however, may propel some clients into the next stage, contemplation. During this stage. they begin to process information regarding their illnesses.

Ries (1994) reports that early in treatment, anxiety disordered clients benefit from a low intensity of emotional expression that deals primarily with here-and-now issues. During contemplation, clients should not be urged to engage in tearful acknowledgment of past traumas. Instead, treatment staff should help clients to move slowly into 12-step program participation. Evans and Sullivan (1990) recommend a stepwise approach in which increments of intensity are added to clients' involvement in 12-step programs. For example, clients might begin being observers at a specific number of meetings. Next, they might begin introducing themselves to others. Clients with phobias related to social situations benefit from rehearsing social skills with treatment staff prior to attending meetings.

Moving from contemplation to preparation for action usually involves strong trust in helpers but also a great deal of belief that recent successes are related to the clients' own efforts. Prochaska and DiClemente (1986) describe this stage as one of the most difficult ones for clients. "For clients, taking action tends to mean taking risks with rejections. Knowing that there is at least one person who cares and is committed to helping serves to ease some of the distress and dread of taking life-changing action" (p. 11).

During the action stage, treatment providers should use behavioral strategies such as desensitization for phobias and cognitive restructuring for generalized anxiety and depression. Another important role is that of providing accurate feedback regarding clients' appropriate and inappropriate handling of stress-provoking situations. Biofeedback has proved useful in teaching clients to monitor their own physiological and psychological responses to their environments.

The final stage, maintenance, pulls together all of the previous work. In addition, it is important at this stage for clients to identify possible triggers of relapse. "Perhaps most important is the sense that one is becoming more of the kind of person one wants to be" (Prochaska & DiClemente, 1986, p. 11).

Roberta appears to be in between the precontemplative and contemplative stages of change. Her anxiety symptoms have become so distressful that she seldom is able to cope without abusing substances. Unfortunately, her substance-induced symptoms were not identified during her emergency room visit, so she did not receive insight or support for either chemical dependency treatment or long-term treatment of her anxiety.

HELPING RELATIONSHIP

Treatment providers should be kind and patient advocates who are allies and supporters of the client's successes. They should not force clients into premature psychological probing or pressure clients to express deep feelings. Clients with anxiety disorders and substance-related disorders might already be focused too much inwardly. They need help in relating to their immediate external environments in socially appropriate ways.

Traditional forms of confrontation that label clients and force them into admitting humiliating behaviors not only are inappropriate but also might be harmful. Instead, clinicians should help to create a relaxed and nonthreatening milieu. Appropriate helper roles include those of educator, trainer, facilitator, advocate, and counselor.

Roberta seems to be the perfect candidate for a helping relationship with a counselor trained in both mental health and chemical dependency issues. She has reached out for help in general medical settings, but her physician has responded only with increasing doses of benzodiazepines. She is unclear about the nature of her illnesses and has withdrawn further into herself and her addictions. She has turned away from friends and coworkers who have confronted her about her increasingly dysfunctional behaviors.

PSYCHOPHARMACOLOGICAL CONSIDERATIONS

Medications that have been used to treat anxiety symptoms have (paradoxically) increased anxiety in some individuals and have created new drug dependencies in others. For persons with coexisting anxiety and substance-related disorders, cognitive and behavioral therapies may be more appropriate than medication interventions (Ries, 1994).

On the other hand, some clients relapse without relief from anxiety symptoms, especially persons suffering from panic disorders, generalized anxiety disorder, and posttraumatic stress disorder. The tricyclics usually are the treatment of choice because there are no dietary restrictions, as with the monoamine oxidase inhibitors (Austrian, 1995). Some people also need a beta-blocker such as Inderal to avoid a stimulant response that increases feelings of panic.

Problems with dependency most frequently have been linked to benzodiazepines often given to persons with generalized anxiety disorder. Other drugs with fewer risks of dependency are buspirone and fluoxetine, which are serotonergic drugs. Medication treatment usually is not prescribed for specific phobias. However, monoamine oxidase inhibitors often are prescribed for severe social phobias (Gitlin, 1990). When symptoms subside, the medication is gradually tapered off.

Ries (1994) points out that dietary considerations also are drug-related considerations. For example, too much caffeine and sugar may bring on anxiety and depressive symptoms. Some clients use chocolate to restore the previous highs of chemical abuse. In fact, diet problems often mimic the cycle of both anxiety and addictions.

Roberta, like many women, seeks help from her general physician even when her problems are primarily psychiatric and substance related. Because her physician does not perform a comprehensive assessment, he is unaware of many of her problems related to addictions. In addition, he is not trained in prescribing and monitoring medications such as the benzodiazepines. Roberta cannot stop taking her medications at this point without experiencing painful withdrawal symptoms. In addition, she continues to abuse alcohol and to eat primarily carbohydrates and sweets.

COGNITIVE-BEHAVIORAL DIMENSIONS

Many believe that maladaptive cognitions are at the heart of anxiety disorders, particularly chronic worry and apprehension (Chorpita & Barlow, 1998). Substance use may silence internal negative statements temporarily but increase them during intoxication and withdrawal. Some effective cognitive interventions, which take into account clients' readiness for change, begin with consciousness raising. Clients should have written and verbal explanations of their illnesses in clear terms appropriate to their backgrounds, educations, and ethnicities. Information should explain how anxiety and substance-related issues interrelate and act to remove client control.

Furthermore, clients should be taught how general health habits (e.g., exercising regularly, getting enough sleep, eating healthy foods) affect mental health. For some clients, such as Roberta, receiving information about the nature of their problems may free them to seek change.

In chemical dependency treatment programs, treatment providers should avoid heavy confrontation and forced deep insights. A more effective approach is to engage clients slowly through helping them to relate to other clients, to the helping staff, and to the immediate environment.

Once clients are in the action stage of desiring change, self-liberation strategies help them to understand how to regain control over their lives. Some of the processes involve forming new cognitive propositions such as with cognitive restructuring techniques. Others help clients to refocus attention away from self and toward new pleasurable activities. Treatment packages that include a variety of cognitive and behavioral techniques seem to be the most effective for anxiety and substance-related disorders, but the particular best combination is not yet clear (Ries, 1994).

In addition, 12-step programs can provide enormous help and relief to anxious persons. It is important, however, to match clients to appropriate groups in terms of similar cultural backgrounds, ages, and genders. Many women, such as Roberta, would not be comfortable in groups with primarily male members.

Ries (1994) maintains that relaxation therapies also help to refocus clients' thoughts away from anxiety and depressive statements and toward healthier and more valuable interactions with others including treatment staff.

Counterconditioning and stimulus control provide clients with ways in which to identify triggers of substance use and of anxiety symptoms and to lessen their power through using new coping techniques. A major trigger of anxiety is central nervous system arousal such as muscle tension and sweat gland activity. Biofeedback has been used effectively to provide information to clients regarding how their bodies respond to simulated stress. Once identified, relaxation techniques are taught so that clients feel as if they have control over somatic responses to stress. There is evidence that biofeedback helps persons to transform psychosomatic information into new cognitive propositions (Barlow, 1988), for example, "I feel more confident with new information about my body and how it interacts with my emotions."

Triggers of substance use and abuse may take more time and effort to identify than do triggers of anxiety. Clients need the support and guidance of trained counselors during this action stage of change. Counselors should help clients to identify errors that they might be making in their attempts (Prochaska & DiClemente, 1986). Roberta, for example, is a college graduate but knows little about addictions except for what she hears or sees in the media. She needs feedback regarding her efforts and needs continuing psychoeducation to help her feel as if she is a self-changer rather than a victim.

Once triggers have been identified, clients need tools for maintaining the gains that they have achieved. Counterconditioning is a behavioral technique of changing responses to persons, settings, and events that elicit substance use. Behavioral techniques such as desensitization, in vivo role rehearsals, and role-plays are common counterconditioning techniques. These approaches are most helpful for persons with panic disorder with agoraphobia and generalized anxiety disorder (Winokur & Coryell, 1991).

FAMILY RELATIONSHIPS

Many clients, such as Roberta, misinterpret communications with family and friends. Similarly, family and friends find behaviors such as constant agitation and complaints of worry to be extremely difficult to tolerate, especially in the absence of any observable threats in the clients' lives. Family psychoeducation has been used effectively with families that have members with schizophrenia, but little is known about its usefulness with other mental disorders.

The most traditional form of family support for alcohol and other drug dependencies has been Al-Anon groups, self-help support groups stressing that dependencies are family problems. Today, addiction experts such as Budd and Hughes (1997) suggest that these self-help family groups might not be as beneficial as family treatment, education, and support. A family can be especially supportive if a person has experienced a real event such as posttraumatic stress often seen in war veterans and victims of sexual or physical abuse. Part of recovery might be in the family and treatment team's ability to alleviate feelings of guilt and shame, a reason why many abuse drugs.

ENVIRONMENTAL INTERVENTIONS

In the absence of family or friends living in the household with Roberta, she needs other strong forms of social support. Individual support groups, meaningful work, ties in community projects, and leisure time activities are critical avenues of environmental support. Whereas psychoeducation and feedback are preferred interventions during contemplation of change, environmental changes often are necessary during the action and maintenance stages of change.

Roberta needs a therapist's support to identify triggers of alcohol and drug abuse in her current social environment. Because she is hypersensitive to the environment, she often generalizes stress to her entire life. However, some of her triggers are very specific. For example, when she eats too many sweets and skips regular meals, she takes friends' pills (e.g., Valium) to avoid feeling out of control. When the feelings of helplessness persist, she turns to alcohol. She would benefit from counterconditioning techniques to use when confronted with the desire to self-medicate to alleviate symptoms of anxiety.

Her current network of friends does not invite her to share in healthy leisure time activities, and her coworkers leave her out of social functions at work. One of her treatment goals is to develop new friendships. She also would like to change jobs.

AFFECTIVE DIMENSIONS

In working with clients with severe and chronic mental illnesses, much has been written about high expressed emotions of family caretakers who are overstressed with the burden of coping with their family members' mental illnesses (Lefley, 1992). High emotional expressions include expressions of frustration, overprotectiveness, and criticism of mentally ill family members' behaviors. When families use highly charged emotional expressions with clients, the clients may rapidly deteriorate and relapse into alcohol and substance use.

Although most of the literature on expressed emotions has focused on persons with schizophrenia, similar findings are emerging with clients with anxiety disorders. Ries (1994) extends the notion of highly expressed emotion from the family to members of treatment teams. He recommends that therapists avoid using emotions as the focus of intervention. This is especially important immediately following detoxification and during the early stages of contemplation of change. Treatment teams should avoid pressing for histories of traumas and should remain focused on current functional aspects of treatment such as daily exercise, good nutrition, and healthy social interactions.

SUPPORT GROUPS

Anxious persons, such as Roberta, often view group activities as additional reasons to feel apprehensive. Yet, to maintain control over her sobriety and over her anxiety disorder, she needs the support of self-help groups such as Alcoholics Anonymous (AA). Some programs offer AA and other self-help groups in-house, with members consisting of staff and clients. "This process makes it possible to frequently stop the meeting, discuss various meeting components, examine group methods, and allow participants to observe and practice" (Ries, 1994, p. 51). Another helpful practice is to accompany anxious clients to meetings early so that they can view the environment and begin meeting other participants and to stay late so that they can join others for coffee, snacks, and conversation. These efforts may help persons such as Roberta to establish new groups of friends with similar problems and similar goals for recovery.

Evans and Sullivan (1990) suggest that practice, staff support, and incremental steps toward group participation may break through denial, enabling persons to move from contemplation of change into preparedness to take action to change. For many persons, self-help groups are a lifelong need to maintain both mental health and sobriety.

EVALUATION OF
TREATMENT EFFECTIVENESS

Anxiety disorders, and especially those with comorbid substance-related disorders, were redefined during the 1980s and 1990s. Changes occurred in the classification of anxiety disorders from the *DSM-III*, to the *DSM-III-R*, to the *DSM-IV*. These changes make it very difficult to have outcome studies regarding treatment effectiveness and treatment efficacy. Most researchers suggest that a treatment package is the most effective intervention. However, is it the most cost-efficient and viable strategy to use in the current managed care environment?

If treatment is tied to accurate diagnoses and comprehensive biopsychosocial assessments, then assessment strategies provide the basis for treatment evaluation. For example, have the type, severity, and/or duration of symptoms lessened? Have daily living situations improved? Are clients satisfied with quality of life indicators such as job satisfaction, satisfaction with living arrangements, and psychological feelings of competence? Outcomes should reflect goal attainment of both relapse prevention objectives and psychiatric rehabilitation objectives. Single-subject designs can be implemented in practice settings with little extra expense (Lewellen, 1993).

SUMMARY

Despite the fact that anxiety disorders are the most prevalent mental disorders among the general population, they might be the least understood. When combined with substance-related disorders, they present complex physiological and psychosocial issues for treatment providers. This chapter presented strategies for differential diagnosis of coexisting anxiety disorders and substance-related disorders, short- and long-term assessment considerations, treatment goals, and a treatment model based on 10 relapse prevention processes at five different stages of readiness for change (Prochaska & DiClemente, 1986).

◼ *QUESTIONS FOR DISCUSSION*

1. What conditions must be met to differentiate between a primary anxiety disorder and a disorder related to substance intoxication or withdrawal?

2. What medications used to treat anxiety can worsen anxiety-like symptoms?

3. What treatment goals are most likely to succeed during the early stages of readiness for change?

4. How do gender-related issues affect the course of coexisting anxiety and substance-related disorders?

5. Do race and ethnicity play a role in the selection of treatment goals throughout the stages of recovery?

9 *Primary Substance Abuse Disorders*

Much of the previous discussion of dual diagnosis has focused on the complicating impact of substance use by persons having mental disorders. This chapter focuses on the treatment of persons whose substance abuse is the major and/or initially occurring disorder.

DEFINITION

Although the *Diagnostic and Statistical Manual of Mental Disorders* (*DSM-IV*) (American Psychiatric Association [APA], 1994) section on substance-related disorders includes side effects of a medication and toxin exposure, this chapter addresses only the substance use disorders, that is, those disorders related to ongoing current use of drugs, whether prescription, over-the-counter, illegal street drugs or legally available ones such as alcohol and inhalants. The *DSM-IV* includes two categories of substance use disorders: substance dependence and substance abuse.

Substance dependence and substance abuse both entail maladaptive patterns of substance use that result in significant adverse consequences. In addition, a diagnosis of substance dependence requires three or more of the following elements: development of tolerance for the substance, withdrawal symptoms in the absence of the substance, substance use in larger amounts or over longer periods of time than intended, desire or unsuccessful efforts to cut down or control the substance use, expenditure of a great deal of time in procuring or using the substance or recovering from its use, loss or reduction of important social/occupational/recreational activities, and continued substance use despite knowledge of consequential physical or psychological problems (APA, 1994).

It has been estimated that two thirds of persons with substance abuse disorders have coexisting mental disorders, most frequently depression

(Seligman, 1990). These coexisting disorders might have preceded the substance abuse but have become unnoticed or of secondary concern because of the severity of the substance abuse disorders. For example, it sometimes is suggested that many chronic cocaine users are self-medicating mental problems such as depression and attention deficit disorder. In other instances, the coexisting disorder is the result of the substance abuse. For example, extensive use of marijuana, or inhalant abuse, can cause hallucinations, delusions, and paranoia. Many diagnoses of antisocial personality disorder may be attributable to behaviors that are a result of chronic substance abuse.

Recent research has begun to explore differences in substance use patterns between those dually diagnosed persons whose mental disorders are primary and those whose substance use disorders are primary. Alcohol disorders are most prevalent among the latter, and overall severity of other substance use is less among those persons whose mental disorders are not a result of organic damage (Cuffel, 1996; Lehman, Myers, & Corty, 1989). It now is believed that primary drug use disorders tend to be more severe than those occurring with primary psychiatric disorders (Cuffel, 1996). Regardless of mental diagnosis, the most severe substance abusers generally are young males.

UNIQUE PROBLEMS

A major obstacle to effective treatment of the dually diagnosed client whose substance abuse is the primary disorder is the complications presented by the accompanying mental disorder. Regardless of which disorder came first, dual disorders are difficult to treat because of the vicious cycle of the substance abuse worsening the coexisting disorder, which in turn increases the client's tendency to use drugs to relieve the discomfort of the coexisting disorder. Furthermore, the substance use often masks the accompanying disorder, making assessment and appropriate treatment more difficult.

The risk of suicide is high among persons who are substance abusers, and particularly among those who also have coexisting disorders such as depression and the various Cluster B personality disorders. The drugs themselves are potentially lethal, and overdoses can bring death through either deliberate misuse or accident. Street drugs vary widely in purity and in the toxicity of substances with which the drugs are cut, making accidental death an ever present possibility. Combinations of psychotropic substances (e.g., alcohol and barbiturates) sometimes are superadditive, thereby raising the risk that an accidental overdose will occur.

ASSESSMENT CONSIDERATIONS

Drake, Rosenberg, and Mueser (1996) identify three primary functions of assessment in substance use disorders: detection, diagnosis, and specialized assessment for treatment planning. As part of the specialized assessment, an accurate social history of the client is needed to determine whether the mental disorder preceded the substance abuse because this information is relevant to the mental state that may be expected following long-term abstinence from the substances. If the onset of mental problems followed the substance abuse, then there is a greater likelihood of their receding once the substance use has ended. However, if the mental disorder came first, then it will remain after the cessation of substance use and will be a primary threat to continued abstinence from drugs. It has been suggested that persons whose psychiatric illnesses have resulted from substance use might need different treatment approaches from those whose two disorders occurred independently (Lehman, Myers, Thompson, & Corty, 1993).

It often is necessary to talk with relatives or friends of the client to get a clear picture of the client's pre-substance abuse functioning. Even then, there is some danger that a retrospective assessment of the client's pre-substance abuse functioning will be colored by intervening events.

The type of mental disorder that accompanies the substance abuse will differentially affect efforts to achieve and maintain a drug-free life. It is important that mental states that tend to increase the desire to use drugs (e.g., anxiety, specific moods) be identified early so that the client can be helped from the beginning of treatment so as to recognize and be prepared to deal with the triggering mental states.

CASE EXAMPLE

Elena sought therapy for depression related to responsibilities of single parenthood and conflictual relationships with her family of origin. She grew up in an affluent family with an alcoholic father and a mother who was addicted to prescription pain medication. Her brother killed himself during his teens in an episode of alcohol intoxication. Her sister was addicted to street drugs during her teens and early adulthood but subsequently recovered sufficiently to develop a professional career. Elena first attempted suicide at 11 years of age when she heard that her drug dealer had left town. During her teen years, the family home was the hangout for drug-abusing youths of the town. Elena's two marriages were characterized by drug abuse and violence. During periods of abstinence from alcohol and drugs, Elena functioned well in a technical field and functioned competently as a parent. Life stresses frequently resulted in feelings of depression and a return to drug abuse. She became known as the black sheep of the family.

TREATMENT GOALS

Corcoran and Grinnell (1992) list the six components usually considered as part of the change process: (a) setting goals, (b) setting objectives, (c) selecting appropriate interventions, (d) structuring the interventions, (e) establishing a contract, and (f) monitoring and evaluating the outcomes of the intervention.

Professionals in the substance abuse treatment field generally enter the treatment process with a goal of their clients' eventual abstinence from all alcohol and nonprescribed drug use. Clients, on the other hand, often enter the process feeling too dependent on the substance to commit to abstinence. "Setting vague or unreasonably high goals subjects your clients to a cruel and destructive experience in disappointment, frustration, and erosion of their confidence" (Corcoran & Grinnell, 1992, p. 3). Therefore, goals need to be negotiated so that there is agreement between the goals toward which the client and the professional are working. Meyers and Smith (1995) suggest sobriety sampling, that is, an agreement by the client to abstain from alcohol and drugs for 3 months (or less, depending on the length of time to which the client can commit). This is a compromise between the professional's goal of permanent abstinence and the client's resistance to giving up the substance use. This modified goal increases the client's chances for success and gives sufficient time to assess the client's mental status when he or she is clear of drugs. It is important that staff not be allowed to impose their own agendas that might undermine this cooperative effort between the client and the treatment program.

The initial treatment goal, then, is to interrupt the pattern of substance abuse so that the client can begin to function without the biopsychosocial distortions of psychotropic substance use. Once the client is stabilized (at least temporarily) in abstinence from psychotropic substances, the residual mental disorders can be assessed and addressed. Relief from the coexisting mental disorder greatly reduces the risk of a return to substance abuse, thereby ending the vicious cycle of abuse-recovery-relapse.

TREATMENT MODEL

Target problems of clients with primary substance abuse disorders and coexisting mental illnesses include cognitive distortions, emotional turmoil, and social isolation or discomfort. Any of these factors may precipitate substance use. The specific nature and combination of these three elements is unique to the individual client. Within these three elements are relationships with others, substance-abusing behaviors, and self-concept. The major factors that converge to create disorders of mental illness and substance abuse sometimes require extensive change efforts. Long-term intense treatment no longer is available to most dually diagnosed clients because of the exorbitant costs of such treatment. Furthermore, much of the change that needs to occur involves elements of personal growth, which cannot be rushed. Therefore, current treatment models are likely to involve short-term intensive treatment followed by long-term relapse prevention services provided by either professional staffs or self-help groups.

The treatment model begins with developing a helping relationship between the clinician and the client. As that relationship builds, it provides support and motivation for the development of behavioral methods to interrupt the substance abuse (Carey, 1996b). Efforts to change client behaviors are stressful for the client and often are unsuccessful initially. Stresses and failures in behavioral change lead to an examination of what kept this from working at this time. Analysis of the client's experience with stressful or unsuccessful efforts to change behaviors is likely to reveal maladaptive cognitions, social stressors, family dysfunction, or underlying emotional problems that are feeding the dependence on the alcohol or other drugs. Appropriate interventions directed at those problem areas might be necessary to achieve long-term behavioral change (Prochaska & DiClemente, 1986). Therefore, both the substance abuse behavior and any underlying contributing factors must be dealt with as part of a total treatment package.

The first focus of treatment is interrupting the substance-abusing behavior. This is followed by exploring the thoughts and feelings contributing to the client discomfort that, in turn, triggers substance abuse. Interrupting the substance-abusing behavior is achieved through the change-directed processes of stimulus control, counterconditioning, contingency management, and self-liberation, all supported by the development of a therapeutic bond or helping relationship as described by Prochaska and DiClemente (1986).

As the client's body becomes free of the psychoactive substances, thinking becomes clearer and emotions that have been distorted or deadened by the substances begin to emerge. Individual differences among clients (especially including the nature of the coexisting mental disorders) bring to the fore different constellations of disturbing thoughts and feelings. This requires differential use of the change processes of consciousness raising, self-reevaluation, environmental reevaluation, social liberation, and dramatic relief as well as further use of the processes used in achieving initial sobriety (Prochaska & DiClemente, 1986).

Most clients experience one or more relapses into substance abuse, and the rate of relapse among clients with mental illnesses is higher than average. It is important that temporary slips and relapses not be interpreted as treatment failures. Both the client and treatment personnel should view relapses as opportunities to better understand the factors that are directing the client's behavior so that the next effort to end the substance use will have a higher probability of success. Often, several fine-tunings of the treatment strategy are needed before long-term recovery is achieved. "With appropriate treatment, follow-up, and client motivation, the prognosis is good for significant improvement, if not complete remission, of behavioral symptoms (Seligman, 1990, p. 168).

READINESS FOR CHANGE

Denial is a major theme in professional literature about substance-abusing clients. Although the pejorative sense in which the term often is used might be inappropriate, the client's dependence on the substance of abuse and fears of inability to cope with life without the substance often contribute to resistance to facing the reality of the damaging effects of substance abuse. Therefore, the substance abuser unconsciously and consciously distorts the extent of his or her use of and dependence on the substance.

> People seeking . . . treatment bring with them widely varying degrees of motivation or commitment to change. Lack of motivation can be problematic. . . . Even voluntary clients may need their motivation enhanced. . . . Even the voluntary client often asks to change some antecedent condition or a consequence of a behavior, but says "don't change my behavior." It is not until the client comes to terms with the need to change some specific action, affect, or cognition that he or she is motivated. We believe that one way to help motivate clients is to use structured interventions. . . . [These involve] setting specific and realistic goals, and you might need to discuss with clients the need to focus on some behavior of theirs rather than of someone else. (Corcoran, 1992, pp. 12-13)

During the precontemplative stage, clients are less inclined to process information about their problems. They spend little time and energy reevaluating themselves, and they experience fewer emotional reactions to the negative aspects of their problems. They tend to be less open with others about their problems, and they do little to shift their attention or their environment in the direction of dealing with their problems (Prochaska & DiClemente, 1984). A dually diagnosed client with a primary substance abuse disorder might not have conscious awareness of either disorder, or the client might be aware of one disorder but in denial about the other.

The client who still is in precontemplation regarding both disorders most often is brought into contact with the clinician through difficulties with the client's health, the law, family relationships, or other dimensions of social functioning. In such cases, the connection must be made between these difficulties and the substance-abusing behavior through the process of consciousness raising. If the client is aware of the mental problems (e.g., anxiety or mood disorders) but not the substance abuse, then the therapist can relate the mental problems to the substance abuse and suggest abstinence as a way of getting a handle on the mental problems. If the client is aware of the substance abuse disorder but not the mental disorder, then work can begin immediately on the substance abuse, and once the substance use has ended, the mental problems will be more apparent. In either case, a functional analysis of current behavior and its repercussions (Meyers & Smith, 1995) can provide a basis for a cost-benefit consideration of continuing the problematic behavior (Carey, 1996b).

HELPING RELATIONSHIP

It is the responsibility of the clinician to facilitate the development of a relationship that will be supportive of and motivating to the client, regardless of his or her stage in readiness for change. This relationship is the working variable that connects the client to the therapeutic process.

Clients often connect with clinicians on the basis of one or more of the following factors. The clinician may be perceived by the client as a person of authority based on his or her level of education, position of power in the treatment setting or community at large, or professional expertise. Just as most physically ill persons rely on the authority of their physicians, chemically dependent clients usually will assume a trusting role toward the professional persons they are seeing for treatment. A second possible foundation for the development of a helping relationship is the client's identification with the clinician (i.e., recognizing commonalities that lend credibility to the clinician's understanding of the client and the client's situation). For this reason, it has been assumed that matching of clients and clinicians on factors such as race, gender, and cultural background will facilitate the development of the helping relationship, although research in this area has brought mixed results. It often is assumed that the presence of persons in recovery on staff will facilitate the client's acceptance of the helping relationship. However, research has not demonstrated that "recovering chemical dependence counselors have an easier time, are better liked by recovering clients, or do a better job than counselors who have not used drugs" (Buelow & Buelow, 1998, p. 4).

A third basis for the client's investing in the helping relationship is his or her belief in the problem-solving abilities of the clinician. For this reason, it often is useful to provide some visible benefit to the client, such as connecting the client with some relevant community resource or providing simple, commonsense advice early in the relationship to demonstrate problem-solving abilities. A systematic approach to information gathering and processing also demonstrates a structured way of proceeding that is confidence inspiring.

A fourth possible thread tying the client to the clinician is the more nebulous personal attraction, or "likability," factor. If the clinician appears to be hostile, disinterested, or preoccupied with problems of his or her own, then the client is not likely to waste energy in working with the clinician. By contrast, empathy, authenticity, personality, and the courage to support and confront are qualities that contribute to treatment success with substance-abusing clients (Buelow & Buelow, 1998; Seligman, 1990).

Most treatment teams in substance abuse programs provide opportunities for clients to relate on more than one of these dimensions. Diplomas on the wall, degree designations on name tags, and the like encourage confidence in the staff's authority. The use of recovering persons on staff and cultural diversity among staff permit easier identification with the staff, the structured intake process and program consistency inspire confidence in the facility's problem-solving ability, and a pleasant and empathic staff is an inviting group of persons with whom to work.

Clinicians working with dually diagnosed clients who have primary substance abuse problems must be able to be both supportive and confrontive. The supportiveness includes empathic responses to clients' situational difficulties, frustrations regarding the inability to control their lives, anger at persons with whom they are in conflict, and acceptance of their resentment of involuntary treatment.

> [Clinicians] also need to handle appropriately their own reactions to clients' reluctance to change, continuing to communicate empathy and acceptance to even the most hostile and resistant clients. . . . One of the challenges facing the therapist is the reversal of these patterns and the development of an honest relationship. (Seligman, 1990, p. 171)

Confrontation does not imply hostility or callousness. Rather, it means bringing to the client's awareness information or connections between elements in the client's behavior or situation that the client has not fully comprehended before. Confrontation can be as subtle as a raised eyebrow in response to a client's distortion or as heavy-handed as exerting external controls when a client is at high risk of harming himself or herself or others.

Support and confrontation usually are used in an alternating fashion. Initial support reassures the client and allows a client-therapist bond to begin to be developed. Confrontation, which is necessary to increase client awareness of his or her behavior and its consequences, nevertheless threatens the client and elicits defensiveness. Support is then needed to reduce defensiveness and reconnect the client to the therapeutic process, at which time more confrontation can be provided. Thus, a sandwiching effect of alternating support and confrontation moves the client forward toward greater awareness of the problem and increased motivation to address it through change.

The helping relationship during the precontemplative stage gives the client the support necessary to consider the possibility that the client's problems might reside within the client and his or her behavior. During the contemplative stage, the relationship anchors the client while he or she struggles with inevitable ambivalence about moving into action to address the substance abuse and mental disorders. During the action stage, the therapist becomes a coach who assists in directing the client's change efforts, offering constructive critiques of what is working and what is not working, and encouraging the client in the step-by-step movement toward recovery. During the maintenance/relapse prevention stage, the helping relationship is used to facilitate treatment generalization, foster self-management skills for handling future problems, and ease the transition to further progress with decreasing involvement with professional helpers and increasing involvement with natural helping networks and self-help groups.

PSYCHOPHARMACOLOGICAL CONSIDERATIONS

Medication seldom is the primary method of treatment for substance abuse disorders. However, medications that reduce craving and withdrawal sometimes are valuable components of treatment (Buelow & Buelow, 1998). In some cases of alcoholism, lithium reduces the craving, the level of intoxication from drinking, and the rate of relapse. Similarly, naltrexone has been effective in reducing craving and relapse in alcoholics and narcotic addicts (Doweiko, 1999). Librium, the first true benzodiazepine (used for relief of anxiety), often is used during detoxication from alcohol (and narcotics) to prevent delirium tremens (Hanson & Venturelli, 1995). Medications are sometimes used to reduce or eliminate the pleasure associated with drug or alcohol use. Methadone, naltrexone hydrochloride, and buprenorphine all have been used to block the euphoria of narcotics use, although each has some offsetting negative attributes. L-alpha-acetylmethadol, like methadone, prevents withdrawal symptoms in opiate addicts and holds some promise as part of a broader treatment package.

A number of medications, such as flupenthixol, bromocriptine, buprenorphine, imipramine, bupropion, and desipramine hydrochloride, have shown some promise for reducing craving during or after cocaine withdrawal, but none has received wide acceptance because of questions concerning health risks, research validity, and possible addictive qualities in the medicine. Some authorities question the necessity for such pharmacological treatment given that withdrawal symptoms from cocaine addiction are mild and craving is short term in comparison to the withdrawal process in opiate addiction (Doweiko, 1999).

Disulfiram (Antabuse) often is used for persons with alcohol dependency. The combination of disulfiram and alcohol generally produces flushing, heart palpitations, difficulty in breathing, nausea, vomiting, and possibly a serious drop in blood pressure, all of which reduce the desirability of further drinking. One major limitation to the use of disulfiram is the medical risks involved that preclude its use with persons who are not generally in good health. Another drawback is the lag time between drinking and the effects of the combined drugs. Still another is clients' resistance to taking medication that they know will interfere with their drinking pleasure (Doweiko, 1999).

Medication more often is used as part of the treatment of psychiatric disorders, and the prescriptions of medications for dually diagnosed clients clearly must take into account the prioritization of disorders (i.e., which disorder is the immediate focus of intervention). Often in the case of persons who have primary substance abuse disorders, halting the substance abuse is the initial priority. Sometimes, the same medication may be helpful with relation to both disorders, as in the case of Librium, which assists with both anxiety disorders and substance withdrawal difficulties. In other situations, medication for the secondary mental disorder might need to be postponed until abstinence from substance abuse is achieved. Two general rules must guide the use of medication with dually diagnosed clients. First, close medical supervision always is required in these complex situations. Second, medication should not be relied on as the sole method of treatment.

COGNITIVE-BEHAVIORAL DIMENSIONS

The term *substance abuse* refers to specific behavior, that is, ingesting psychotropic substances to an extent that brings significant negative consequences. Therefore, treatment success is dependent on changing that behavior.

The behavioral component of the larger biopsychosocial issue of substance abuse is explained by Donovan (1988):

> The changes that are induced when the individual engages in the addictive behavior serve as an unconditioned stimulus. Through repeated association with these changes, a wide variety of other stimuli acquire the power of conditioned stimuli . . . , mood states, cognitive expectations, and levels of physiological arousal, as well as more specific features of the social or physical environment in which the behavior typically occurs. . . . The changes induced by the addictive experience also serve to reinforce those behaviors associated with it; those behaviors instrumental in the individual's engaging in the addictive experience become more frequent, vigorous, and persistent. These reinforcement processes, in conjunction with physiological factors, contribute to the development of acquired tolerance, psychological dependence, and/or physical dependence on the addictive experience. The individual may experience withdrawal distress when unable to engage in the addictive behavior. . . . The effects of withdrawal that appear consistent across addictive behaviors include craving, emotional distress, and disruption of behavior. . . . Finally, the experience of this distress generates a state of disequilibrium that may motivate continued involvement in the addictive behavior. (pp. 7-8)

Three of the processes of change identified by Prochaska and DiClemente (1986) are particularly helpful in bringing the substance abuse behavior under control: stimulus control, counterconditioning, and contingency management. "Stimulus control procedures involve clients or therapists restructuring the environment so that the probability of a particular conditional stimulus occurring is significantly reduced" (Prochaska & DiClemente, 1984, p. 11). Substance abusers and their therapists can identify situations and mental states that tend to trigger the substance use, and strategies for avoiding those triggers can be developed. Triggers usually include being in the presence of others who are using the addictive substances; emotional states such as anger, anxiety, and depression; and times and locations that have been associated with past substance use.

Strategies for stimulus control might include avoiding persons who themselves are substance abusers, staying away from the client's favorite site of substance use during the times when the use most often occurs, and modifying one's mood when it moves into a triggering state. Client training in assertiveness skills, effective communication, and handling criticism can increase the client's ability to prevent relationship-based depression, thereby eliminating one source of emotional state triggers (Rohsenow, Monti, Binkoff, Leipman, & Nirenberg, 1991). Similarly, substance abuse triggering anxiety can be reduced through behavioral methods such as systematic desensitization and cognitive restructuring (Persons, 1989).

Stimulus control sometimes is difficult because of the paucity of acquaintances who do not drink or do drugs, the near impossibility of avoiding some places where one has used drugs (e.g., home, work), and the intractability of some emotional states (especially in the dually disordered client). Nevertheless, avoiding temptation when feasible is a necessary first step in getting substance use under control.

Counterconditioning refers to relearning or developing nondestructive means of handling triggering stimuli when they are unavoidable. Techniques might include, at the situational level, learning skills in "just saying *no*" to invitations to participate in substance use behavior and developing automatic thoughts such as "I'm going to remain clean today" to redirect cognitions away from substance use. Cognitive techniques are most effective with those persons who have the ability to recognize their automatic thoughts, can recognize and label their own emotional states, and can accept personal responsibility for change (Safran & Segal, 1990). When psychological states (e.g., anxiety, depression) are triggers, as most often is the case with dually diagnosed persons, the client must develop non-substance-using ways of coping with those states. For example, anxiety often can be reduced through strenuous physical activity, relaxation exercises, or interaction with a supportive companion. The client relearns how to respond to the triggering psychological state in a nondestructive manner.

Contingency management, or changing the payoff for the substance-abusing behavior, is more difficult to apply due to the reinforcing nature of the substance use and the lack of control the therapist has over most of the contingencies in the client's environment. The most common use of contingency management is the training of enablers to no longer reward the substance abuser with the responses that the abuser has found reinforcing in the past. The depressed substance abuser, for example, may customarily find gratification in the sympathy that he or she receives when coming down from a cocaine high. Stopping the gratifying sympathy reduces the client's positive payoff for substance abuse.

COPING

There is a need to help substance abusers develop constructive coping skills. Research on substance-abusing and non-substance-abusing populations revealed the substance abusers to be more depressed and to use suppression, help seeking, substitution, and blaming as coping styles more often as compared to non-substance abusers. Women substance abusers had increased passivity, depression, and conflict and had lower levels of functioning than did their male counterparts (Conte, Plutchik, Picard, & Galanter, 1991).

When in the treatment and relapse prevention stages, substance abusers must learn to cope with the idea of a future without the substance on which they have relied. This brings forth a variety of emotions analogous to the grief process. Related to this loss of their habitual coping mechanism, clients need assistance in finding new ways of structuring their time and developing new recreational and social outlets. Furthermore, they must adopt the identities of recovering persons, declining drinks or drugs in settings where such refusal might be conspicuous. Such changes in identity usually take months or years after the achievement of abstinence from drugs and alcohol.

PSYCHOEDUCATION

Psychoeducation is a standard part of the treatment package in most intensive treatment programs for substance abusers and in a growing number of programs that treat mental illness. In substance abuse treatment, psychoeducation groups most often provide basic information about the influence of psychoactive substances on the individual and the addiction process and include only the clients themselves. "Information and education are almost always a part of treatment. Clients are taught about the negative impact of their behaviors on their physical and emotional adjustment and learn new and more effective behaviors to replace the old ones" (Seligman, 1990, p. 166). In mental health settings, psychoeducation is more likely to be directed at families of the clients. Simon (1997) states,

> Problems of various magnitudes often arise in families with mentally ill family members. If familial stress is to be reduced, family members must be equipped with skills and knowledge that allow them to handle problems effectively. The ability to handle problems and crises that occur has a major impact on family functioning and intrafamilial stress. (p. 132)

The information provided by psychoeducation assists in consciousness raising. Because the setting is a group of persons with similar problems, the client or family feels less threatened and defensiveness is minimized. This approach can be used to educate audience members about the nature of substance abuse, mental disorders, and the combination of the two; to inform them of the purposes and procedures of the treatment program; and to alert them to factors that might threaten recovery and lead to relapse. Psychoeducation is a valuable part of treatment of persons with primary substance disorders, but educational intervention alone seldom is sufficient to bring about behavioral change (Carey, 1996b).

INTERPERSONAL SKILLS

Problems in interpersonal relationships are inevitable in persons with primary substance abuse disorders. In some cases, premorbid interpersonal problems might have contributed to the development of substance abuse behaviors (Prochaska & DiClemente, 1986). Once the individual has developed dependence on substance use, interpersonal relationships are negatively affected in several ways. The substance abuser becomes less reliable and more focused on meeting drug dependency needs than on meeting social role obligations. In some cases, dishonesty and crimes against family and friends are perpetrated either when under the influence of drugs or in desperate efforts to get resources for more drugs. "People who use drugs or alcohol to excess may have learned to cope by lying to others or by placating or abusing others, and these patterns may be carried into their therapy" (Seligman, 1990, p. 170). In addition, the acquisition of new social skills is halted as the substance abuser increasingly relies on the alcohol or drugs to cope with problems of living. Consequently, social relationships are deficient and damaged at the time the client gets into a treatment setting.

Social skills training often is helpful in maintaining abstinence from alcohol and drug abuse. The substance abuser's frequent use of extreme passivity or hostile aggression (either of which undermines healthy social functioning) can be replaced by constructive interactions through assertiveness training. The new skills also are effective in reducing depression and anxiety, the most common accompaniments to substance abuse in dually diagnosed clients. Prochaska and DiClemente (1986) state that assertiveness and anxiety are incompatible and that assertiveness training deconditions anxiety responses and is rewarded by more successful social interactions. In some cases, passive clients resist the use of assertiveness because of their fears of not being nice persons if they demand respect from others. In these cases, values clarification (self-reevaluation) is appropriate because these clients might have to decide whether their recovery is worth the sacrifice of an appeasing style of interacting with others. Research shows that highly anxious and less educated clients benefit particularly well from social skills training (Rohsenow et al., 1991).

Sometimes, the cause of poor social relationships is prejudice or intolerance within the society for specific subpopulations. For example, members of racial minority groups, lesbians and gay men, and persons with visible physical disabilities often have difficulty in establishing normal interpersonal relationships because of attitudinal barriers imposed by the larger society. Prochaska and DiClemente (1984) refer to these as individuo-social conflicts, and persons confronted with such negative responses from their social environments are particularly vulnerable to both substance abuse and mental disorders. Therapeutic intervention in these situations is dual focused, addressing the need for social change in the environment (social liberation) and assisting the individual client in learning techniques for transcending the negativism in the environment (self-liberation).

FAMILY RELATIONSHIPS

Like other social relationships, unsatisfactory family relationships may be part of the cause, and almost always are a result, of long-term substance abuse. Family conflict often involves issues relating to intimacy and sexuality, communication, hostility, and control of others (Prochaska & DiClemente, 1984). As substance abuse increases, so do family conflicts. Often, the substance abuse becomes the focal point in the family, and all members learn some means of coping with it, achieving some balance. Cessation of the substance abuse disrupts that balance and brings a new period of fluidity in family roles. Unsuccessful adjustment of other family members to the new abstinence may raise stress levels that threaten the client's recovery. Therapeutic intervention should include all family members involved in the conflicts and should include a renegotiation of family rules and roles, establishing appropriate boundaries between individuals and generations and clarification of reasonable expectations for each member.

The change process of consciousness raising is active as families learn more about the dynamics of substance abuse, and contingency management is used when families stop reinforcing substance abuse behavior. "When family members are helped to change patterns that reinforce and provide secondary gains for the negative behavior, the likelihood of the client's improvement is increased and the family members also benefit (Seligman, 1990, p. 167). Environmental reevaluation occurs as the substance abuser receives feedback about how his or her substance abuse has affected each member of the family. Altogether, family therapy offers a rich opportunity for positive change.

ENVIRONMENTAL
INTERVENTIONS

Because of the role of environmental stressors in contributing to substance abuse and mental disorders, it sometimes is necessary to intervene at the environmental level during the action stage and often at the relapse prevention stage of recovery. Intervention during the action stage might include (a) suggesting that the client change employment to a less psychologically stressful work setting to diminish the overall stress level during early stages of treatment, (b) relocating to an area absent of known drug dealers, or (c) moving out of a relationship that is contributing to the substance abuse (as in the case of a woman who is living with a drug abuser or an alcoholic).

Many clients need assistance with furthering their educations, career development, socialization, communication skills, parenting, and developing drug-free leisure activities. During the relapse prevention stage, environmental intervention is likely to involve upgrading of education and enhancing job skills in an overall plan to give greater economic opportunities. "Always provide a bridge back into the workforce by addressing career and work concerns as a normal part of therapy" (Buelow & Buelow, 1998, p. 9). Achievement of educational career advancement might be dependent on developing linkages to community resources, especially in the case of clients with low socioeconomic status.

AFFECTIVE DIMENSIONS

In addition to problems presented by the mood, personality, or anxiety disorder that may accompany the dually diagnosed client with a primary substance abuse disorder, the client will have a reservoir of intense feelings that have built up during the lengthy development of the substance abuse disorder. These are likely to include feelings of guilt, frustration, anger, and defensiveness. Problem solving and other cognitive tasks cannot be accomplished until there is some reduction in the feelings that are overwhelming the client at the beginning of therapeutic contact. Ventilation of feelings brings dramatic relief that frees the client to begin using psychological resources for more rational consciousness raising and problem solving.

During later stages of treatment, intense emotions again will surface as long repressed feelings begin to emerge and as abstinence from alcohol and drugs takes away the client's usual means of escaping from the frustrations of daily living. Unless these feelings are dissipated through dramatic relief, they will be a threat to recovery. The development of new social skills will provide new and healthier means of dealing with powerful emotional reactions to problems of living.

The role of the clinician is to permit the client to ventilate feelings in the safety of the helping relationship. This requires nonjudgmentalism, nondefensiveness, and empathy.

Psychotherapeutic skills, in addition to counseling competence, are needed for successful work with dually diagnosed clients. A deep understanding of the clients' internal worlds is required so as to bring about the intrapersonal changes often needed in clients who have mental disorders as well as chemical dependence (Buelow & Buelow, 1998).

SUPPORT GROUPS

Persons with primary substance abuse disorders are good candidates for 12-step and other support groups. During the precontemplative stage, the client's consciousness of his or her problems with substance abuse is raised through identification with group members whose symptoms and experiences are similar to those of the client. During the contemplative stage, the shared successful experiences of group members give hope that the client too can gain control over substance abuse. During the active stage of treatment, change is facilitated by learning specific techniques of attaining abstinence that have worked for others. During the relapse prevention stage, the group support and shared learning are important in sustaining recovery.

Clear advantages to support groups include their success in overcoming the sense of alienation that is typical of substance abusers, information sharing among peers, and the group acceptance that validates the work of the individual. Since the establishment of Alcoholics Anonymous (AA) in 1935, 12-step groups have helped more substance users attain sobriety than have any other methods, and it is estimated that there are 2 million members of AA worldwide (Bender & Leone, 1998). This model continues to prevail in the United States both as a stand-alone treatment method and as a support to professional treatment services, and some researchers attest to their effectiveness (Gorski, 1998).

On the other hand, Fox (1998) argues that relatively few problem drinkers (roughly 6.4%) become members of AA, four out of five of those soon drop out, and a very small percentage of AA members succeed in staying sober. Fox concludes that the 12-step method of treatment is simply not acceptable to the majority of persons who have substance abuse problems. The fact that many substance abusers do not find 12-step programs helpful probably is due to poor fits between the needs of the individuals and the group's principles and methods. The 12-step programs are deeply influenced by the evangelical Protestantism of the 1930s (Makela et al., 1996), and their spiritual focus is objectionable to increasing numbers of people. Furthermore, many professionals in the substance abuse field, in the light of research that does not support substance abuse as a disease (Kishline, 1998), object to the disease model that AA and its sister groups promote. These professionals are hesitant to refer to groups that emphasize the physiological causation when research has suggested that environmental factors may be a more powerful influence on substance-using behavior (Kishline, 1998). Also, the concept of powerlessness of the individual to change his or her behavior is believed by some to undermine cognitive-behavioral treatment methods. Some of these concerns have resulted in the recent development of alternative forms of support groups (e.g., rational recovery, smart management, recovery training) that avoid religious attribution to individual change and emphasize the ability of the individual to change behavior through cognitive-behavioral methods.

There is no formula for determining which clients will benefit from 12-step groups and which will not, so an effort should be made to assess the probability of a fit between the client and available support groups. A major factor for consideration is the nature of the coexisting mental disorder of the client. For example, will the depressed client be further distressed by accepting having an additional disease of addiction? Or, will such acceptance relieve guilt and diminish stress? It is imperative that the decisions about the use of support groups be made on the basis of the needs and preferences of the client rather than the dogmas and biases of treatment personnel.

❏ *QUESTIONS FOR DISCUSSION*

1. In view of the importance of methods such as the teaching of social skills and psychoeducation, is there really a need for therapy for the primary substance abuser?

2. What are possible pitfalls of dependence on the use of disulfiram or other medications for taking care of the problem of alcohol abuse?

3. Why is the clinician's personal history regarding substance use of importance in the treatment of clients with substance abuse problems in addition to psychiatric disorders?

4. How may cultural differences complicate the process of diagnosis of substance abuse in the primary substance-related disorders?

5. Does the disagreement about the value of 12-step programs contribute to or detract from the delivery of effective services? How?

10 Conclusion and Treatment Grid

Substance abuse, especially when long term, results in diminished cognitive effectiveness, inappropriate or exaggerated mood states, increased anxiety, and behavioral problems involving interpersonal relationships. Mental illness generally is characterized by one or more of those same elements. Therefore, the coexistence of a mental illness with substance abuse does not bring anything new or unfamiliar to the treatment situation except in degree. Substance abuse treatment personnel need thorough knowledge of cognitive, affective, and behavioral problems to treat not only the dually diagnosed but their single-disordered clients as well. If they are incapable of working effectively with the mentally ill, then they might very well be equally incapable of working with single-disordered substance abusers who are experiencing cognitive, affective, and behavioral problems as a result of their substance abuse.

Mental health treatment personnel, likewise, need to generalize their expertise to better treat dually diagnosed persons. It is almost universally accepted by mental health professionals that mental illness is largely due to biochemical factors over which the client has little control. Consequently, clinicians do not react judgmentally when a client with schizophrenia regresses to hallucinations or when a person with major depression again goes into a depressed state. Yet, these same professionals often want to wash their hands of responsibility for persons with substance abuse disorders because such clients "don't comply with the treatment expectations." Unlike mental illness, substance abuse disorders still are too often regarded as personal failures of the individual, with minimal credence given to the biochemical factors that perpetuate the patterns of abuse. As numerous other authors (notably Evans & Sullivan, 1990) have concluded, cross-training of personnel in mental health and substance abuse treatment programs is essential to effective service delivery. We would add that such cross-training is needed for effective service to single-disordered clients as well as the dually diagnosed population.

Much of the professional literature decries the fact that dually diagnosed clients do not respond well in treatment programs that are designed for persons with substance abuse problems only or with mental illnesses only. The accommodations that are required for dually diagnosed clients are, in many cases, advantageous to single-disordered clients as well. In experimentation to better treat the special population of dually diagnosed persons, insights have been gained in how to treat those with single disorders. The following are some conclusions that would seem to apply to substance abuse and mental health treatment generally as well as to the special population of persons with coexisting mental illnesses and substance abuse disorders.

ASSESSMENT

Assessment is problematic when the client is under the influence of alcohol or other drugs. In the context of contemporary funding crises, it is impractical to wait until the client is dried out or clean to begin the assessment process. One can proceed with a vigilant assessment of the degree to which the client's condition is acute. Is there a medical crisis or high suicide/homicide potential that would necessitate immediate hospitalization or other authoritative intervention? Also, differential treatment of symptoms can be done prior to a final and formal diagnosis. Intervention with family members need not be delayed until an ideal assessment is accomplished. Action taken on the basis of tentative and partial assessments must be cautious, symptom directed, and carefully monitored.

READINESS FOR CHANGE

Professionals cannot work successfully during the action or maintenance stage when the client still is in precontemplation or contemplation. It seems that much of the disgruntlement of professionals and third-party payers is based on the unrealistic expectation that clients are ready to take action as soon as they enter a treatment milieu. The current practice of evaluating the effectiveness of service on the sole basis of the extent to which total abstinence is achieved is self-defeating to the professionals and is demoralizing to the clients. Professionals must begin to recognize that readiness must be developed over time and that efforts put into moving clients toward readiness for change are as important (and as worthy of third-party payments) as are the techniques used during the action stage. Furthermore, we must educate health insurance organizations about the process of achieving readiness and must lobby for reimbursement for this essential part of treatment. Our researchers need to assist us in developing better measurements of readiness so that we can document client progress in the absence of abstinence from alcohol and drugs. Progress toward this end has been made in the United Kingdom by Rollnick, Heather, Gold, and Hall (1992), who have developed a brief Readiness to Change Questionnaire, but treatment personnel in the United States have been distressingly slow to adopt innovations from abroad that might challenge our treatment traditions. Mental health professionals must recognize that readiness for change is relevant to mental illnesses as well as to substance abuse. Dually diagnosed clients may be at one stage of readiness for change regarding one disorder and at another stage of readiness with regard to the other disorder. The clinician must work at the client's levels of readiness in both situations simultaneously.

In addition, clients do not necessarily move in a straight line sequence from the precontemplation stage, to the contemplation stage, to the action stage, to the maintenance stage. Instead, there often is movement back and forth between stages as internal and external factors shift the client's motivation and defensiveness. Therefore, therapeutic work often is iterative, reworking issues that already have been addressed, in a "three steps forward and two steps back" manner. Acceptance of this concept puts slips and relapses in more appropriate perspective as sometimes essential parts of an arduous process toward meaningful and lasting recovery.

With the dually diagnosed client, the nature of the mental disorder affects the level of motivation for change, the client's ability to interpret data in consciousness raising, and the cognitive and affective resources available for efforts at change.

HELPING RELATIONSHIP

There are long traditions of "we know best, and if you do not agree, then you are resisting" in both mental health and substance abuse treatment settings. Such attitudes often led to adversarial relationships between staff and clients as staff tried to break through clients' denial. In some substance abuse treatment settings, consciousness raising took the form of aggressive—even hostile—group confrontations. Psychologically fragile dually diagnosed clients decompensated when targeted by such methods. Mental health settings experienced client revolts in the form of client advocacy and self-help organizations that grew out of clients' perceptions that they were shown little respect in the treatment process.

More recently developed methods are based on a collaborative relationship between the client and staff, as described by Meyers and Smith

(1995) and Miller and Rollnick (1991). This relationship includes respect for the client and acceptance of his or her limitations, a nonthreatening approach, and a vision of wellness tempered with cautious realism. The client is the expert on his or her experience of illness, and the clinician must have the flexibility to work compatibly with the client's view of reality.

PSYCHOPHARMACOLOGICAL CONSIDERATIONS

Many persons with coexisting mental illness and substance abuse disorders will need medications to maintain wellness. The medications must be selected on the basis of their abuse potential, what characteristics they have that might help the client to maintain control over his or her mental illness, what characteristics might help to maintain abstinence from substances of abuse, and characteristics that might hinder wellness (Ries, 1993). Psychosocial services are needed to work with the client around resistance to medication compliance that sometimes results from unpleasant side effects of the medication, ambivalence about the necessity of medication (particularly during the contemplative stage of change), or fears that the medication will contribute to continuing drug dependence.

COGNITIVE-BEHAVIORAL DIMENSIONS

The concept of self-liberation contributes a major sense of hope and empowerment to persons with either mental illness or substance abuse disorders or the two in combination. Removing the victimhood from clients enables them to define their illness in their own terms and to take responsibility for their own wellness including decisions about the use of medications.

Behavioral methods are particularly useful in the treatment of dually diagnosed clients. Stimulus control has long been a technique used by substance abusers attempting to stop their addictive behavior, but it has equally useful potential for persons with mental illness. They can learn to recognize both internal and external stimuli that tend to lead to mental destabilization and can either avoid those stimuli or use counterconditioning measures to react less destructively to the triggers. Contingency management has broad implications. It is important to discover with the client what effects reinforce symptomatic behavior and to minimize that reinforcement. Allowing the client to suffer reasonable negative consequences for symptomatic behavior while withholding positive payoffs removes the reinforcing quality of the behavior. In the case of dually diagnosed persons with severe mental illness, natural consequences of relapse behavior are not always reasonable. For example, letting the person with schizophrenia go to jail for disorderly conduct is likely to do more harm than good. However, giving in to unreasonable demands of the client is not prudent either.

PSYCHOEDUCATION

Dually diagnosed clients and their families need accurate information about disorders, their causes, their consequences, and their interactions. It is essential that clients and their families understand that family members are not to blame for disorders of mental illness or substance abuse. Psychoeducation can cover these topics as well as issues of daily living such as interpersonal interactions, vocational preparation, and input regarding how to maximize clients' participation in the community. The more impersonal presentation that psychoeducation provides is more palatable than individual discussions to many persons with a variety of disorders. Psychoeducation tends to be nonjudgmental and nonthreatening to both clients and their family members. Its popularity is growing, and research strongly supports its further development (Simon, 1997).

SELF-REEVALUATION

As dually diagnosed clients become more aware of the nature of their disorders, they need assistance in redefining themselves in less pejorative terms than they have used previously. Both rational and emotional appraisals of their disorders, with their pros and cons, will help to stabilize clients' self-perceptions and facilitate client progress toward living well even within their illnesses. A shift of focus from "ill self" to "self with some illness" comes when clients are helped to recognize and value the healthy parts of themselves. This focus is good practice for single-disordered clients as well as dually disordered clients.

INTERPERSONAL
RELATIONSHIPS

Environmental reevaluation highlights the impact of client behaviors on other persons around the client, often stirring up guilt that may serve as motivation to change and bringing a desire to improve relationships with those who have suffered from client actions. The dually diagnosed client, however, might feel helpless in ameliorating any of the damage done to interpersonal relationships. Interpersonal relationships traditionally have been good grist for the therapeutic mill, but discussion alone often is insufficient for major change. Interpersonal skills training (including explanation, demonstration, and rehearsal) is needed, especially with the dually diagnosed client who might have diminished capacity for insight. This training will increase the client's ability to function appropriately in social situations, thereby reducing the risk of harmful isolation.

CULTURAL SENSITIVITY

Although this topic has been referred to sporadically in the preceding chapters, it seems important to stress here the necessity to take seriously issues of gender and subcultural group membership. Most of our treatment literature and experience have come from an expectation that the client population is homogeneous, specifically male and of Western European cultural heritage. There is a major need for adapting our theories and methods to females and clients of racial and ethnic diversity.

There is an ever expanding research base demonstrating that cultural expectations for females are different from those for males; that the pathways to substance abuse for females are different than those for males; that women's bodies respond to substances differently than do men's; and that the physiological, psychological, and social consequences of substance abuse are different for women than for men. Two conclusions may be drawn from this information. First, treatment needs are likely to be different for women as well. Women's issues must be an integral part of services to females. Second, because of historic and extant dynamics governing the social interactions between males and females, it often is advantageous to females that they be treated separately from males.

Males and females also are affected differently by mental illness, as evidenced by different rates of incidence by diagnostic categories, age of onset, and paths to recovery. With the many other disadvantages faced by the dually diagnosed client, gender bias or discrimination must not be added.

Similarly, the cultural contexts within which mental and substance abuse disorders occur and are treated are extremely diverse. A sub rosa theme of this book has been to "start where the client is," and nowhere is this axiom more important than in relation to the culture that the client brings to the treatment situation. Assessment can go awry when the client expresses psychological problems in somatic terms, as people do in many cultures. Treatment is impeded when the therapeutic regimen is culturally biased, as in cases where behavior that is normative in the client's culture is labeled pathological by staff from the core culture. Cultural conflicts may play a major role in the development of mental and substance abuse disorders, as in immigrant populations (Yu, 1997) or in members of oppressed minority groups (McNeil & Kennedy, 1997). Refugees often bring histories of severe trauma that increase their risk for multiple disorders (Yu, 1997). It is important that the clinician assess the cultural status of the client and the impact of that culture on daily living, stress levels, coping strategies, and appropriate direction for treatment.

CONCLUSION

In view of the many dimensions of coexisting disorders and multiple implications for treatment, we provide a treatment grid (Table 10.1) that we hope will be useful as a guide to therapeutic service to persons having coexisting mental illness and substance abuse disorders.

TABLE 10.1 Treatment Grid

Topic	Schizophrenia	Bipolar Disorder	Major Depression	Personality Disorder	Primary Substance Abuse	Anxiety
Unique problems	Cognitive, sensory distortions	Drugs mimic affective symptoms	Drugs mimic affective disorders	Relationship deficits; insight deficits	Substance abuse blocks recognition of other disorder	Substance withdrawal mimics anxiety
Assessment considerations	Confusing psychoses due to drugs with mental illness	Highs from manic state or drugs/alcohol	Determine whether mood is from withdrawal or depression	Masking of disorders via acting out behavior	Accurate assessment often impossible until drug free	Differentiation between withdrawal anxiety and anxiety as a disorder
PRECONTEMPLATIVE STAGE						
Goals	Establish relationship; give concrete help	Establish relationship; set concrete goals; define illness	Establish relationship; set concrete goals; define illness	Use situational discomfort to motivate	Identify client's area of pain as point of focus	Focus on pain as motivation to stay with treatment
Helping relationship	Establish trust through empathy and concrete help	Establish trust through empathy and concrete help	Establish trust through empathy and concrete help	Collaborative, pragmatic, nonemotional	Empathic authority	Establish trust; avoid probing
Pharmacological considerations	Antipsychotic medicines; short-term benzodiazepine for anxiety	Medication; monitor side effects	Antidepressants; monitor side effects	Not usually appropriate	Use only if needed for physical condition	Medication recommended with precautions on dependence and side effects
Cognitive behavior dimensions	Avoid "cold" cognitions	Define symptoms as illness	Define symptoms as illness	Rational consciousness raising begins	Begin questioning maladaptive behavior and thoughts	Define behavior as illness; identify triggers

(continued)

TABLE 10.1 Treatment Grid (*continued*)

Topic	Schizophrenia	Bipolar Disorder	Major Depression	Personality Disorder	Primary Substance Abuse	Anxiety
Coping	Focus on everyday life; teach skills in concrete terms	Stimulus control; identify triggers; keep mood chart	Stimulus control; identify triggers; keep mood chart	Acceptance of consequences	Begin structuring life that is coming apart	Stimulus control; environmental reevaluation
Psychoeducation	Short informational presentation in clear and concrete terms	Consciousness raising about illness	Consciousness raising about illness	Nonthreatening means of consciousness raising	Nonthreatening means of consciousness raising	Consciousness raising about illness
Interpersonal relationships	Use of peer networks	Evaluate networks that support health	Evaluate networks that support health	Likely to be a major means of assessment of the personality disorder	Gather information; gentle questioning	Identify safe relationships
Family relationships	Begin family psychoeducation; focus on information	Solicit input from family regarding client's family role functioning	Solicit input from family regarding client's family role functioning	Solicit input from family regarding client's family role functioning	Solicit input from family regarding client's family role functioning	Solicit input from family regarding client's family role functioning
Environmental intervention	Concrete help with living arrangements, other physical needs	Assess environment	Assess environment	Input from justice, health, and work systems	Input from environmental systems (if needed)	Input from environmental systems (if needed)
Affective dimensions	Avoid ventilation of feelings; provide labels for feelings	Focus on moods as illness; keep mood chart	Focus on moods as illness; keep mood chart	Allow ventilation but avoid affective crowding	Allow ventilation as part of therapeutic bonding	Reframe emotions as illness

	Col 1	Col 2	Col 3	Col 4	Col 5	Col 6
Support groups	Encourage, although client is likely to resist initially	Encourage, although client is likely to resist initially	Encourage, although client is likely to resist initially	Encourage, although client is likely to resist initially	Encourage, although client is likely to resist initially	Encourage, although client is likely to resist initially
CONTEMPLATIVE STAGE						
Goals	Psychoeducation regarding illness	Psychoeducation regarding illness	Psychoeducation regarding illness	Consciousness raising; using situational discomfort to motivate	Consciousness raising; using situational discomfort to motivate	Psychoeducation regarding illness
Helping relationship	Continued helping in concrete ways	Collaborative	Collaborative	Collaborative, pragmatic, nonemotional	Alternating support and pragmatic confrontation	Collaborative
Pharmacological considerations	Antipsychotics; monitor for side effects, compliance	Mood stabilizer; monitor for side effects, compliance	Antidepressants; monitor for side effects, compliance	Not usually used	May use Antabuse as part of sobriety sampling	Monitor for antianxiety medication dependence/side effects, compliance
Cognitive-behavioral dimensions	Do not confront cognitions; work on new behaviors; role-play; skill rehearsals	Confront cognitive distortions	Confront cognitive distortions	Confront maladaptive cognitions and behavior	Weigh pros and cons of change	Confront cognitive distortions
Coping	Continue social skill development	Maintain mood chart; identify triggers	Maintain mood chart; identify triggers	Assist in acceptance of differences from others	Continue providing structure for possible change	Identify triggers; counterconditioning
Psychoeducation	Focus on skills; separate illness from "mind"	Educate about illness; teach social skills	Educate about illness; teach social skills	Nonthreatening means of consciousness raising	Very helpful in consciousness raising and self-liberation	Educate about illness; teach social skills

(continued)

TABLE 10.1 Treatment Grid *(continued)*

Topic	Schizophrenia	Bipolar Disorder	Major Depression	Personality Disorder	Primary Substance Abuse	Anxiety
Interpersonal relationships	Practice communication skills	Practice communication skills	Practice communication skills	Make connections between relationships and client behavior	Make connections between relationships and substance abuse	Practice communication skills
Family relationships	Focus psychoeducation on communication	Focus psychoeducation on communication	Focus psychoeducation on communication	Point out family consequences of behavior	Point out family consequences of substance abuse	Focus psychoeducation on communication
Environmental intervention	Continue concrete assistance; work on employment issues	Environmental reevaluation; contingency management	Environmental reevaluation; contingency management	Begin liaison with justice and other systems regarding client	Help collaterals to refrain from reinforcing addictive behavior	Environmental reevaluation; contingency management
Affective dimensions	Reframe client's self-assessment	Use CBT for self-talk distortions	Use CBT for self-talk distortions	Avoid countertransference reactions	Empathize with ambivalent feelings	Use CBT for self-talk distortions
Support groups	Help in identification and consciousness raising	Help in identification and consciousness raising	Help in identification and consciousness raising	Help in identification and consciousness raising	Help in identification and consciousness raising	Help in identification and consciousness raising
ACTION						
Goals	Social skills development	Halt substance abuse. Begin medication for mood control.	Halt substance abuse. Begin medication for mood control.	Interrupt substance abuse; identify triggers	Halt substance use via behavioral methods	Communication skill development
Helping relationship	Supportive relationships form partnership	Supportive relationships form partnership	Supportive relationships form partnership	Collaborative, pragmatic, nonemotional	Supportive but reality focused	Supportive relationships form partnership

164

Pharmacological considerations	Support taking medication; assist management of side effects	Support compliance; monitor side effects	Support compliance; monitor side effects	Assist with detox, reduce craving; possible methadone	If on Antabuse, support compliance	Support compliance; monitor dependence and side effects
Cognitive-behavioral dimensions	Stimulus control taught in psychoeducation; contingency management	Use CBT to deal with illness/behavior; stimulus control; contingency management	Use CBT to deal with illness/behavior; stimulus control; contingency management	This is strongest mode for intervention; stimulus control, counterconditioning, contingency management	Heavy emphasis on stimulus control, counterconditioning, and contingency management	Self-liberation strategies; CBT for restructuring thoughts
Coping	Empowerment, stimulus control	Come to terms with chronicity of illness	Come to terms with chronicity of illness	Come to terms with future without drugs	Prevent becoming overwhelmed by emerging feelings	Stimulus control techniques
Psychoeducation	Focus on relapse prevention	Focus on relapse prevention	Focus on relapse prevention	Provide for family for supportive purposes	Normalize slips and relapses to prevent giving up	Focus on relapse prevention
Interpersonal relationships	Peer/team support; practice communication skills	Practice communication skills	Practice communication skills	Demand nonexploitative relationships	Make relationships secondary to personal recovery	Practice communication skills
Family relationships	Family psychoeducation; communication skills	Psychoeducation	Psychoeducation	Receive straight feedback and adapt to it	Recognize that these are in flux and will have to be renegotiated	Psychoeducation
Environmental intervention	Social skills training; job assistance	Increase emotional support from environment	Increase emotional support from environment	Continue liaison with environmental systems	Rally support for efforts to change	Environmental triggers need to be identified

(continued)

TABLE 10.1 Treatment Grid (*continued*)

Topic	Schizophrenia	Bipolar Disorder	Major Depression	Personality Disorder	Primary Substance Abuse	Anxiety
Affective dimensions	Provide labels for emotions	Provide labels for emotions; attribute to illness	Provide labels for emotions; attribute to illness	Permit tentative emotional bonding	Prevent overwhelming by surge of unmasked feelings	Deal with emotions through CBT; name feelings; do not probe
Support groups	Continue STEMSS, double trouble	STEMSS, double trouble	STEMSS, double trouble	Helpful adjunct to professional services	Provide supportive stability during change and setbacks	STEMSS, double trouble
MAINTENANCE						
Goals	Relapse prevention	Relapse prevention	Relapse prevention	Focus on predisposing factors to substance use	Relapse prevention	Relapse prevention
Helping relationship	Collaborative, pragmatic	Collaborative, pragmatic	Collaborative, pragmatic	Collaborative, pragmatic, nonemotional	Deemphasize as client establishes natural supportive networks	Collaborative, pragmatic
Pharmacological considerations	Continue medication; manage side effects	Continue medication; manage side effects	Continue medication; manage side effects	Methadone (if appropriate)	Not usually applicable	Same as bipolar disorder and major depressive disorder
Cognitive-behavioral dimensions	Continue affirmative cognitions of self	Continue affirmative cognitions of self; maintain awareness of behavior/illness	Continue affirmative cognitions of self; maintain awareness of behavior/illness	Heavy emphasis on change of behavior and maladaptive cognition	Identify threats to success and cognitive-behavioral strategies for controlling them	Self-affirmation, maintenance awareness of behavior/illness
Coping	Stimulus control to avoid substance and triggers	Keep mood charts	Keep mood charts	Realignment of life with limitations	Acceptance of loss of crutch	Stimulus control

Psychoeducation	Continue with focus on relapse prevention	Continue with focus on relapse prevention	Continue with focus on relapse prevention	Continue with focus on relapse prevention	Continue as needed	Focus on needs for new skills in living	Continue as needed
Interpersonal relationships	Strengthen relationship skills through education and role-playing	Strengthen relationship skills through education and role-playing	Strengthen relationship skills through education and role-playing	Strengthen relationship skills through education and role-playing	Continue expectation of non-exploitative relationships	Develop more honest and nonhostile interactions	Continue expectation of non-exploitative relationships
Family relationships	Continue family support; focus on relapse prevention	Continue family support; focus on relapse prevention	Continue family support; focus on relapse prevention	Continue family support; focus on relapse prevention	Maintain open family interaction; educational and job enhancement	Renegotiate family roles around healthy lifestyle	Maintain open family interaction; educational and job enhancement
Environmental intervention	Identify triggers in environment; social liberation; counter-conditioning	Counter-conditioning	Counter-conditioning	Counter-conditioning	Promote nonexploitative interactions with natural consequences	Facilitate honest and responsible interactions	Counter-conditioning
Affective dimensions	Continue positive affirmations of self; role-playing	Self-reevaluation	Self-reevaluation	Self-reevaluation	Use care and sensitivity during termination phase	Support learning to accept honest emotions in self and others	Self-reevaluation
Support groups	Continue STEMSS, double trouble	In most cases, support groups are very helpful	In most cases, support groups are very helpful	In most cases, support groups are very helpful	In most cases, support groups are very helpful	Maintain on long-term basis for support and growth	In most cases, support groups are very helpful

NOTE: CBT = cognitive-behavioral therapy; STEMSS = Support Together for Emotional and Mental Serenity and Sobriety.

References

Alexander, M. J. (1996). Women with co-occurring addictive and mental disorders: An emerging profile of vulnerability. *American Journal of Orthopsychiatry, 66,* 71.

Alterman, A. I. (Ed.). (1985). *Substance abuse and psychopathology.* New York: Plenum.

American Psychiatric Association. (1993). *APA task force.* Washington, DC: Author.

American Psychiatric Association. (1994). *Diagnostic and Statistical Manual of Mental Disorders* (4th ed.). Washington, DC: Author.

Anderson, C. M., Reiss, D. J., & Hogarty, G. (1986). *Schizophrenia and the family.* New York: Guilford.

Andreasen, N. C. (1994). *Schizophrenia from mind to molecule.* Washington, DC: American Psychiatric Press.

Anthenelli, R. M. (1994). The initial evaluation of the dual diagnosis patient. *Psychiatric Annals, 24,* 407-411.

Anthenelli, R. M., & Schuckit, M. A. (1993). Affective and anxiety disorders and alcohol and drug dependence: Diagnosis and treatment. *Journal of Addictive Diseases, 12*(3), 73-87.

Anthony, W. A., & Liberman, R. P. (1986). The practice of psychiatric rehabilitation: Historical, conceptual, and research base. *Schizophrenia Bulletin, 12,* 542-559.

Appleby, J. D., Dyson, V., Altman, E., McGovern, M. P., & Luchins, D. J. (1996). Utility of the Chemical Use, Abuse, and Dependence Scale in screening patients with severe mental illness. *Psychiatric Services, 47,* 647-649.

Austrian, S. G. (1995). *Mental disorders, medications, and social work.* New York: Columbia University Press.

Barber, J. G. (1994). *Social work with addictions.* New York: New York University Press.

Barlow, D. H. (1988). *Anxiety and its disorders: The nature and treatment of anxiety and panic.* New York: Guilford.

Basco, M., & Rush, A. T. (1996). *Cognitive behavioral therapy for bipolar disorder.* New York: Guilford.

Baxter, E. A., & Diehl, S. (1998). Emotional stages: Consumers and family members recovering from the trauma of mental illness. *Psychiatric Rehabilitation Journal, 21,* 349-355.

Beck, A. T., & Beamesderfer, A. (1974). Assessment of depression: The Depression Inventory. In P. Pichot (Ed.), *Modern problems of pharmacopsychiatry: Psychological measurements in pharmacology* (pp. 151-169). Basel, Switzerland: Karger.

Beck, A. T., & Emery, G. (1985). *Anxiety disorders and phobias: A cognitive perspective.* New York: Basic Books.

Beck, A. T., Rush, A. J., Shaw, B. F., & Emery, G. (1979). *Cognitive therapy of depression.* New York: Guilford.

Bender, D. L., & Leone, B. (Eds.). (1998). *Alcohol: Opposing viewpoints.* San Diego, CA: Greenhaven.

Benes, F. (1995). Is there a neuroanatomic basis for schizophrenia? An old question revisited. *Neuroscientist, 1*(2), 104-115.

Brady, K., & Roberts, J. (1995). Pharmacotherapy of substance abuse: The pharmacotherapy of dual diagnosis. *Psychiatric Annals, 25,* 344-351.

Brady, K. T., & Sonne, S. C. (1995). The relationship between substance abuse and bipolar disorder: Symposium on optimizing treatment in forms of bipolar disorder. *Journal of Clinical Psychiatry, 56*(Suppl. 3), 19-24.

Breakey, W. R., Calabrese, L., Rosenblatt, A., & Crum, R. M. (1998). Detecting alcohol use disorders in the severely mentally ill. *Community Mental Health Journal, 34,* 165-174.

Bricker, M. G. (1988). STEMSS: Support Together for Emotional and Mental Serenity and Sobriety. Milwaukee, WI: DePaul Belleview.

Bricker, M. G. (1989). *STEMSS and 12-step recovery programs: A comparison.* Milwaukee, WI: DePaul Belleview.

Brody, S., Hiam, C. M., Salmann, R., Humbert, L., Fleming, M. Z., & Dawkins-Brickhouse, K. (1996). Dual diagnosis: A treatment model for substance abuse and major mental illness. *Community Mental Health Journal, 32,* 573-578.

Brown, D. R., Ahmed, F., Gary, L. E., & Milburn, N. G. (1995). Major depression in a community sample of African Americans. *American Journal of Psychiatry, 152,* 373-378.

Brown, T. A., & Barlow, D. H. (1995). Diagnostic comorbidity in panic disorder: Effect on treatment outcome and course of comorbid diagnoses following treatment. *Journal of Consulting and Clinical Psychology, 63,* 408.

Budd, R. J., & Hughes, I. C. T. (1997). What do relatives of people with schizophrenia find helpful about family intervention? *Schizophrenia Bulletin, 23,* 341-347.

Buelow, G. D., & Buelow, S. A. (1998). *Psychotherapy in chemical dependence treatment: A practical and integrative approach.* Pacific Grove, CA: Brooks/Cole.

Burland, J. (1995). The Journey of Hope: A family to family self help educational program. *Journal of the California Alliance for the Mentally Ill, 6,* 20-22.

Butler, S. F., Gaulier, B., & Haller, D. (1991). Assessment of Axis II personality disorders among female substance abusers. *Psychological Reports, 68,* 1344-1346.

Cacciola, J. S., Rutherford, M. G., Alterman, A. I., McKay, J. R., & Snyder, E. C. (1996). Personality disorders and treatment outcome in methadone maintenance patients. *Journal of Nervous and Mental Disease, 184,* 234-239.

Carey, K. B. (1996a). Substance use reduction in the context of outpatient psychiatric treatment: A collaborative, motivational, harm reduction approach. *Community Mental Health Journal, 32,* 291-306.

Carey, K. B. (1996b). Treatment of co-occurring substance abuse and mental illness. In R. E. Drake & K. T. Mueser (Eds.), *Dual diagnosis of major mental illness and substance abuse: Vol. 2. Recent research and clinical implications* (pp. 19-32). San Francisco: Jossey-Bass.

Chorpita, B. F., & Barlow, D. H. (1998). The development of anxiety: The role of control in the early environment. *Psychological Bulletin, 124,* 3.

Cloninger, C. R., Svrakic, D. M., & Przybeck, T. R. (1993). A psychobiological model of temperament and character. *Archives of General Psychiatry, 50,* 975-990.

Clopton, J. R., Weddige, R. L., Contreras, S., Fliszar, G. M., & Arredondo, R. (1993). Treatment outcome for substance misuse patients with personality disorder. *International Journal of the Addictions, 28,* 1147-1153.

Cohen, J., & Levy, S. J. (1992). *The mentally ill chemical abuser: Whose client?* Lexington, MA: Lexington Books.

Cone, J. D., & Hawkins, R. P. (Eds.). (1977). *Behavioral assessment: New directions in clinical psychology.* New York: Brunner/Mazel.

Conte, H., Plutchik, R., Picard, S., & Galanter, M. (1991). Sex differences in personality traits and coping styles of hospitalized alcoholics. *Journal of Studies on Alcohol, 52*(1), 25-32.

Cook, B. L., Winokur, G., Garvey, M. J., & Beach, V. (1991). Depression and previous alcoholism in the elderly. *British Journal of Psychiatry, 158,* 72-75.

Corcoran, K. (Ed.). (1992). *Structuring change: Effective practice for common client problems.* Chicago: Lyceum Books.

Corcoran, K., & Grinnell, R. (1992). Defining the structure of change: An introduction. In K. Corcoran (Ed.), *Structuring change: Effective practice for common client problems* (pp. 3-17). Chicago: Lyceum.

Coryell, W., Winokur, G., Keller, M. B., Scheftner, W., & Endicott, J. (1992). Alcoholism and primary major depression: A family study approach to co-existing disorders. *Journal of Affective Disorders, 24*(2), 93-99.

Cowger, C. D. (1992). Assessment of client strengths: The strengths approach to assessment and research. In D. Saleebey (Ed.), *The strengths perspective in social work practice* (pp. 139-146). New York: Longman.

Cuffel, B. J. (1996). Comorbid substance use disorder: Prevalence, patterns of use, and course. In R. E. Drake & K. T. Mueser (Eds.), *Dual diagnosis of major mental illness and substance abuse: Vol. 2. Recent research and clinical implications* (pp. 93-105). San Francisco: Jossey-Bass.

Cutler, D. L. (1993). Substance abuse in severely mentally ill patients: Why is there a problem? *Community Mental Health Journal, 29,* 193-194.

Daley, D. D., & Thase, M. E. (1994). *Dual disorders recovery counseling.* Independence, MO: Herald House/Independence Press.

Devore, W., & Schlesinger, E. G. (1996). *Ethnic-sensitive social work practice* (4th ed.). Boston: Allyn & Bacon.

Dewey, J. (1939). *Intelligence in the modern world: John Dewey's philosophy.* New York: Modern Library.

DiNitto, D. M., & Webb, D. K. (1994). Compounding the problem: Substance abuse and other disabilities. In C. A. McNeece & D. M. DiNitto (Eds.), *Chemical dependency: A systems approach* (pp. 312-348). Englewood Cliffs, NJ: Prentice Hall.

DiNitto, D. M., & Webb, D. K. (1998, November). *Dual diagnosis treatment, research, and a look toward the future.* Paper presented at annual state conference of the National Association of Social Workers/Texas, Austin, TX.

Donovan, D. M. (1988). Assessment of addictive behaviors: Implications of an emerging biopsychosocial model. In D. M. Donovan & G. A. Marlatt (Eds.), *Assessment of addictive behaviors* (pp. 3-48). New York: Guilford.

Dorus, W., Kennedy, J., & Gibbons, R. D. (1987). Symptoms and diagnosis of depression in alcoholics. *Alcohol Clinical Experimental Research, 11,* 150-154.

Doweiko, H. E. (1999). *Concepts of chemical dependency* (4th ed.). Pacific Grove, CA: Brooks/Cole.

Drake, R. E. (1996). Substance use reduction among patients with severe mental illness. *Community Mental Health Journal, 32,* 311-314.

Drake, R. E., Alterman, A. I., & Rosenberg, S. R. (1993). Detection of substance use disorders in severely mentally ill patients. *Community Mental Health Journal, 29,* 175-192.

Drake, R. E., Rosenberg, S. D., & Mueser, K. T. (1996). Assessing substance use disorders in persons with severe mental illness. In R. E. Drake & K. T. Mueser (Eds.), *Dual diagnosis of major mental illness and substance abuse: Vol. 2. Recent research and clinical implications* (pp. 3-18). San Francisco: Jossey-Bass.

Drake, R. E., Rosenberg, S. D., & Mueser, K. T. (1998). Assessing substance disorder in persons with severe mental illness. In R. E. Drake, C. Mercer-McFadden, G. J. McHugo, K. T. Mueser, S. D. Rosenberg, R. E. Clark, & M. F. Brunette (Eds.), *Readings in dual diagnosis* (pp. 123-139). New York: International Association of Psychosocial Rehabilitation Services.

Drake, R. E., & Wallach, M. A. (1989). Substance abuse among the chronically mentally ill. *Hospital and Community Psychiatry, 40,* 1041-1046.

el-Guebaly, N. (1995). Substance use disorders and mental illness: The relevance of comorbidity. *Canadian Journal of Psychiatry, 40*(1), 2-3.

Elkin, I. (1994). The NIMH treatment of depression collaborative research program: Where we began and where we are. In A. E. Bergin & S. L. Garfield (Eds.), *Handbook of psychotherapy and behavior change* (pp. 114-139). New York: John Wiley.

Ellison, J. M., & Adler, D. A. (1990). A strategy for the pharmacotherapy of personality disorders. In D. A. Adler (Ed.), *New directions for mental health services* (No. 47, pp. 43-64). San Francisco: Jossey-Bass.

Evans, K., & Sullivan, J. M. (1990). *Dual diagnosis: Counseling the mentally ill substance abuser.* New York: Guilford.

Feinman, J. A., & Dunner, D. L. (1996). The effect of alcohol and substance abuse on the course of bipolar affective disorder. *Journal of Affective Disorders, 37,* 43-49.

Fine, J., & Miller, N. S. (1993). Evaluation and acute management of psychotic symptomatology in alcohol and drug addictions. In M. S. Miller & B. Stimme (Eds.), *Addictive and psychiatric disorders* (pp. 59-71). New York: Haworth.

Finley, L. Y. (1998). The cultural context: Families coping with severe mental illness. *Psychiatric Rehabilitation Journal, 21,* 230-239.

Fox, V. (1998). Alcoholics Anonymous is ineffective. In D. L. Bender & B. Leone (Eds.), *Alcohol: Opposing viewpoints* (pp. 120-127). San Diego, CA: Greenhaven.

Frank, E., Kupfer, D. J., Perel, J. M., Cornes, C., Jarrett, D. B., & Grochocinski, V. J. (1990). Three year outcomes for maintenance therapies in recurrent depression. *Archives of General Psychiatry, 47,* 1093-1099.

Frank, E., Kupfer, D. J., Wagner, E. F., McEachem, A. B., & Cornes, C. (1991). Efficacy of interpersonal psychotherapy as a maintenance treatment of recurrent depression. *Archives of General Psychiatry, 48,* 1053-1059.

Frank, E., Prien, R. F., Jarrett, D. B., Keller, M. B., Kupfer, D. J., Lavori, P., Rush, A. J., & Weissman, M. M. (1991). Conceptualization and rationale for consensus definitions of terms in major depressive disorders: Response, remission, recovery, relapse, and recurrence. *Archives of General Psychiatry, 48,* 851-855.

Frank, E., & Spanier, C. (1995). Interpersonal psychotherapy for depression: Overview, clinical efficacy, and future directions. *Clinical Psychology Science and Practice, 2,* 349-369.

Frank, J. D. (1974). Therapeutic components of psychotherapy: A 25-year progress report of research. *Journal of Nervous & Mental Disorders, 159,* 325-342.

Gitlin, M. J. (1990). *The psychotherapist's guide to psychopharmacology.* New York: Free Press.

Gitlin, M. J., Swendsen, J., Heller, T. L., & Hammen, C. (1995). Relapse and impairment in bipolar disorder. *American Journal of Psychiatry, 152,* 1635-1640.

Goldberg, J. F., Harrow, M., & Grossman, L. S. (1995). Course and outcome in bipolar affective disorder: A longitudinal follow-up study. *American Journal of Psychiatry, 152,* 379-384.

Goldenberg, I. M., Mueller, T., Fierman, E. J., Gordon, A., Pratt, L., Cox, K., Park, T., Lavori, P., Goisman, R. M., & Keller, M. (1995). Specificity of substance use in anxiety-disordered subjects. *Comprehensive Psychiatry, 36,* 319.

Goldstein, E. (1993). The borderline substance abuser. In S. L. A. Straussner (Ed.), *Clinical work with substance-abusing clients* (pp. 270-290). New York: Guilford.

Goldstein, M. J., & Miklowitz, D. J. (1990). Behavioral family treatment for patients with bipolar affective disorder. *Behavior Modification, 14,* 457-489.

Goodman, L. A., Dutton, M. A., & Harris, M. (1995). Episodically homeless women with severe mental illness: Prevalence of physical and sexual assault. *American Journal of Orthopsychiatry, 65,* 468-478.

Gorski, T. T. (1994). A suggestion for conceptualizing dual diagnosis: A systematic analysis to help cut through the confusion and mismanagement. *Behavioral Health Management, 14,* 50-53.

Gorski, T. T. (1998). Alcoholism should be treated as a disease. In D. L. Bender & B. Leone (Eds.), *Alcohol: Opposing viewpoints* (pp. 98-104). San Diego, CA: Greenhaven.

Grant, B. F. (1995). Comorbidity between DSM-IV drug use disorders and major depression: Results of a national survey of adults. *Journal of Substance Abuse, 7,* 481-497.

Hanson, G., & Venturelli, P. J. (1995). *Drugs and society.* Boston: Jones & Bartlett.

Harrison, P. A., Martin, J. A., Tuason, V. B., & Hoffmann, N. (1985). Conjoint treatment of dual disorders. In A. I. Alterman (Ed.), *Substance abuse and psychopathology.* New York: Plenum.

Haywood, T. W., Kavitz, H. M., Grossman, L. S., Cavanaugh, J. L. J., Davis, J. M., & Lewis, D. A. (1995). Predicting the "revolving door" phenomenon among patients with schizophrenic, schizoaffective, and affective disorders. *American Journal of Psychiatry, 152,* 856-861.

Hepworth, D. H., Rooney, R. H., & Larsen, J. A. (1997). *Direct social work practice: Theory and skills* (5th ed.). Pacific Grove, CA: Brooks/Cole.

Hirschfeld, R. M. A., Hasin, D., Keller, M. B., Endicott, J., & Wunder, J. (1990). Depression and alcoholism: Comorbidity in a longitudinal study. In J. D. Maser & C. R. Cloninger (Eds.), *Comorbidity of mood and anxiety disorders* (pp. 293-303). Washington, DC: American Psychiatric Press.

Hogarty, G. E., & Flesher, S. (1992). Cognitive remediation in schizophrenia: Proceed . . . with caution. *Schizophrenia Bulletin, 18,* 51-57.

Hudson, C. F. (1990). Anxiety disorders and substance abuse. In D. F. O'Connell (Ed.), *Managing the dually diagnosed patient* (pp. 119-136). New York: Haworth.

Hutchinson, D. S., Shrinar, G. S., & Cross, C. (1999). The role of physical fitness in rehabilitation and recovery. *Psychiatric Rehabilitation Journal, 22,* 355-359.

Jerrell, J. M., & Ridgely, S. (1995). Gender differences in the assessment of specialized treatments for substance abuse among people with severe mental illness. *Journal of Psychoactive Drugs, 27,* 347.

Jordan, C., Barrett, M. C., & Lewellen, A. (1997, February). *Psychoeducation with Mexican-American families: A cross-cultural psychosocial rehabilitation model.* Paper presented at "Encuentro de las Americas: De la Exclusión a la Rehabilitación Psicosocial," Mexico City.

Jordan, C., Barrett, M. C., Vandiver, V., & Lewellen, A. (1999). Psychoeducational family practice. In C. Franklin & C. Jordan (Eds.), *Family practice: Brief systems methods for social workers* (pp. 178-198). Pacific Grove, CA: Brooks/Cole.

Jordan, C., Lewellen, A., Vandiver, V., & Barrett, M. C. (1997, April). *Recent studies on family as educator: A cross-cultural psychoeducation model.* Paper presented at the meeting of the National Social Science Association, Las Vegas, NV.

Kantor, M. (1992). *Diagnosis and treatment of the personality disorders.* St. Louis, MO: Ishiyaku EuroAmerica.

Keefe, R. S. E., & Harvey, P. D. (1994). *Understanding schizophrenia: A guide to the new research on causes and treatment.* New York: Free Press.

Keith, R. A., & Lipsey, M. W. (1993). The role of theory in rehabilitation assessment, treatment, and outcomes. In R. L. Gluekauf, L. B. Secrest, G. R. Bond, & E. C. McDonel (Eds.), *Assessment in rehabilitation and health* (pp. 33-58). Newbury Park, CA: Sage.

Keller, M. B., Lavori, P. W., Coryell, W., Andreasen, N. C., Endicott, J., Clayton, P. J., Klerman, G. L., & Hirschfeld, R. M. (1986). Differential outcome of pure manic, mixed/cycling, and pure depressive outcomes in patients with bipolar illness. *Journal of the American Medical Association, 255,* 3138-3142.

Kessler, R. C., McGonagle, K. A., Nelson, C. B., Hughes, M., Swartz, M., & Blazer, D. G. (1994). Sex and depression in the National Comorbidity Survey: II. Cohort effects. *Journal of Affective Disorders, 30*(1), 15-26.

Kirst-Ashman, K. K., & Hull, G. H. (1997). *Understanding generalist practice.* Chicago: Nelson & Hall.

Kishline, A. (1998). Alcoholism should not be treated as a disease. In D. L. Bender & B. Leone (Eds.), *Alcohol: Opposing viewpoints* (pp. 105-119). San Diego, CA: Greenhaven.

Klerman, G. L., Leon, A. C., Wickramaratne, P., Warshaw, M. G., Mueller, T. I., Weissman, M. M., & Akiskal, H. (1996). The role of drug and alcohol abuse in recent increases in depression in the U.S. *Psychological Medicine, 26,* 343-351.

Klerman, G. L., Weissman, M. M., Markowitz, J., Glick, I., Wilner, P. L., Mason, B., & Shear, M. K. (1994). Medication and psychotherapy. In A. E. Bergin & S. L. Garfield (Eds.), *Handbook of psychotherapy and behavior change* (pp. 743-782). New York: John Wiley.

Kopp, R. G., & Ruzicka, M. F. (1993). Women's multiple roles and psychological well-being. *Psychological Reports, 72,* 1351-1354.

Kosten, R., & Ziedonis, D. M. (1997). Substance abuse and schizophrenia: Editors' introduction. *Schizophrenia Bulletin, 23,* 181-186.

Kulkarni, J. (1997). Women and schizophrenia: A review. *Australian and New Zealand Journal of Psychiatry, 31,* 46-56.

Lamb, H. R. (1994). A century and a half of psychiatric rehabilitation in the U.S. *Hospital and Community Psychiatry, 45,* 1015-1019.

Lara, M. C., Ferro, T., & Klein, D. N. (1997). Family history assessment of personality disorders: Association with measures of psychosocial functioning in direct evaluations with relatives. *Journal of Personality Disorders, 11,* 137.

Layne, G. S. (1990). Schizophrenia and substance abuse. In D. F. O'Connell (Ed.), *Managing the dually diagnosed patient* (pp. 163-181). New York: Haworth.

Lefley, H. P. (1990). Cultural and chronic mental illness. *Hospital and Community Psychiatry, 41,* 277-286.

Lefley, H. (1992). Expressed emotion: Conceptual, clinical, and social policy issues. *Hospital and Community Psychiatry, 43,* 591-598.

Lehman, A. F. (1996). Heterogeneity of person and place: Assessing co-occurring addictive and mental disorders. *American Journal of Orthopsychiatry, 66,* 32-41.

Lehman, A. F., & Burns, B. J. (1996). Severe mental illness in the community. In B. Spilker (Ed.), *Quality of life and pharmacoeconomics in clinical trials* (2nd ed., pp. 919-924). Philadelphia: Lippincott-Raven.

Lehman, A. F., Myers, C. P., & Corty, E. (1989). Assessment and classification of patients with psychiatric and substance abuse syndromes. *Hospital and Community Psychiatry, 40,* 1019-1025.

Lehman, A. F., Myers, C. P., Thompson, J. W., & Corty, E. (1993). Implications of mental and substance abuse disorders: A comparison of single and dual diagnosis patients. *Journal of Nervous and Mental Disease, 181,* 365-370.

Leibenluft, E. (1996). Women with bipolar illness: Clinical and research issues. *American Journal of Psychiatry, 153,* 163-173.

Lewellen, A. (1993). *An information processing model of women with chronic anxiety: An integrative treatment approach.* Ann Arbor, MI: UMI Dissertation Abstracts.

Liberman, R. P. (1998). International perspectives on skills training for the mentally disabled. *International Review of Psychiatry, 10*(1), 5.

Lin, K.-M., & Cheung, F. (1999). Mental health issues for Asian Americans. *Psychiatric Services, 50,* 774-780.

Lipton, R. (1997). Relationship between alcohol, stress, and depression in Mexican-Americans and non-Hispanic whites. *Behavioral Medicine, 23*(3), 101-111.

Littrell, K. H. (1998). Assessment of lethality in potentially suicidal persons with schizophrenia. *Probe, 3*(1), 1-3. (Tucker, GA: Promedica Research Center)

Lopez, S. R., Groves, P., Holland, D., Johnson, M. J., Kalin, C. D., Kanel, K., Mellins, A., & Rhyne, M. D. (1989). Development of culturally sensitive psychotherapists. *Professional Psychology: Research and Practice, 20,* 369-376.

Magnavita, J. J. (1997). *Restructuring personality disorders: A short-term dynamic approach.* New York: Guilford.

Makela, K., Arminen, I., Bloomfield, K., Eisenback-Stangl, I., Bergmark, K. H., Kurube, N., Mariolini, N., Olafsdottir, H., Peterson, J., Phillips, M., Rehm, J., Room, R., Resenqvist, P., Rosovsky, H., Stenius, K., Swaitkiewscz, G., Woronosicz, B., & Zielinshi, A. (1996). *Alcoholics Anonymous as a mutual-help movement: A study in eight societies.* Madison: University of Wisconsin Press.

Manson, S. P., Shore, J. H., & Bollin, J. D. (1985). The depressive experience in American Indian communities: A challenge for psychiatric theory of diagnosis. In A. Kleinman & B. Good (Eds.), *Culture and depression* (pp. 331-368). Berkeley: University of California Press.

Markowitz, J. C. (1997). *Interpersonal psychotherapy for dysthymic disorder.* Washington, DC: American Psychiatric Press.

Markowitz, J. C., & Kocsic, J. H. (1994). Dysthymia. In L. Grunhaus & J. F. Greden (Eds.), *Severe depressive disorders* (pp. 209-219). Washington, DC: American Psychiatric Press.

Marlowe, D. B., Kirby, K. C., Festinger, D. S., Husband, S. D., & Platt, J. (1997). Impact of comorbid personality disorders and personality disorder symptoms on outcomes of behavioral treatment for cocaine dependence. *Journal of Nervous and Mental Disease, 185,* 483-490.

Maser, J. D., & Dinges, N. (1993). Comorbidity: Meaning and uses in cross-cultural clinical research. *Culture, Medicine, and Psychiatry, 16,* 409-425.

Mayfield, D., McLeod, G., & Hall, P. (1974). The CAGE questionnaire: Validation of a new alcoholism screening instrument. *American Journal of Psychiatry, 131,* 1121-1123.

McBride, A. B. (1988). Mental health effects of women's multiple roles. *Image: The Journal of Nursing Scholarship, 20*(1), 57-64.

McCown, W. G. (1988). Multi-impulsive personality disorder and multiple substance abuse: Evidence from members of self-help groups. *British Journal of Addiction, 83,* 431-432.

McGovern, M. P., & Morrison, D. H. (1992). The Chemical Use, Abuse, and Dependence Scale (CUAD): Rationale, reliability, and validity. *Journal of Substance Abuse Treatment, 9,* 27-38.

McHugo, G. J., Drake, R. E., Burton, H. L., & Ackerson, T. H. (1995). A scale for assessing the stage of substance abuse treatment in persons with severe mental illness. *Journal of Nervous and Mental Disease, 183,* 762.

McLellan, A. T., Luborsky, L., Woody, G. E., & O'Brien, C. P. (1980). An improved diagnostic evaluation instrument for substance abuse patients: The Addiction Severity Index. *Journal of Nervous and Mental Diseases, 168*(1), 26-33.

McNeil, J., & Kennedy, R. (1997). Mental health services to minority groups of color. In T. Watkins & J. Callicutt (Eds.), *Mental health policy and practice today* (pp. 235-257). Thousand Oaks, CA: Sage.

Meichenbaum, D. (1995). The evolution of a cognitive-behavior therapist. In J. K. Zeig (Ed.), *The evolution of psychotherapy: The third conference* (pp. 95-104). New York: Brunner/Mazel.

Meyers, R. J., & Smith, J. E. (1995). *Clinical guide to alcohol treatment: The community reinforcement approach.* New York: Guilford.

Miklowitz, D. J., & Goldstein, M. J. (1997). *Bipolar disorder: Why family treatment? A family-focused treatment approach.* New York: Guilford.

Miklowitz, D. J., Goldstein, M. J., Nuechterlein, K. H., Snyder, K. S., & Mintz, J. (1988). Family factors and the course of bipolar affective disorder. *Archives of General Psychiatry, 45,* 225-231.

Milby, J. B., Schumacher, J. E., Raczynski, J. M., Caldwell, E., Engle, M., Michael, M., & Carr, J. (1996). Sufficient conditions for effective treatment of substance abusing homeless persons. *Drug and Alcohol Dependence, 43*(1-2), 39.

Miller, R. N., Faulkner, L. R., & Craig, J. M. (1994). Problems in the recognition and treatment of patients with dual diagnoses. *Journal of Substance Abuse Treatment, 11,* 267-271.

Miller, W. R., & Rollnick, S. (1991). *Motivational interviewing: Preparing people to change addictive behavior.* New York: Guilford.

Minkoff, K. (1996). Discussion of "Substance Use Reduction in the Context of Outpatient Psychiatric Treatment." *Community Mental Health Journal, 32,* 307-310.

Mirowsky, J. (1985). Disorder and its context: Paranoid beliefs as thematic elements, thought problems, hallucinations, and delusions under threatening social conditions. *Community and Mental Health, 5,* 185-204.

Montrose, K., & Daley, D. C. (1995). *Celebrating small victories: A primer of approaches and attitudes for helping clients with dual disorders.* Center City, MN: Hazelden.

Morrison, J. (1995). *DSM-IV made easy.* New York: Guilford.

Moxley, D. P., & Freddolino, P. P. (1990). A model of advocacy for promoting client self-determination in psychosocial rehabilitation. *Psychosocial Rehabilitation Journal, 14*(2), 68-81.

Mueser, K. T., Drake, R. E., & Noordsy, D. L. (1998). Integrated mental health and substance abuse treatment for severe psychiatric disorders. *Journal of Practical Psychology and Behavioral Health, 4,* 129-139.

Nace, E. P. (1990). Substance abuse and personality disorder. *Journal of Chemical Dependency Treatment, 3*(2), 183-198.

Nace, E. P., Davis, C. W., & Gaspari, J. P. (1997). Axis II comorbidity in substance abusers. *American Journal of Psychiatry, 148,* 118-120.

National Center for Health Statistics. (1991). *Health, United States, 1990* (DHHS Pub. No. PHS 91-1232). Hyattsville, MD: U.S. Department of Health and Human Services.

National Institute on Drug Abuse. (1991). *Drug abuse and drug abuse research: The third triennial report to Congress from the secretary, Department of Health and Human Services.* Washington, DC: Author.

Nikkel, R. E. (1994). Areas of skill training for persons with mental illness and substance use disorders: Building skills for successful community living. *Community Mental Health Journal, 30,* 61-72.

Nunes, E. V., Deliyannides, D., Donovan, S., & McGrath, P. J. (1996). The management of treatment resistance in depressed patients with substance use disorders. *Psychiatric Clinics of North America, 19,* 311-327.

O'Boyle, M. (1993). Personality disorder and multiple substance dependence. *Journal of Personality Disorders, 7,* 342-347.

O'Boyle, M., & Hirschfeld, R. M. A. (1994). Recurrent depression: Comorbidity with personality disorder or alcoholism and impact on quality of life. In L. Grunhaus & J. F. Greden (Eds.), *Severe depressive disorders* (pp. 141-158). Washington, DC: American Psychiatric Press.

O'Connell, R. A., Mayo, J. A., Flatow, L., Cuthbertson, B., & O'Brien, B. E. (1991). Outcome of bipolar disorder in long-term treatment with lithium. *British Journal of Psychiatry, 159,* 123-129.

O'Hare, T. (1992). The substance-abusing chronically mentally ill client: Prevalence, assessment, treatment, and policy concerns. *Social Work, 37,* 185-187.

O'Malley, S., Kosten, T., & Renner, J. (1990). Dual diagnosis: Substance abuse and personality disorders. In D. Adler (Ed.), *Treating personality disorders* (New Directions for Mental Health Services, No. 47, pp. 115-137). San Francisco: Jossey-Bass.

O'Nell, T. D. (1993). "Feeling worthless": An ethnographic investigation of depression and problem drinking at the Flathead Reservation. *Culture, Medicine, and Psychiatry, 16,* 447-469. (Special issue)

Onken, L. S., Blaine, J., Genser, L., & Horton, A. M. (Eds.). (1997). *Treatment of drug-dependent individuals with comorbid mental disorders.* Rockville, MD: National Institute on Drug Abuse.

Orlin, L., & Davis, J. (1993). Assessment and intervention with drug and alcohol abusers in psychiatric settings. In S. L. A. Straussner (Ed.), *Clinical work with substance-abusing clients* (pp. 50-68). New York: Guilford.

Osher, F. C., & Kofoed, L. L. (1989). Treatment of patients with psychiatric and psychoactive substance abuse disorders. *Hospital and Community Psychiatry, 40,* 1025-1030.

Patrick, D. L., & Bergner, M. (1990). Measurement of health status in the 1990's. *Annual Review of Public Health, 11,* 165-184.

Penn, D. (1991). Cognitive rehabilitation of social deficits in schizophrenia: A direction of promise or following a primrose path? *Psychosocial Rehabilitation Journal, 15*(1), 27-41.

Pepper, B., & Ryglewicz, H. (1984, June). *Schizophrenia: A constant brain disorder in a changing world.* Paper presented at the annual meeting of the American Psychiatric Association, Chicago.

Perlman, H. H. (1957). *Social casework: A problem-solving process.* Chicago: University of Chicago Press.

Persons, J. B. (1989). *Cognitive therapy in practice: A case formulation approach.* New York: Norton.

Pies, R. W. (1993). *Clinical manual of psychiatric diagnosis and treatment: A biopsychosocial approach.* Washington, DC: American Psychiatric Press.

Preston, J. D., O'Neal, J. H., & Talaga, M. C. (1997). *Handbook of clinical psychopharmacology for therapists* (2nd ed.). Oakland, CA: New Harbinger.

Prochaska, J. O., & DiClemente, C. C. (1984). *The transtheoretical approach: Crossing the traditional boundaries of therapy.* Homewood, IL: Dow Jones/Irwin.

Prochaska, J. O., & DiClemente, C. C. (1986). Toward a comprehensive model of change. In W. R. Miller & N. Heather (Eds.), *Treating addictive behaviors: Processes of change* (pp. 3-27). New York: Plenum.

Prochaska, J. O., DiClemente, C. C., & Norcross, J. C. (1992). In search of how people change: Applications to addictive behaviors. *American Psychologist, 47,* 1102-1114.

Rapp, C. A. (1998). *The strengths model: Case management with people suffering from severe and persistent mental illness.* New York: Oxford University Press.

Rapp, C. A., Shera, W., & Kisthardt, W. (1993). Research strategies for consumer empowerment of people with severe mental illness. *Social Work, 38*(6), 727-735.

Rauch, J. (1993). Introduction. In J. Rauch (Ed.), *Assessment: A sourcebook for social work practice* (pp. xii-xxi). Milwaukee, WI: Families International.

Read, M. R., Penick, E. C., & Nickel, E. J. (1993). Treatment for dually diagnosed clients. In E. M. Freeman (Ed.), *Substance abuse treatment: A family systems perspective* (pp. 123-156). Newbury Park, CA: Sage.

Regier, D. A., Farmer, M. E., Rae, D. S., Locke, B. Z., Keith, S. J., Judd. L. L., & Goodwin, F. K. (1990). Comorbidity of mental disorders with alcohol and other drug abuse. *Journal of the American Medical Association, 264,* 2511-2518.

Ridgely, M. S., & Jerrell, J. M. (1996). Analysis of three interventions for substance abuse treatment of severely mentally ill people. *Community Mental Health Journal, 32,* 561-572.

Ries, R. K. (1993). The dually diagnosed patient with psychotic symptoms. *Journal of Addictive Diseases, 12*(3), 103-122.

Ries, R. K. (1994). *Assessment and treatment of patients with coexisting mental illness and alcohol and other drug abuse* (DHHS Pub. No. 94-2078). Rockville, MD: U.S. Department of Health and Human Services.

Riso, L. P., Thase, M. E., Howland, R. H., Friedman, E. S., Simons, A. D., & Tu, X. M. (1997). A prospective test of criteria for response, remission, relapse, recovery. *Journal of Affective Disorders, 43,* 131-142.

Rogers, C. R. (1951). *Client-centered therapy: Its current practice, implications, and theory.* Boston: Houghton Mifflin.

Rohsenow, D., Monti, P., Binkoff, M., Leipman, M., & Nirenberg, T. (1991). Patient treatment matching for alcoholic men in communication skills versus cognitive-behavioral mood management training. *Addictive Behaviors, 17,* 63-69.

Rollnick, S., Heather, N., Gold, R., & Hall, W. (1992). Development of a short "readiness to change" questionnaire for use in brief, opportunistic interventions among excessive drinkers. *British Journal of Addiction, 87,* 743-754.

Ross, H. E., Glaser, F. B., & Germanson, T. (1988). The prevalence of psychiatric disorders in patients with alcohol and other drug problems. *Archives of General Psychiatry, 45,* 1023-1031.

Rubinstein, L., Campbell, F., & Daley, D. (1990). Four perspectives on dual diagnosis: An overview of treatment issues. In D. F. O'Connell (Ed.), *Managing the dually diagnosed patient* (pp. 97-116). New York: Haworth.

Ryglewicz, H., & Pepper, B. (1992). The dual disorder client: Mental disorder and substance use. In S. Cooper & T. H. Lentner (Eds.), *Innovations in community mental health* (pp. 270-290). Sarasota, FL: Professional Resource Press.

Safran, J. D., & Segal, Z. V. (1990). *Interpersonal process in cognitive therapy.* New York: Basic Books.

Saleebey, D. (1992). Power in the people: The philosophy of the strengths perspective. In D. Saleebey (Ed.), *The strengths perspective in social work practice* (pp. 3-17). New York: Longman.

San Blise, M. L. (1995). Radical positive reframing. *Journal of Psychosocial Nursing, 33*(12), 18-25.

Schmidt, L. (1991). Specialization in alcoholism and mental health residential treatment: The "dual diagnosis" problem. *Journal of Drug Issues, 21,* 859-874.

Schutte, K. K., Hearst, J., & Moos, R. H. (1997). Gender differences in the relations between depressive symptoms and drinking behavior among problem drinkers: A three-wave study. *Journal of Consulting and Clinical Psychology, 65,* 392-404.

Schutte, K. K., Moos, R. H., & Berman, P. L. (1995). Depression and drinking behavior among women and men: A three wave longitudinal study of older adults. *Journal of Consulting and Clinical Psychology, 63,* 810-822.

Sciacca, K. (1987). New initiatives in the treatment of the chronic patient with alcohol/substance use problems. *TIE-Lines, 4*(3), 1-6. (The Information Exchange of Young Adult Chronic Patients)

Seivewright, N., & Daly, C. (1997). Personality disorder and drug use: A review. *Drug and Alcohol Review, 16,* 235-250.

Seligman, L. (1990). *Selecting effective treatments: A comprehensive, systematic guide to treating adult mental disorders.* San Francisco: Jossey-Bass.

Selzer, M. L. (1971). Michigan Alcohol Screening Test: The quest for a new diagnostic instrument. *American Journal of Psychiatry, 127,* 89-94.

Selzer, M. L., Vinokur, A., & Van Rooijen, L. (1975). A self-administered Short Michigan Alcoholism Screening Test (SMAST). *Journal of Studies on Alcohol, 36,* 117-126.

Simon, C. E. (1997). Psychoeducation: A contemporary approach. In T. Watkins & J. Callicutt (Eds.), *Mental health policy and practice today* (pp. 129-145). Thousand Oaks, CA: Sage.

Skinner, H. A. (1984). The Drug Abuse Screening Test. *Addictive Behaviors, 7*, 363-371.

Smith, G., Schwebel, A. I., Dunn, R. L., & Melver, S. D. (1993). The role of psychologists in the treatment, management, and prevention of chronic mental illness. *American Psychologist, 48*, 966-971.

Sobell, M. B., Maisto, S. A., Sobell, L. C., Cooper, A. M., Cooper, T., & Sanders, B. (1980). Developing a prototype for evaluating alcohol treatment effectiveness. In L. C. Sobell, M. B. Sobell, & E. Ward (Eds.), *Evaluating alcohol treatment effectiveness* (pp. 129-150). New York: Pergamon.

Solomon, P. (1998). The cultural context of interventions for family members with a seriously mentally ill relative. *New Directions for Mental Health Service, 77*, 5-16.

Sonne, S. C., Brady, K. T., & Morton, W. A. (1994). Substance abuse and bipolar affective disorder. *Journal of Nervous and Mental Disease, 182*, 349-351.

Spanier, C., & Frank, E. (1997). Maintenance interpersonal psychotherapy: A preventive treatment for depression. In J. C. Markowitz (Ed.), *Interpersonal psychotherapy* (pp. 67-97). Washington, DC: American Psychiatric Press.

Sperry, L. (1995). *Handbook of diagnosis and treatment of the DSM-IV personality disorders*. New York: Brunner/Mazel.

Spielberger, C. D. (1985). Anxiety, cognition, and affect: A state-trait perspective. In A. H. Tumas & J. D. Maser (Eds.), *Anxiety and the anxiety disorders*. Hillsdale, NJ: Lawrence Erlbaum.

Spitzer, R. L., Williams, J. B. W., Gibbon, M., & First, B. B. (1990). *Structured clinical interview for DSM-III-R patient version*. New York: New York State Psychiatric Institute.

Swann, A. C. (1997). Manic-depressive illness and substance abuse. *Psychiatric Annals, 27*, 507-511.

Thase, M. E., Greenhouse, J. B., Frank, E., Reynolds, C. F., Pilkonis, P. A., Hurley, K., Grochocinski, V., & Kupfer, D. J. (1997). Treatment of major depression with psychotherapy or psychotherapy-pharmacotherapy combinations. *Archives of General Psychiatry, 54*, 1009-1015.

Thompson, K. S., Griffith, E. H., & Leaf, P. J. (1990). A historical review of the Madison model of community care. *Hospital and Community Psychiatry: A Journal of the American Psychiatric Association, 41*, 625.

Toner, B. B., Gillies, L. A., Prendergast, P., Cote, F. H., & Browne, C. (1992). Substance use disorders in a sample of Canadian patients with chronic mental illness. *Hospital and Community Psychiatry, 43*, 251-254.

Tsuang, D., Cowley, D., Ries, R., Dunner, D. L., & Roy-Byrne, P. P. (1995). The effects of substance use disorder on the clinical presentation of anxiety and depression in an outpatient clinic. *Journal of Clinical Psychiatry, 56*, 549.

Vogel, H. S., Knight, E., Laudet, A. B., & Magura, S. (1998). Double trouble in recovery: Self help for people with dual diagnoses. *Psychiatric Rehabilitation Journal, 21*, 356-364.

Wallace, J. (1993). Modern disease models of alcoholism and other chemical dependencies: The new biopsychosocial models. *Drugs and Society, 8*(1), 69-87.

Ware, J. E., & Sherbourne, C. D. (1992). The MOS 36 item short-form health survey (SF-36). *Medical Care, 30,* 473-483.

Ware, N. C., & Kleinman, A. (1992). Culture and somatic experience: The social course of illness in neurasthenia and chronic fatigue syndrome. *Psychosomatic Medicine, 54,* 546-560.

Weiss, R. D., Mirin, S. M., Griffin, M. L., Gunderson, J. G., & Hufford, C. (1993). Personality disorders in cocaine dependence. *Comprehensive Psychiatry, 34*(3), 145-149.

Weissman, M. M., & Markowitz, J. C. (1994). Interpersonal psychotherapy: Current status. *Archives of General Psychiatry, 51,* 599-606.

Westermeyer, J. (1985). Substance abuse and psychopathology: Sociocultural factors. In A. I. Alterman (Ed.), *Substance abuse and psychopathology* (pp. 45-68). New York: Plenum.

Westermeyer, J. (1995). Cultural aspects of substance abuse and alcoholism: Assessment and management. *Cultural Psychiatry, 18,* 589-605.

Wilson, W. H. (1997). Neuroscientific research in mental health. In T. R. Watkins & J. W. Callicutt (Eds.), *Mental health policy and practice today* (pp. 89-106). Thousand Oaks, CA: Sage.

Winokur, G., & Coryell, W. (1991). Familial alcoholism in primary unipolar major depressive disorder. *American Journal of Psychiatry, 148,* 184.

Winokur, G., Coryell, W., Akiakal, H. S., Maser, J. D., Keller, M. B., Endicott, J., & Mueller, T. (1995). Alcoholism in manic-depressive (bipolar) illness: Familial illness, course of illness, and the primary-secondary distinction. *American Journal of Psychiatry, 152,* 365-372.

Woody, G. (1996). The challenge of dual diagnosis. *Alcohol Health and the Research World, 20,* 76-80.

Woolf-Reeve, B. S. (1990). A guide to the assessment of psychiatric symptoms in the addictions treatment setting. In D. F. O'Connell (Ed.), *Managing the dually diagnosed patient* (pp. 71-95). New York: Haworth.

Wright, O. L., & Anderson, J. P. (1998). Clinical social work practice with urban African American families. *Families in Society: The Journal of Contemporary Human Services, 79,* 197-205.

Young, D. M. (1997). Depression. In W. Tseng & J. Streltzer (Eds.), *Culture and psychopathology: A guide to clinical assessment* (pp. 28-43). New York: Brunner/ Mazel.

Yu, M. (1997). Mental health services to immigrants and refugees. In T. Watkins & J. Callicutt (Eds.), *Mental health policy and practice today* (pp. 164-181). Thousand Oaks, CA: Sage.

Ziedonis, D. M., & Trudeau, K. (1997). Motivation to quit using substances among individuals with schizophrenia: Implications for a motivation-based treatment model. *Schizophrenia Bulletin, 23,* 229-238.

Index

About the Authors

TED R. WATKINS earned graduate degrees in social work at Louisiana State University and the University of Pennsylvania after receiving his bachelor's degree in psychology at the University of North Texas. His practice experience includes work with substance abusers and persons with mental illness in a variety of settings including community mental health centers, residential treatment programs, private psychiatric hospitals, addictive disease clinics, family counseling agencies, and private practice. He has taught social work at the B.S.W., M.S.W., and Ph.D. levels and has held administrative positions as B.S.W. program director, director of criminal justice programs, chair of the Department of Sociology, Anthropology and Social Work, and graduate adviser, all at the University of Texas at Arlington. He is now director of the B.S.W. program at Southwest Texas State University.

ARA LEWELLEN is Associate Professor in the Department of Social Work at Texas A&M University–Commerce, where she has taught for 7 years. She earned her Ph.D. degree in the School of Social Work at the University of Texas at Arlington in 1993. Prior to pursuing her doctorate, she worked in community mental health, serving the severe and persistently mentally ill in both public and private settings. She has numerous publications regarding individual and family psychoeducation and the special concerns of women with mental disorders. She is a licensed master social worker–advanced clinical practitioner in the state of Texas.

MARJIE C. BARRETT earned her Ph.D. degree at Texas Woman's University in 1978 with a focus on early childhood education and child development. Her M.S. degree in social work was obtained at the University of Texas at Austin in 1962, and her B.A. degree was obtained at Texas Christian University in 1959. She has been continuously licensed by the state of Texas since the inception of licensing. Currently, she is Associate Professor in the School of Social Work at the University of Texas at Arlington. She teaches graduate courses in the human behavior and social environment content area. She has been a professional social worker for 40 years; has practiced social work continuously with individuals, families, and groups; and has done extensive consultation and training. Her interest in this topic grows out of her research and clinical practice with families and couples, but particularly with women and women's groups. She speaks from the practice setting that is community based; nonprofit; and serving individuals, families, and children.